AF473787

GEORGE INNESS *and the Visionary Landscape*

Art is a subtle essence. It is not a thing of surfaces, but a moving spirit. . . . Like the humanity of God, it is personal only to love; unknown to the worldling; a myth to the searching intellect.

—George Inness

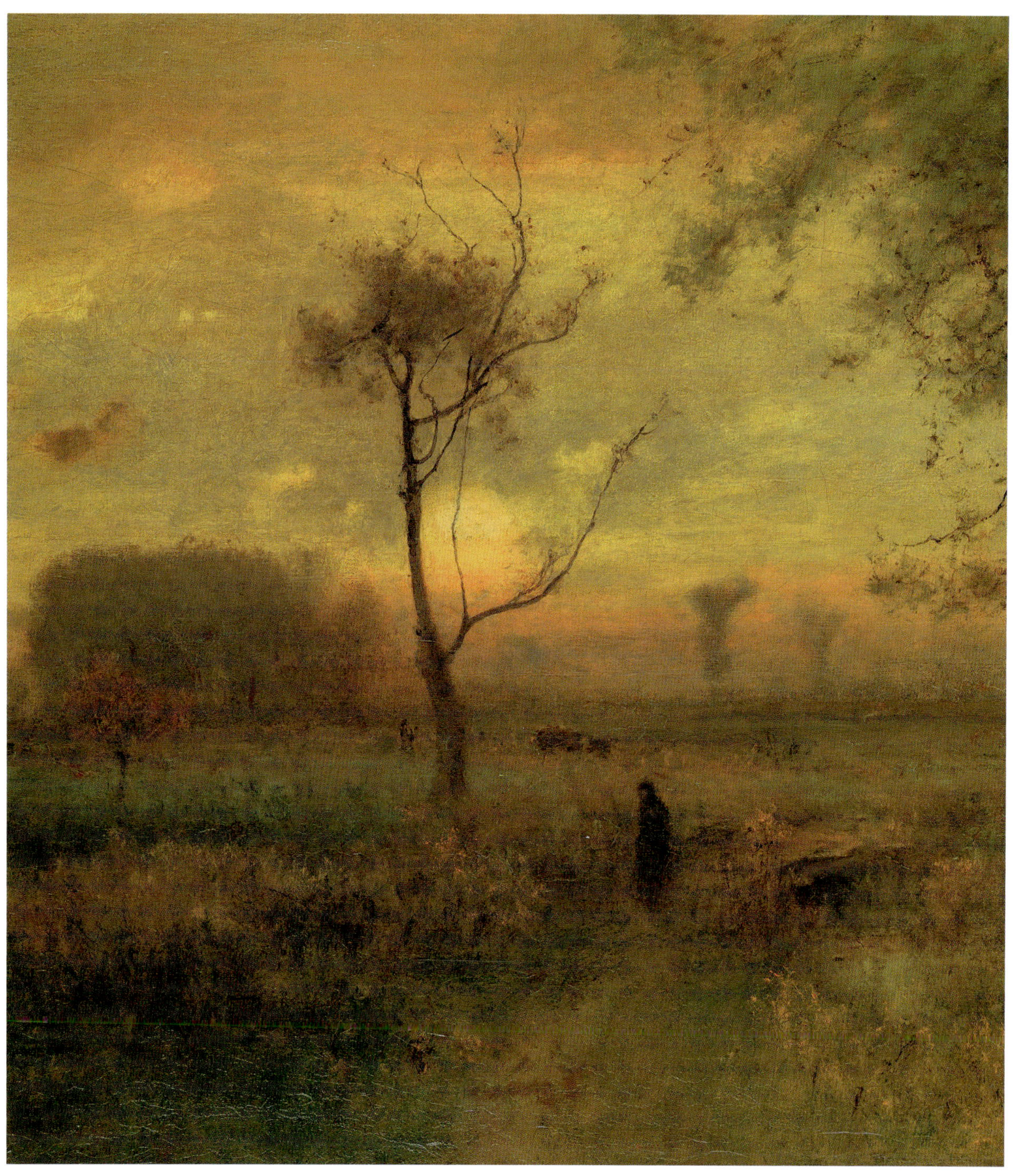

GEORGE INNESS
and the Visionary Landscape

ADRIENNE BAXTER BELL

George Braziller, Publishers
NEW YORK

Support for this publication has been generously provided by Frank and Katherine Martucci,
by Furthermore: a program of the J. M. Kaplan Fund, and by one anonymous donor.

Published on the occasion of the exhibition "George Inness and the Visionary Landscape"
Organized by the National Academy of Design, New York

Published in 2003 by George Braziller, Inc., New York

For information, please address the publisher:
George Braziller, Inc.
90 Broad Street, Suite 2100
New York, NY 10004

Library of Congress Cataloging-in-Publication Data
Bell, Adrienne Baxter.
George Inness and the visionary landscape / Adrienne Baxter Bell.–Second edition.
pages cm
Includes bibliographical references.
ISBN 978-0-8076-0009-2
1. Inness, George, 1825-1897–Exhibitions. 2. Landscapes in art–Exhibitions. I. Inness, George, 1825-1894.
Paintings. Selections. II. National Academy of Design (U.S.) III. San Diego Museum of Art. IV. Title.
ND237.15A4 2015
759.13–dc23
2014042413

Half-title page quotation: George Inness in E., "Mr. Inness on Art-Matters," *The Art Journal* 5 (1879): 377
Frontispiece: George Inness, *Sunrise* (detail), 1887, oil on canvas, 30 x 45¼",
The Metropolitan Museum of Art, New York. Anonymous gift in memory of Emile Thiele, 1954 (54.156).

Designed by Rita Lascaro

First Edition
First Printing, 2003
Second Printing, 2004
Third Printing, 2004
Fourth Printing, 2006
First Printing in paperback, 2006

Second Edition
First Printing, 2015
Second Printing, 2021
Printed and bound in China

Contents

Preface to the Second Edition

OVERVIEW OF THE PUBLICATION

THE CLAIM OF "VISIONARY" in the title of *George Inness and the Visionary Landscape* stems first from my reading of Inness's paintings.[1] In works such as *Sunrise* (1887; Pl. 37) and *Hazy Morning, Montclair* (1893; Pl. 39), objects bear little resemblance to their normative identities; they seem incorporeal. Likewise, spaces seem paradoxically substantial. "Visionary" also speaks to Inness's role as one of our great artist-philosophers, a man as deeply invested in the philosophy of art as in the art of philosophy. As noted here (p. 18), his friends, colleagues, and family members regularly described him as devoted to metaphysical speculations. Referring to Inness, the critic George Sheldon put it succinctly: "Passionate as is his fondness for painting, he is most passionately of all a metaphysician."[2] After decades of exploring the topic in art, in interviews, and in his essays and poems, Inness focused squarely on this theme in his final remarks to the press. He declared, "I am seventy years of age, and the whole study of my life has been to find out what it is that is in myself; what is this thing we call life, and how does it operate."[3] In short, George Inness, a leading American landscape painter of the nineteenth century, grappled throughout his life with the inscrutable question of *how life operates*.

These allusions to metaphysics are simultaneously informative and elusive. Plentiful as they are, they may seem incidental, at face value, to Inness's project. This volume aims to shed light on that relevance. After "Inness's Artistic Self-Education," in which I describe how Inness trained on the landscape paintings of Claude Lorrain, Thomas Cole, Asher B. Durand, and the Barbizon School, I analyze the dramatic shift in his painting style during the mid-1860s, when his work became at once more emblematic and enigmatic. I attribute this shift in part to his growing devotion to the ideas of the Swedish scientist-turned-visionary Emanuel Swedenborg (1688–1772), author of theological treatises on the relationships between the natural and spiritual realms. Inness joined a wide circle of European and American artists and writers who derived inspiration from Swedenborg's work. Swedenborg's description of "spiritual influx" as a continual inflowing of God's divine love and wisdom—of life—from the spiritual into the natural realms aligned with Inness's desire to convey nature's "living motion," not her "fixed material condition," through his art.[4]

Another goal of *George Inness and the Visionary Landscape* is to highlight an extraordinary and near-simultaneous confluence: Inness's creation of "visionary" landscapes and William James's landmark writings on the nature of consciousness, including the historical and philosophical underpinnings of mysticism. Paul Jerome Croce has argued that James sought to retrieve a sense of belief in an age of increasing uncertainty; the same could be said of Inness.[5] In his efforts to provide a more thorough and more accurate understanding of our immensely complex and nuanced range of psychological experiences, including those so ineffable as to defy expression, James called for "the reinstatement of the vague to its proper place in our mental life."[6] Along a parallel track, Inness criticized science for its inability to "conceive of spirit" and for the fact that it "ignores the reality of the unseen."[7] He asserted his own claim to "reinstate the vague" as forcefully as James: "You must suggest to me reality," Inness declared, "you can never show me reality."[8] Confident in the omnipresence of the divine, Inness invented a new language of landscape painting to challenge the growing secularism of the Gilded Age.

INNESS AND EMBODIMENT

Concordances between the philosophies of Inness and James necessarily involved their equally innovative understanding of the role of the body in producing knowledge. I touch on these ideas in the introduction to this volume and in the section entitled "The Rhythm of the Working Hand." As I discussed elsewhere after the publication of this book, Inness joined several Gilded Age American artists, including Albert Pinkham Ryder and Abbott Handerson Thayer, in overturning traditional modes of artistic production. These artists exhibited a new appreciation—hitherto unseen in American art—for the communicative properties of paint and the physical act of painting.[9] They painted more aggressively, more corporeally, than their predecessors, and the art world took notice. Their actions coincided with new identities of the body writ large during the Gilded Age—namely, of the laborer, of the outsider, and, according to James, of the body as an instrument in formulating knowledge and experience. Inness's practice of ruminating before painting, of regularly scraping out and repainting his compositions, of daubing paint with his fingers, and of scoring with his brush handle all signal a break from the traditions of his American predecessors. They call to mind alliances with succeeding generations of artists, for whom the very process of applying paint to canvas sparked radical invention.

The works of Ryder, Thayer, and Inness suggest that all three artists were intuitively aware of and exploited the expressive potential of the body in painting. Psychologists have extensively investigated the central role of touch in human interactions and have shown that it functions as a powerful and often overlooked means of communication—a means of embodied knowledge. The "synoptic forms" in Inness's paintings that I discuss in this volume (see, for example, pages 38–47) represent a type of embodied knowledge in that, as indexes of actions, they convey the illusion of objects in nature—a branch, an animal, a human being—without actually representing them. Given Inness's heightened emotional state when painting, and given the depth and complexity of his operations as a painter, further research into Inness's work may involve neuroaesthetics, which foregrounds physiological and neurological activity in determining aesthetic judgment. As David Freedberg has shown, we experience "embodied engagement" with art when we see it; when we see the walls of a sculpture by Richard Serra, for example, "In our bones we feel a sense of scale and weight and a pressure to move around or within them. The sculptures command attention because they involve our bodies." Such reactions transcend the physicality of sculpture and extend into the realm of pictorial expression. Here, Freedberg points specifically to "the beholder's corporeal sense of the artisan's movement behind the mark, indeed the action itself, the creative work in other words, behind the mark." Taking into account the wealth of scientific research in this field in recent years, he adds, "We are now in a position to plot the cortical motoric responses to the movements of the hand implied by [Chinese] calligraphy."[10] Transposing this analysis only slightly from Chinese calligraphy to Inness's brushwork, we may ask, for example, to what extent did kinesthetic communication inform Inness's artistic agenda? To what extent do we engage now with his paintings because they display traces of the artist's vascular efforts and because, when we see these traces, we are neurologically inclined to rehearse the artist's actions?

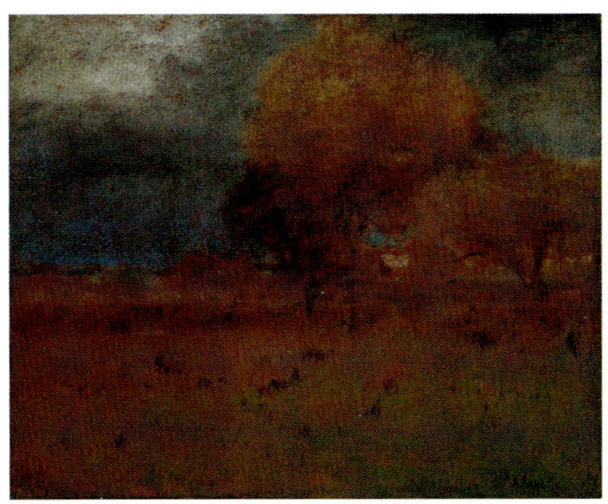

George Inness, *Autumn in Montclair,* c. 1894, oil on canvas, 29 x 35⅞", Sterling and Francine Clark Art Institute, Williamstown, Massachusetts. Gift of Frank and Katherine Martucci, 2013.1.8. Image © Sterling and Francine Clark Art Institute, Williamstown, Massachusetts (photo by Michael Agee).

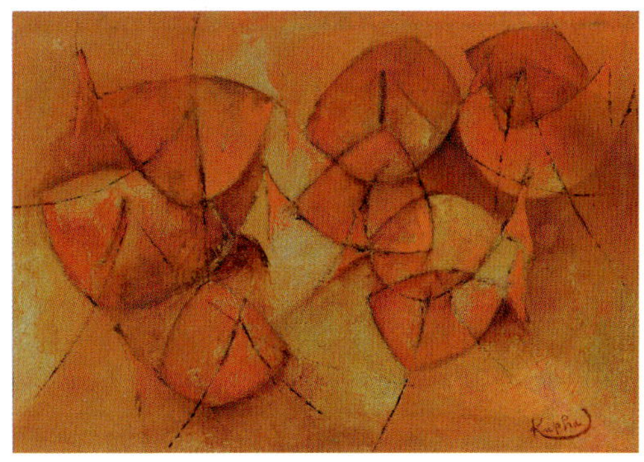

František Kupka (1871–1957), *Untitled,* ca. 1910–13, oil on canvas, 15½ x 22⅜", Joslyn Art Museum, Omaha, Nebraska, Gift of Steve and Susie Kupka, 2004.16.

INNESS AND COLOR THEORY

While it will always be valuable to consider Inness's work within its American historical and art historical contexts, and within the context of metaphysics, we find innumerable avenues for further research beyond the Hudson River School and Tonalism. His treatment of color, for example, invites comparison to the work of twentieth-century European artists. The belief that colors have meanings beyond their normative identities—spiritual meanings, for example—anchors the work of the Fauves, the Blue Rider and Bauhaus groups, the Synchromists, and Orphists. For his part, František Kupka translated his visionary experiences into his painting as a transperceptual realm in which, according to Maurice Tuchman, "color is imaginary, space is infinite, and everything appears to be in a state of constant flux," a statement that evokes the Swedenborgian principle of spiritual influx.[11] As with Wassily Kandinsky, Kupka studied Theosophy and developed ideas on the intimate relationship between music and painting. Kandinsky is viewed, by Michael T. H. Sadler, as "a prophet of an art of spiritual harmony."[12] The word "prophet" is not fortuitous; as Donald Kuspit has reminded us, Kandinsky came to the idea of the spiritual in art—to the realization that "the sensations of color on the palette" could be "spiritual experiences"—through his memories of walking through a Russian Orthodox church. In these spaces, Kuspit asserts, "color and feeling were inextricable: sense experience was spiritual experience and spiritual experience took sensuous form. That is, the external, visible phenomenon of color seemed to be a spontaneous manifestation of the internal, invisible phenomenon of feeling."[13]

To be sure, the dynamism of Kandinsky's and Kupka's paintings is compelling—so much so that it can overwhelm comparisons to other works of art. Still, we are doing an injustice to the very powerful history of the spiritual in American art when we fail to analyze—when we fail even to recognize—the ideas of its leading spokesmen, one of whom was Inness. The strikingly pervasive orange-red tonalities of Inness's *Autumn in Montclair* (c. 1894), for example, do more than identify subject matter. As Michael Quick has shown, Inness gave the work a "bath" of a single color to create the sense of "unity" that the artist long identified as "an essential quality of the best art."[14] This treatment might initially call to mind Tonalism, a branch of the Aesthetic movement exemplified by the works of James Abbott McNeill Whistler. However, in this case, the "bath" of color foretells a spiritual component.[15] As Inness studied color theory through a Swedenborgian lens, he interpreted orange as "the color of the most delicious fruits, the color of the pure, celestial flame that warms as it illumines."[16] Therefore, the pervasive orange-red throughout *Autumn in Montclair* corresponds not only to autumnal colors and physical heat from the sun but also to heavenly warmth from the divine. In *Untitled* (c. 1910–13), Kupka used a technique akin to Inness's "bath" of color with an equally spiritual goal in mind. "Atmosphere in a painting is achieved through bathing the canvas in a single scale of colors," he declared. "Thus one achieves an *état d'âme* (state of being) exteriorized in luminous form."[17] Although Inness never entirely abandoned the scaffolding of mimesis on which he built his artistic education, toward the end of his life, and committed as he was to both the spiritual in art and the spiritual identity of colors, he anticipated two key ideas of European modernism.

While Inness has received attention in books and exhibitions since 2003, much lies ahead in Inness studies. He remains a touchstone for artists and writers engaged with the future of landscape representation. Those who pursue his devotion to the spiritual in nature find as deep a resource as those who press the issues of land use and intersections between art and ecology.[18] An extraordinary and lasting characteristic of Inness's work is that it cultivates such inquiry and, at the same time, retains its inscrutable capacity to astonish and to inspire.

—A.B.B., March 2015

Endnotes

1. For a more extensive treatment of all of the subjects discussed in *George Inness and the Visionary Landscape,* see Adrienne Baxter Bell, "George Inness: Painting Philosophy," Ph.D. diss., Columbia University, 2005. See also Adrienne Baxter Bell, ed., *George Inness: Writings and Reflections on Art and Philosophy* (New York: George Braziller, 2006) (hereafter: Bell 2006).
2. G. W. Sheldon, "George Inness," *Harper's Weekly Magazine* 26:1322 (22 April 1882): 246; reprinted in Bell 2006, p. 183.
3. Inness quoted in "His Art His Religion," *New York Herald* (12 August 1894): 9; reprinted in Bell 2006, p. 91.
4. In *George Inness and the Science of Landscape* (Chicago: University of Chicago Press, 2005), Rachael Ziady DeLue takes a kindred approach to Inness's work in that she also examines it through the lens of metaphysics. However, she argues that Inness's agenda was shaped by questions concerning visual function and that it represents an investigation of the larger problems of perception. Ultimately, for DeLue, Inness's goal was the "construction of a model of spiritual sight, the means by which to discern and then see with God" (p. 3).
5. Paul Jerome Croce, *Science and Religion in the Era of William James: Eclipse of Certainty, 1820–1880* (Chapel Hill and London: The University of North Carolina Press, 1995).
6. William James, "On Some Omissions of Introspective Psychology," *Mind: A Quarterly Review of Psychology and Philosophy* 9:33 (January 1884): 16; reprinted in William James, *The Principles of Psychology* (1890; reprint Cambridge, Mass.: Harvard University Press, 1950), vol. 1, p. 254.
7. Inness quoted in E., "Mr. Inness on Art-Matters," p. 377; reprinted in Bell 2006, p. 79.
8. Ibid.
9. Adrienne Baxter Bell, "Body-Nature-Paint: Embodying Experience in Gilded Age American Landscape Painting," *The Cultured Canvas: New Perspectives on American Landscape Painting* (Durham, NH: University of New Hampshire Press, 2011), pp. 241–85. Recent studies of Inness's painting techniques include Judy Dion, "A Technical Comparison of Two Paintings from Inness's First Italian Trip," *Inness and Italy* (Philadelphia Museum of Art, 2011), pp. 45–60; Lance Mayer and Gay Myers, "George Inness: Glazing, Alternation, and Intuition," *American Painters on Technique, 1860-1945* (Los Angeles, CA: Getty Publications, 2013), pp. 131–55.
10. David Freedberg, "Movement, Embodiment, Emotion," in *Histoire de l'art et anthropologie* (Paris: INHA / Musée du Quai Branly, 2009); URL: http://actesbranly.revues.org/330.
11. Maurice Tuchman, "Hidden Meanings in Abstract Art," *The Spiritual in Art: Abstract Paintings 1890–1985* (New York: Abbeville Press Publishers, in association with the Los Angeles County Museum of Art, 1986), p. 35.
12. Michael T. H. Sadler, "Introduction" to Wassily Kandinsky, *Concerning the Spiritual in Art* (original English translation 1914; reprint New York: Dover Publications, 1977), p. xx.
13. Donald Kuspit, "Reconsidering the Spiritual in Art," *Blackbird: An Online Journal of Literature and the Arts* 2:1 (Spring 2003). URL: http://www.blackbird.vcu.edu/v2n1/gallery/kuspit_d/reconsidering.htm.
14. Michael Quick, *George Inness: A Catalogue Raisonné* (New Brunswick, NJ: Rutgers University Press, 2007), vol. 2, p. 424.
15. The exhibition "Like Breath on Glass: Whistler, Inness, and the Art of Painting Softly" provisionally

returned Inness to the aesthetic arena of Tonalism, though the essays in the exhibition's catalogue (Williamstown, MA: Sterling and Francine Clark Art Institute, 2008) provided a more nuanced view of the affiliation. For example, Leo Mazow made it clear that Inness was "no Whistlerian formalist"; instead, he emphasized Inness's ties to cultural history (p. 54). Another important exhibition catalogue on Inness is Maureen Johnson Hickey, Cornelia Brooke Gilder, and Sarah Lees, *A Walk in the Country: Inness and the Berkshires* (Williamstown, MA: Sterling and Francine Clark Art Institute, 2005).

16. George Inness, "Colors and their Correspondences," *New Jerusalem Messenger* 13:20 (13 November 1867): 79; Bell 2006, p. 113.
17. Quoted on the website for Kupka's *The Yellow Scale*, ca. 1907, Museum of Fine Arts, Houston. URL: http://www.mfah.org/art/detail/yellow-scale. Christian Carey's selection of Inness's *Sunset* (1892; Montclair Art Museum) as inspiration for his chamber music piece "Innesscapes" (2008) calls to mind Kandinsky's description of the intimate bonds between music and color: "Colour is the keyboard, the eyes are the hammers, the soul is the piano with many strings. The artist is the hand which plays, touching one key or another, to cause vibrations in the soul." See Kandinsky, p. 25.
18. Connections between nineteenth-century and contemporary landscape representations, including Inness's work, were discussed at the session "Still on Terra Firma? The American Landscape in Contemporary Art," chaired by the author and sponsored by the Association of Historians of American Art (AHAA), College Art Association Conference, Chicago, 14 February 2014. I thank Douglas Giebel, Regan Golden, Maggie Puckett, and Emily Eliza Scott for their contributions to this lively and informative panel discussion.

Acknowledgments

In preparing the book and exhibition bearing the title *George Inness and the Visionary Landscape*, I have benefited from the generosity of numerous friends and colleagues. I am grateful to them all for their advice, assistance, and support.

In the early stages of the exhibition, I received enthusiastic reactions to its intentions from several scholars. For their invaluable encouragement, I offer my thanks again to Nicolai Cikovsky, Jr., Senior Curator Emeritus of American and British Painting, National Gallery of Art; Paul Jerome Croce, Professor and Chair of American Studies, Stetson University; David B. Dearinger, Chief Curator, National Academy of Design; Richard Murray, Senior Curator, Smithsonian American Art Museum; Barbara Novak, Altschul Professor of Art History Emerita, Barnard College and Columbia University; Sally M. Promey, Professor of American Art, University of Maryland; David Rosand, Meyer Schapiro Professor of Art History, Columbia University; and Philip Yenawine, Co-Director, Visual Understanding in Education. I also thank Dr. Cikovsky for his prescient work on Inness and for his astute guidance on matters of Inness scholarship and connoisseurship.

My many thanks go to Annette Blaugrund, Director of the National Academy of Design, for graciously guiding me through every stage of my curatorial tenure. It has been a pleasure to work with her and with the entire staff of the Academy. I am grateful to the Academy's exhibition committee for endorsing the initial idea of an exhibition of Inness's work. I reiterate Dr. Blaugrund's thanks to all of the donors who helped to fund the project and to the public collections and private collectors who generously lent their paintings. My special thanks go to Frank Martucci for his unwavering support, and to Frederick D. Hill and Bruce Weber of Berry-Hill Galleries, Inc.; Thomas Colville and Deborah Cressler of Thomas Colville Fine Art; Martha Long and Meredith Long of Meredith Long & Company; Inness Hancock and Ira Spanierman of Spanierman, LLC;

and Robert C. Vose III, Abbot W. Vose, and Siobhan M. Wheeler of Vose Galleries, Inc., for helping to secure loans of paintings in private collections.

Many museum directors, curators, and librarians gave me permission to study Inness's paintings and review curatorial files in their collections; curatorial and research assistants unlocked doors to storage rooms and provided copies of bibliographic and archival materials. For their many kindnesses, I thank Susan Faxton, Addison Gallery of American Art; Judith A. Barter, The Art Institute of Chicago; Diana Larsen and Theodore E. Stebbins, Jr., Fogg Art Museum; Thomas Ford and Jennie Rathbun, Houghton Library, Harvard University; Joel Smith, Frances Lehman Loeb Art Center, Vassar College; Cheryl Adams, The Library of Congress; Kevin J. Avery and H. Barbara Weinberg, The Metropolitan Museum of Art; Mary Birmingham and Gail Stavitsky, Montclair Art Museum; Susanna Sabolcsi, Le Brun Library, Montclair Art Museum; Pamela A. Fosdick, Montclair Historical Society; the staff of the Montclair Public Library; Patrick Murphy, Museum of Fine Arts, Boston; Heidi Applegate and Anne Halpern, National Gallery of Art; and Betsy Anderson, Smithsonian American Art Museum. I am grateful to Col. Merl M. Moore, Jr., for assembling his extraordinary clipping files on American artists, now located at the Smithsonian American Art Museum; to Ross Merrill of the National Gallery of Art for generously answering questions concerning the condition and conservation of Inness's paintings and for providing insight into the artist's painting techniques; and to Michael Quick, author of the forthcoming Inness catalogue raisonné, for his thoughtful advice.

While researching at Bryn Athyn College of the New Church in Bryn Athyn, Pennsylvania, I was liberally assisted by Joyce Bradley, Nicole Hill, and Carroll Odhner at the Swedenborg Library; Bret Bostock, Registrar/Collections Manager, Glencairn Museum; Anne Synnestvedt; and the scholars Robert W. Gladish, Martha Gyllenhaal, and Jane Williams-Hogan. Dr. Williams-Hogan kindly read and offered helpful suggestions on portions of this manuscript concerning Swedenborg. The Reverend Robert E. McCluskey of The New Church (Swedenborgian), New York, provided generous access to the church's archives and library.

A President's Grant and an Associates of American Art Grant at Columbia University, as well as the Sheila W. and Richard J. Schwartz Fellowship at the Smithsonian American Art Museum, provided welcome support for research for my dissertation on Inness, of which this publication is an extension. I thank the funders of these grants and hope they will continue to support graduate work in American art history. The Smithsonian grant provided many valuable opportunities to discuss this project with Fellows in residence during the 2000–2001 academic year and to profit from the sound advice and encouragement of Curators Virginia Mecklenburg and Richard Murray.

I thank all those who helped to bring this book to fruition: Richard G. Gallin, for his sensitive copyediting; Rita Lascaro, for her elegant design; Mary Taveras, for her expert handling of all editorial and production concerns; and especially George Braziller, for his unwavering faith in this project.

I will always be grateful to Caroline Houser, Professor of Art History at Smith College, for encouraging my initial efforts in the field. Finally, my sincere and lasting gratitude goes to Barbara Novak and David Rosand. The superlative models of their scholarship and their unstinting support serve as permanent sources of inspiration.

I dedicate this book to the memories of Dr. and Mrs. James E. Baxter, Justin Baxter, and Jeannie Bell, and especially to my husband, Richard L. Bell.

—A. B. B.

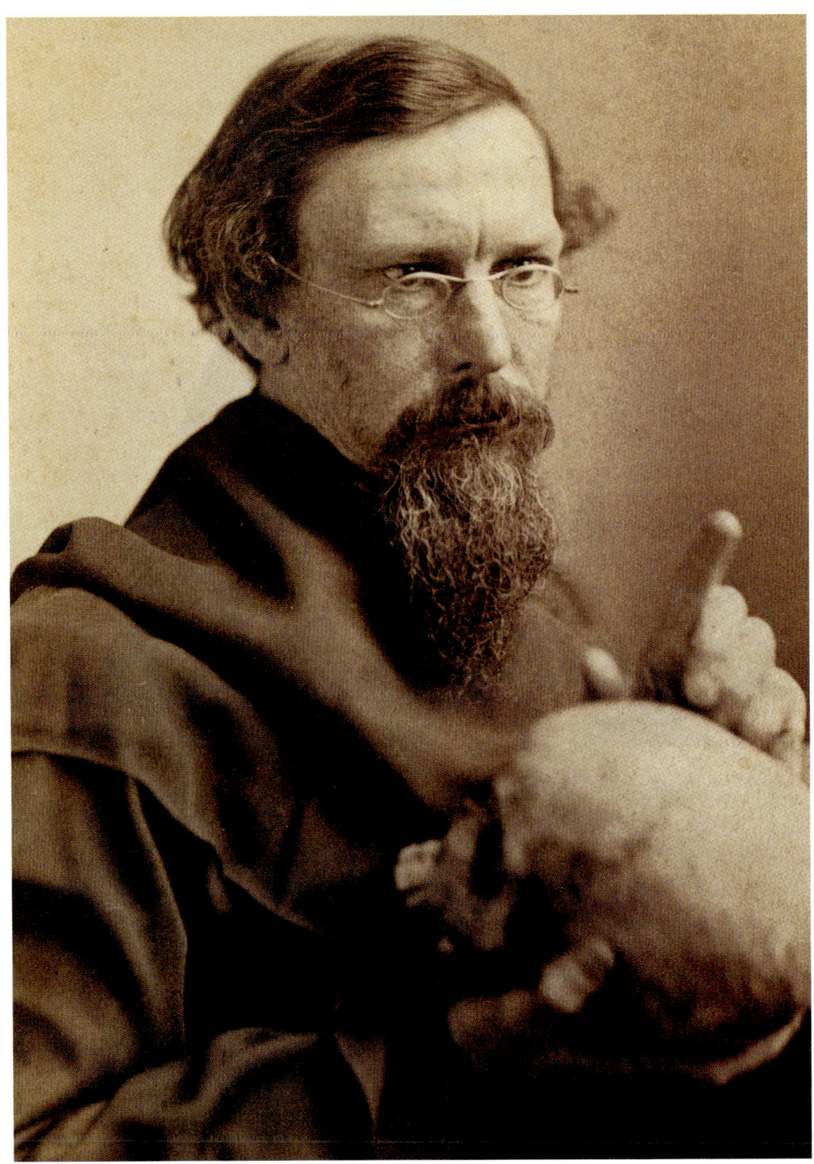

FIG. 1.
Napoleon Sarony, *George Inness,* c. late 1870s, albumen print, 6 x 4⅜", Culver Pictures, New York.

George Inness and the Visionary Landscape

"You must suggest to me reality—you can never show me reality."
—George Inness[1]

Hamlet. ". . . there is something in this more than natural, if philosophy could find it out." —Shakespeare, *Hamlet,* Act II, Scene II

DRAMATIS PERSONA

WE IMAGINE that he hesitated only briefly before donning the sacerdotal wool cloak, cupping the skull in his right hand, pointing toward it with his censorious left index finger, and investing it with his penetrating gaze (fig. 1). A painter attuned to the rituals of academic drawing, George Inness (1825–1894) would have immediately recognized the skull as the enduring memento mori, archetypal symbol of fragile, mortal life. As the photographer's light blazed, Inness's alter ego, his doppelgänger, imprinted on the albumen surface. Perhaps, in this moment, Inness sensed an equally illuminating alliance: his kinship with Hamlet.[2]

Inness's photographic incarnation probably occurred in the late 1870s, possibly between 1876 and 1878, when he rented a painting studio in the Booth Theater building at Twenty-third Street and Sixth Avenue in New York. Inness may even have seen Edwin Booth, owner of the theater, portray Hamlet there between 21 and 26 January 1878.[3] Despite the uncertainties of its conception, the photograph makes one thing clear: Inness bound himself for posterity to this most metaphysical of literary characters.

The choice of identity could not have been arbitrary. Debates on the distinctions between appearance and reality, the seen and the unseen, the natural and spiritual realms, the waking and unconscious states, and on the filaments entwining sleep, dreams, and death continuously preoccupied both Inness and Hamlet. Hamlet's obsessions are renowned; less familiar are those of Inness. In fact, for every hour that Inness spent painting, he seems to have spent another hour harvesting metaphysical problems and ideas from the domains of philosophy, psychology, mathematics, and especially theology. By his own account, he wrote "piles upon piles of manuscripts" on these subjects, although none of them has survived intact.[4] Furthermore, critics, friends, and family members regularly described Inness as "devoted to mystical speculations"[5] and engaged in "metaphysical labors."[6] For the art critic George Sheldon, Inness was, quite simply, a "metaphysician,"[7] admittedly, an unusual appellation for a nineteenth-century American landscape painter. Toward the end of his life, Inness himself acknowledged this passion when he described his investigations of art and theology as kindred pursuits. Asked what he did when he grew "weary of painting," Inness replied,

> Then I take to theology. That is the only thing except art which interests me. In my theory, in fact, they are very closely connected. That is, you may say it is theology, but it has resolved itself gradually into a scientific form and that is the development which has become so very interesting to me.[8]

In this cogent description of the reciprocity between his art and theology, Inness alluded to his invention, during the last quarter of his life (1877–94)—his 'resolution' into "a scientific form"—of a new and ambitious mode of landscape painting. Shaped in large part by Inness's devotion to metaphysical ideas, especially to theological ones, these paintings encourage viewers to think in new ways about themselves and about their relationships to nature and to the divine. Seen as a group, they remain some of the most thought-provoking and inspiring works in the history of art. Their authority and the mystery of their effectiveness remain as powerful today as they did more than a century ago.

THE SACRED WAY

> The purpose of man's first speech was an address to the unknowable.... [His] hand traced the stick through the mud to make a line before he learned how to throw the stick as a javelin. —Barnett Newman[9]

Inness's quest to 'resolve' his "theology" into "a scientific form" lays claim to a place within the long and complex history of similar quests. The first Indian mandalas;

pictures of spirit houses in prehistoric rock engravings; ancient Egyptian wall paintings of Ammon-Ra; images of Mamaragan, the lightning spirit in Aboriginal bark paintings—such representations and abstract forms have long served as vehicles to expand lines of communication between man and the divine, however that force may be defined in each culture and to each person. In our more modern history, and in addition to the countless artistic renderings of scenes from religious texts, we recall Francesco di Giorgio's plan for a church based on the proportions of the human body and Sandro Botticelli's drawings of Beatrice and Dante viewing the dance of the stars in the nine heavens of the Primum Mobile. Despite his ironic statement that Dutch painters "had hardly any imagination or fantasy," Vincent van Gogh extolled Rembrandt's representations of angels: "he knew them; he felt them there," Vincent insisted.[10] Among Inness's contemporaries, Albert Pinkham Ryder revealed, in word and image, perhaps the closest ties to the mystical. Ryder once described himself as "an inch worm" at the end of a leaf or twig, "trying to find something out there beyond the place on which I have a footing."[11] Tethered to the realm of the profane, Ryder, like so many of his artistic predecessors, aspired to the sacred. Inness did as well.

Inness's works, especially his late landscape paintings, are visionary for their prescience. Grounded in the lessons and traditions of their time, they transcend those lessons and offer wholly new pictorial forms for contemplation. They are visionary, too, in that the process of examining their forms and compositional structures tends to alter our ordinary, waking state of consciousness. This process can induce a type of reverie akin to the religious experience. Our psychological shift prompts us to consider metaphysical questions, questions familiar to Hamlet, Inness, and other visionaries: What do we see and what do we know? How is our world constructed? What relationships might it maintain to other, unseen realms?

THE SUBJECTIVE MYSTERY OF NATURE IN AMERICAN LANDSCAPE PAINTING

> Several years before I went to Europe . . . I had begun to see that elabourateness [*sic*] in detail did not gain me meaning. . . . I could not sustain it everywhere and produce the sense of spaces and distances and with them that subjective mystery of nature with which wherever I went I was filled.
>
> —George Inness[12]

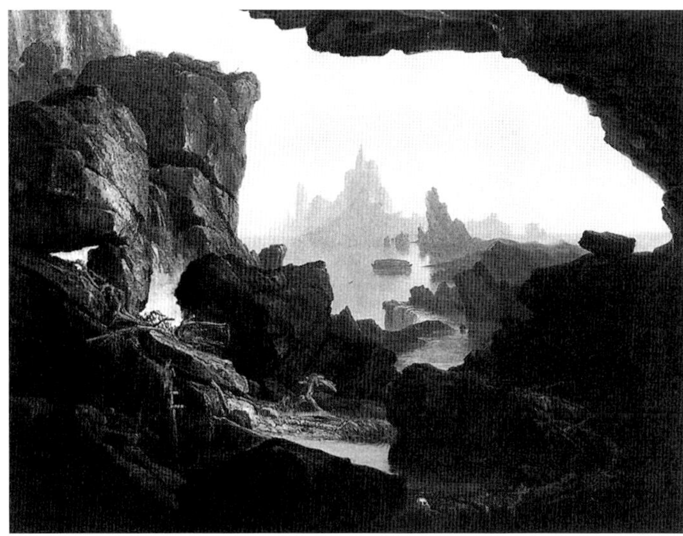

FIG. 2.
Thomas Cole (1801–1848), *Subsiding of the Waters of the Deluge,* 1829, oil on canvas, 36 x 48", Smithsonian American Art Museum, Washington, D.C. Gift of Mrs. Katie Dean in memory of Minnibel and James W. Dean and Museum Purchase through S. I. Collections Acquisitions Program.

Examined in the context of the history of nineteenth-century American landscape painting, Inness's understanding of the reciprocal relationship of art and theology seems entirely conventional. The overarching mission of most of Inness's colleagues—American landscape painters of the mid- to late nineteenth century—was to represent nature as a manifestation and revelation of the divine. God and the American landscape maintained a steady affiliation throughout the century. Writers and artists alike described America's vast, mostly uncharted terrain as the Garden of Eden and the New Jerusalem; her settlement became an "errand into the wilderness."[13] As an essentially religious site, as "God's second book," the primal American landscape "could be read as a sacred story as authentic and compelling as that recorded in Christian Scriptures," or "God's first book."[14] With this identification established, it became the responsibility of artists to "paint the natural landscape in a way that allowed the beholder to discern this divine communion."[15]

American landscape painters championed the idea of the sacred identity of the domestic terrain from a variety of perspectives. Thomas Cole envisioned an oneiric postdiluvian world in *Subsiding of the Waters of the Deluge* (1829; Smithsonian American Art Museum, Washington, D.C.; fig. 2) and, at the opposite end of the eschatological spectrum, illustrative scenes of angels guiding the bark of life in *The Voyage of Life* (1838; National Gallery of Art, Washington, D.C.; 1839–40; Munson-Williams-Proctor Institute, Utica, New York). Anchoring his work in meticulous studies from nature, that is, in the empirical truths of science, Frederic Edwin Church envisioned Creation in the iceberg-strewn waters of Newfoundland and in the lush, volcanic mountains of Central and South America. In *The Mountain of the Holy Cross* (1875; Gene Autry Western Heritage Museum, Los Angeles), Thomas Moran celebrated the seemingly miraculous appearance of a naturally formed cross etched into the northernmost peak of the Sawatch Range. For countless new settlers to this region, this cross represented divine approbation for their right to develop the land, in short, for Manifest Destiny.[16] Although it was painted for commercial purposes (a commission from the Delaware, Lackawanna, and Western Railroad), Inness's *The Lackawanna Valley* (c. 1855; National Gallery of Art, Washington, D.C.; fig. 3) encapsulated the conflicting responses from American artists to industry's growing assault on God's wilderness. Here, a lone figure, reclining on a sloping coulisse, blithely contemplates how the construction of a new railroad station has reduced the surrounding Edenic fields to patches of unsightly tree stumps.[17]

Although the narrative tenor of *The Lackawanna Valley* represents something of an exception for Inness, the allusions to the divine in nature remain ever present in his corpus of landscape paintings. On the whole, Inness filtered his approach to this subject not through storytelling devices but through a wide range of pictorial techniques. In this way, his initial forays into landscape painting, conducted during the mid- to late 1840s and early 1850s, resonate with the pictorial approach of the American followers

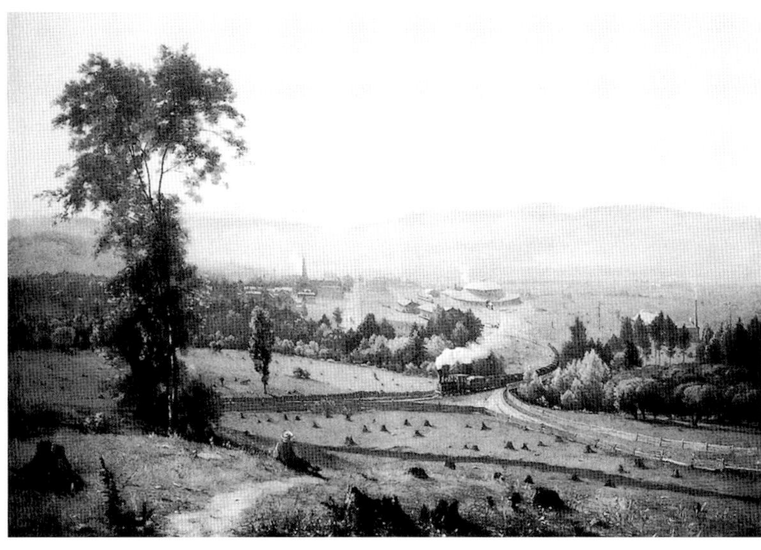

FIG. 3.
The Lackawanna Valley,
c. 1855, oil on canvas,
33⅞ x 50¼",
National Gallery of Art,
Washington, D.C., Gift of
Mrs. Huttleston Rogers.

of John Ruskin, the artists of the New Path, who meticulously represented each detail in nature as though it were an integral reflection of God's handiwork.

Signs of this scrupulous attitude toward representation appear in a delightful pastoral landscape inspired by Inness's first European foray, a trip to Italy in 1851–52. For the basic compositional structure of *A Bit of the Roman Aqueduct* (1852; Plate 1), Inness followed the overall blueprint established by the French landscape painter Claude Lorrain and maintained by the majority of Inness's Hudson River School colleagues. Here, two massive sets of trees frame a centrally located body of water in the foreground and a small mountain range in the distance. Shepherds and cattle represent standard compositional accessories. In keeping with Ruskin's aesthetics, Inness carefully delineated the physiognomies of individual leaves and subtle gradations of light and shade across the fields. One discreetly rebellious detail shows how, even during this early stage in his career, Inness diverged from the habitual practices of his Hudson River School colleagues. He placed relatively little value on the identity of the aqueduct, the eponymous subject of the painting, representing it only in miniature in the middle distance. The tendency to depreciate famous sites—ones whose conspicuous representation would maintain strong commercial value—and to emphasize such emotive qualities as mood and self-expression will become a trademark of Inness's later body of work.

At the end of his first trip to Europe, Inness stopped off briefly in Paris to visit the Salon of 1852. He deepened his knowledge of contemporary French paintings when he visited Paris again in 1853–54. His exposure to the work of the Barbizon School surely confirmed what he later identified as his instinctive sense that "elabourateness [*sic*] in detail did not gain me meaning" and bolstered his desire to capture "the subjective mystery of nature with which wherever I went I was filled." During the late 1850s and 1860s, Inness would have opportunities in America to study, in his words, the "inspirational power" of Jean-Baptiste-Camille Corot and the "pure ideas" expressed in the paintings of Théodore Rousseau and Charles-François Daubigny.[18] The Francophile George Ward Nichols, a friend of Inness's and an early champion of his work, exhibited and sold Barbizon paintings at the Crayon Art Gallery, which he founded and operated in New York.[19]

Many of Inness's landscape paintings of the late 1850s and early 1860s reflect his admiration for the Barbizon aesthetic. In *Hackensack Meadows, Sunset* (1859; Plate 2), Inness used loose brushstrokes to capture subtle plays of light and shade across the fertile, bucolic terrain. He used an even looser brushstroke technique in *Landscape* (1860; Plate 3), which he donated to the National Academy of Design to fulfill a requirement for his election to Member in 1868. Here, tiny dots of white paint at the middle left of this painting create the illusion of houses on the opposite side of the pond. Using far more rapid, calligraphic brushstrokes, ones that will become a hallmark of his late landscapes, Inness nearly ignored representational integrity in *The Huntsman* (1859; Plate 4). He allowed the bodies of the huntsman and his prey to trail off into the forest floor while he pursued the essence of a vibrant, capricious dialectic between light and shade deep in the heart of nature. In *Evening Landscape* (1862; Plate 7), where a warm, lambent sunset invokes ethereal tranquility, Inness appears to have achieved Rousseau's definition of the purpose of art: to represent objects not for themselves but "in order to embody, under a natural appearance, the echoes they have placed in our soul."[20]

Inness's instinctive attraction to the emotionalism and painterly practices of the Barbizon School placed him at odds with the prevailing artistic tendencies of his native land. His loyalty did not lie, as it did for the majority of his American colleagues, with the empirically based object in art. In the body of Inness's work, we do not find figural works on the order of Winslow Homer's architectonic croquet players of the 1860s. There is little of the love of graphic realism that allowed Thomas Eakins to plot, with mathematical precision, the geographical coordinates of his rowers in single sculls during the 1870s. Although it may be argued that Inness probed the dialectic between reality and illusion as effectively as did William Michael Harnett and John Frederick Peto in their trompe l'oeil paintings of the 1880s and 1890s, he felt none of their allegiance to the demands of mimetic representation.[21]

Instead, Inness's paintings shared an affinity with the works of numerous American artists, writers, and philosophers who derived inspiration from visionary beliefs and ideas. (Again, in using the word *visionary*, I am excluding artists who offered pictorial renditions of familiar *religious* scenes in literature, notably scenes from the Bible. I am aligning the efforts of visionary American artists with those artists and artisans worldwide who sought, in Inness's words, to 'resolve' their theology into "a scientific form.")[22] The complex history of this search in American art has yet to be comprehensively described.[23] One such account might include Washington Allston's investigation of Masonic beliefs and his periodic representation of mystical events, such as *Saul and the Witch of Endor* (1820–21; Amherst College, Amherst, Massachusetts).[24] It might incorporate the role of spiritual symbols in Shaker artifacts and Native American pictographs. It could include William Sidney Mount's and Harriet Goodhue Hosmer's commitment to Spiritualism and its role in shaping the character of their art. It would certainly discuss most of Ryder's work—again, not his explicitly religious scenes (*The*

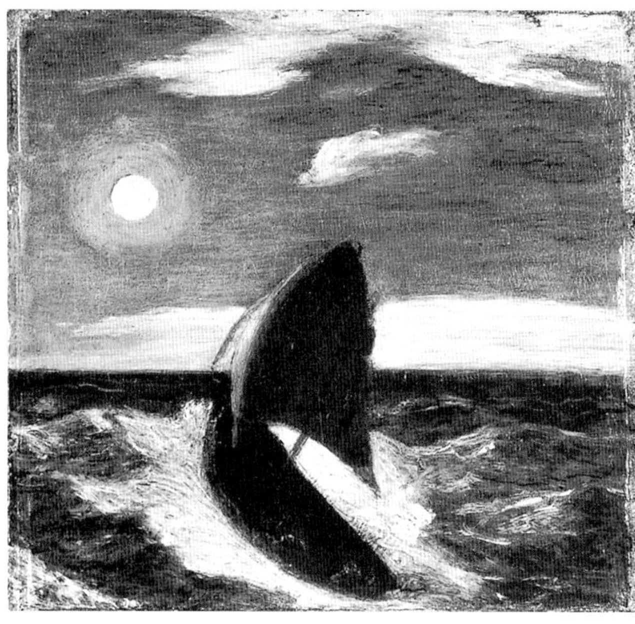

FIG. 4.
Albert Pinkham Ryder (1847–1917), *Toilers of the Sea*, c. 1890s, oil on panel, 11½ x 12", The Metropolitan Museum of Art, New York. George A. Hearn Fund, 15.32. Photo Credit: Image copyright © The Metropolitan Museum of Art. Image source: Art Resource, NY

Resurrection, Christ Appearing to Mary, The Story of the Cross) but, rather, his highly enigmatic—and highly mystical—paintings, such as *The Dead Bird* (c. late 1870s; The Phillips Collection, Washington, D.C.), *The Temple of the Mind* (1887; Albright-Knox Art Gallery, Buffalo, New York), and *Toilers of the Sea* (c. 1890s; The Metropolitan Museum of Art, New York; fig. 4). It would probe the implications of Elihu Vedder's *Memory* (1870; Los Angeles Country Museum of Art) and Ralph Albert Blakelock's dark, nearly cryptic scenes of Indian encampments.[25] It would investigate the dedication, expressed by John Flaxman, William Blake, George Inness, Hiram Powers, William Page, Miner Kellogg, William Keith, Thomas Anshutz, and others to the doctrines of the Swedish scientist-turned-visionary, Emanuel Swedenborg (1688–1772). Inness belonged to this less prominent, but no less influential, visionary tradition in American history.

INNESS AND SWEDENBORG

Although Inness was perhaps the most famous American artist identified as a Swedenborgian, we still do not know precisely when he gained his initial exposure to Swedenborg's writings.[26] A profile on Inness that appeared in the 13 July 1867 issue of

Harper's Weekly, in which he is described as "a disciple of Swedenborg," marks the first public affiliation.[27] In November 1867, Inness published an article on the spiritual significance of colors in the Swedenborgian newspaper the *New Jerusalem Messenger.*[28] The following year, on 4 October 1868, the Reverend John Curtis Ager baptized Inness and his wife, Elizabeth Abigail Hart Inness, as Swedenborgians. Ager was affiliated with the Brooklyn Society of the New Church, based in the Church of the New Jerusalem, then located at Clark Street and Monroe Place in Brooklyn, New York.[29] In his eulogy for Inness, delivered at the National Academy of Design on 23 August 1894, Ager alluded to the artist's initial attraction to Swedenborgian doctrine. He recalled,

> It was my lot to know [Inness] at the somewhat critical point in his life when he was drifting away from every definite belief and had just begun to find in the writings of Swedenborg a solution of [*sic*] his difficulties.

Later in his eulogy, Ager described his sense of what Inness gained from these writings:

> In Swedenborg George Inness found the basis for his theories of art. He found there the true solution for all the problems of expression. To him all nature was symbolic—full of spiritual meaning. He prized nothing in nature that did not stand for something.[30]

Although the *Harper's Weekly* account and Inness's publication of his color analysis in the *New Jerusalem Messenger* have led several scholars to support the notion that Inness became interested in Swedenborgian doctrine during the mid-1860s, it seems likely that he was exposed to and began thinking about Swedenborgian doctrine much earlier.[31] During his first trip to Italy, in 1851–52, Inness rented a studio on the Via Sant'Apollonia in Florence. Working directly below him was the portraitist William Page (fig. 5).[32] Page had been introduced to Swedenborgian doctrine the previous year by the sculptor Hiram Powers.[33] By the time Inness arrived in Florence in April 1851, Page was avidly studying the subject. By September 1851, he could be found reading Swedenborgian texts aloud to the poet James Russell Lowell during Lowell's visit to Florence.[34] Later, in the 1860s and 1870s, Page would lecture on art at the Athenaeum Club and at the National Academy of Design in New York. His topics, such as "The Measure of a Man" and "Equilibrium of Nature and the Palette and 'How To Do It,'" were all infused with basic principles of Swedenborgian doctrine. Joshua C. Taylor, Page's chief biographer, observed that

Page "seems always to have looked upon art as a branch of religion. . . ."[35] Inness may have found either in Page's approach to art and theology or, specifically, in his Swedenborgian theories, a way to address—perhaps even to 'resolve'—philosophical and theological dilemmas through the art of landscape painting. It is worth considering the possibility that Inness's landscapes from even the mid-1850s reflect his engagement with the mystical doctrines to which he would devote himself for the rest of his life.

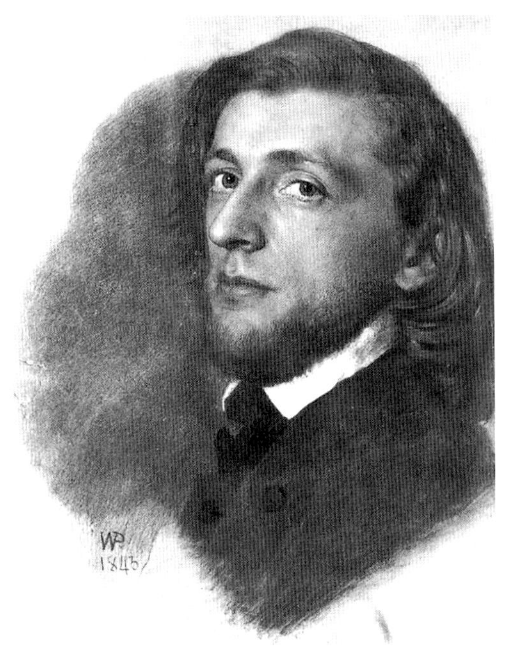

FIG. 5.
William Page (1811–1885), *Self-Portrait*, black and white chalk and graphite on tan wove paper, lined, 18 x 14½", Princeton University Art Museum, Gift of Frank Jewett Mather, Jr.

How, we may ask, might Swedenborgian doctrine have helped to shape the character of Inness's landscape paintings, especially those late, visionary landscape paintings that we have already identified as radically inventive and thought provoking? What might Reverend Ager have meant when he explained that, in Swedenborg's ideas, Inness found "the true solution for all the problems of expression"? First, I would like to suggest that Inness, as an amateur metaphysician—an enthusiastic student of philosophy, science, mathematics, evolutionary history, psychology, spiritualism, numerology, and theology—was probably drawn to Swedenborg's unusual *identity*. At the core of this identity lay a sense of dedication, in equal measure, to the sciences and to the visionary.

One could hardly anticipate, from an examination of Swedenborg's early life, the influential legacy he would leave in the history of visionary experiences.[36] As Ralph Waldo Emerson would later remark in his profile of Swedenborg for *Representative Men* (1849), "This man, who appeared to his contemporaries a visionary, and elixir of moonbeams, no doubt led the most real life of any man then in the world."[37] Born in 1688 into a wealthy Swedish family, Swedenborg, by all accounts, possessed an extremely inquisitive mind. As a young man, he studied with some of the leading scientists of his day, including John Flamsteed (1646–1719) and Edmund Halley (1656–1742); he published the fruits of his research in scholarly texts on geology, chemistry, mining, anatomy, and physiology.[38] He designed prototypes for a submarine and fixed-wing airplane, inventions far ahead of their time. In 1740, as a tribute to his achievements in the sciences, Swedenborg was awarded membership in the Swedish Academy of Sciences, joining Carl von Linné (Carolus Linnaeus), the founder of modern botany.

Swedenborg's commitment to the sciences was severely shaken when, at the age of fifty-seven, he began to experience a series of "vastations," or crises of selfhood.[39] He recorded his visionary experiences in his *Journal of Dreams*.[40] These epiphanic incidents quickly assumed a religious guise. On one such occasion, Swedenborg claimed that the Lord appeared to him; His task, according to Swedenborg, was to "explain to me the spiritual meaning of Scripture."[41] Swedenborg soon abandoned his scientific work and dedicated the rest of his life—some twenty-seven years—to his revelatory spiritual experiences, Bible study, and extensive writing on theological and metaphysical subjects.

The authenticity of all visionary experiences, including Swedenborg's, will continue to be debated. Some people will accept them unconditionally; others will dismiss them outright; still others will remain open-minded. Given the evidence of Inness's engagement with this subject, we focus on Swedenborg's ideas for the ways in which they help to clarify Inness's complex, provocative theories on art and, perhaps, for how they help to unravel those especially enigmatic facets of his paintings, notably his late landscapes. Later, I will suggest resonances between Swedenborg's ideas, Inness's paintings, and William James's groundbreaking and highly influential theories on consciousness and the religious experience.[42] A son of the leading antiecclesiastical Swedenborgian philosopher Henry James, Sr. (1811–1882), the psychologist-philosopher William James (1842–1910) published his theories during the last quarter of the nineteenth century, that is, concurrently with the production of Inness's late landscape paintings. James's insights into the human mind illuminate the transformative effects on viewers of Inness's later work.[43]

Given Swedenborg's fundamental commitment to the sciences, it is not surprising that he would present his findings on spiritual matters within highly methodical contexts. The systematic nature of Swedenborg's worldview is reflected in the doctrine of correspondence, which undergirds much of his writing. It is clear, from Inness's article on "Colors and Their Correspondences," that the artist studied this principle and its various manifestations. Indeed, the doctrine of correspondence constitutes a primary field of study for all philosophically minded Swedenborgians.

The principle of correspondence is based on Swedenborg's belief that there is a spiritual world lying beyond the realm of bodily senses but within a realm of the most substantial being and reality. This world is not above the natural world in space but is an *interior* world, lying within the realm of the natural, "as the soul in man pervades his bodily organs."[44] According to Swedenborg, that which is interior, or spiritual, is more real—and precedes—that which is exterior, or natural. Man is not formed in body and then *imbued* with spirit; on the contrary, the body is the evolution of the spirit, just as an architect's building is the physical manifestation of an idea that first appeared in his mind (his own spiritual realm) and then descended to the exterior world. For Swedenborg, the relationship between the interior and the exterior is, therefore, correspondential, in that every thing and every quality from the natural world first possesses a spiritual identity, a *correspondence* at the level of the soul.[45]

In addition to Inness's engagement with the principle of the correspondential (spiritual) identity of colors, there is evidence, too, that he devoted much time and attention to the spiritual significance, or "science," of numbers. George Sheldon informs us that,

> For years, [Inness] studied the science of numbers,—into which Swedenborg also made many incursions,—and in several of his manuscripts he demonstrated that the number one represents the infinite; the number two, conjunction; the number three, potency; the number four, substance; the number five, germination; the number six, material condition; and so on. And wherever these numbers occurred in the Bible, he was ready, in conversation or with his pen, to prove their symbolical significance.

"So fond was [Inness] of these speculations," Sheldon added, "that, had he been rich, he said, he would have pursued them to the exclusion of painting."[46]

Whether or not Inness's explanations of the spiritual meaning of colors exerted an influence on his choice of colors for his landscape paintings, and whether or not his interest in the spiritual significance of numbers played a role in the invention of his visionary late landscape paintings remain topics for more extended analyses of Inness's work. I mention them here to allude to the depth of Inness's engagement with Swedenborgian ideas. For now, I would like to suggest that a feature of Swedenborgian doctrine that is related to correspondence theory may have helped Inness, during the

1860s, to formulate one of his most inventive—indeed, most visionary—concepts of pictorial space. That feature is the principle of spiritual influx.

SPIRITUAL INFLUX

Swedenborg defined the mysterious process of spiritual influx as the continual inflowing of God's divine love and wisdom—of life—from Him through the spiritual world, the "world of causes," into nature, the "world of effects." According to Swedenborg, all natural objects are intrinsically inanimate until imbued with life through the influx of spirit. Swedenborg described the corresponding process that occurs in the natural world when light nourishes all living organisms.[47] Moreover, just as natural light provides human beings with physical sight, spiritual light, in the form of love and wisdom, provides their minds with divine insight.[48] Walt Whitman evoked the enlightening character of influx when offering one of his many self-portraits in *Leaves of Grass*. (Whitman also refers to *efflux,* a Swedenborgian term that characterizes acts of kindness that a person performs in gratitude for spiritual *influx*.) Whitman wrote of himself,

> Howler and scooper of storms, capricious and dainty sea,
> I am integral with you, I too am of one phase and of all phases.
>
> Partaker of influx and efflux I, extoller of hate and conciliation,
> Extoller of amies and those that sleep in each others' arms . . .[49]

Whitman, who once wrote that Swedenborg "will probably make the deepest and broadest mark upon the religions of future ages here, of any man that ever walked the earth,"[50] envisioned himself as a metaphysical vessel for divine influx. For Inness, the artist's calling was to reflect the omnipresence of divine influx in nature.

Swedenborg described the highly mystical process by which divine influx enlivened nature and invisibly embodied nature's continuously changing state. Inness alluded to this concept in his own definition of the purpose of art. "The true end of Art," according to Inness, "is not to imitate a fixed material condition, but to represent a living motion." He added, "The intelligence to be conveyed by it is not of an outer fact, but of an inner life."[51] In other words, Inness was not especially engaged by the challenge of capturing, through his art, the fleeting, physical appearances of scenes in nature, of representing nature according to information derived through physical sight. He attempted, instead, to express something far more difficult to discern: a sense of nature's "inner life," a sense of those invisible forces—those divine forces of influx—that generated nature's "living motion."

Inness's visionary quest may have helped to determine the idiosyncratic character of forms, spaces, and light in such middle-period paintings as *Christmas Eve (Winter Moonlight)* (1866; Plate 9) and *Winter, Close of Day (A Winter Sky)* (1866; Plate 10). It may not be coincidental that Inness painted both works during a particularly active period of Swedenborgian research. *Christmas Eve* remains one of his most haunting landscapes. A modest, somewhat fragile painting, it resonates with the mystical character of Swedenborgian influx. A lone figure, seen only from the back in silhouette, walks down a snowy path in a frozen, roughly hewn terrain. The full moon pierces an irregular, somewhat ovoid patch of blue in the cloud-strewn sky. A dark bank of trees, also represented in silhouette, blocks our wandering gaze; a gaunt, leafless tree in the middle distance embodies the pervasive spectral aura of the scene. Here, nature seems suspended in time and space. Only Inness's flickering brushstrokes in the foreground, his depiction of snow scattered on the ground, convey light's chaotic activities. Yet light, paradoxically, fails to accommodate itself to the illusion of the scene; Inness's strokes of yellowish-white paint seem to rest, somewhat awkwardly, on the surface of the canvas. With these strokes of paint, Inness telegraphs *the force* of light's activity without actually representing its contouring effects in nature.

For *Christmas Eve,* Inness left the practice of representing the "outer facts" of nature to his New Path and Impressionist contemporaries. In the equally haunting scene entitled *Winter, Close of Day,* Inness again alludes to *the force* of nature's vitality without ever conveying it through the trope of naturalism. Absent is the sense of naturalistic clarity that we would expect to see from Inness's Hudson River School colleagues. Absent, too, is the sense of naturalism gained by capturing the transitory effects of light through a rich variety of brushstrokes in a multitude of optically exacting colors. Instead, Inness kept his forms limited in color and clarity; in so doing, he challenges our sense of spatial location. The setting and details of his scene allude to the familiar while remaining wholly ambiguous. Even the flock of migrating birds seems frozen in uncertainty in the incandescent, alizarin yellow sky. By dislocating the familiar from its home in naturalism, Inness isolated its essentiality. He captured, from out of the whirlwind of experiences and sensations received in such snowy scenes, the most emblematic, most representative qualities—the strength of the feelings that constituted the essence of his personal experiences, in short, of his own "inner life."

Inness extended these visionary ideas into several of his most striking late landscape paintings. *Sunset at Montclair* (1892; Plate 12) remains one of his finest and most engaging works, a painting that commands and deserves extended contemplation. Here, spaces seem even more uncertain than those of *Christmas Eve* and *Winter, Close of Day*. Inness's light permeates forms without illuminating them, without clarifying their identities. We are offered only suggestions: a sky infused with golden sunlight; an anonymous terrain; a house with a smoking chimney at the far left; two or, possibly, three figures in red beside it; a leafy tree in the distance and, somewhat paradoxically, two additional trees almost entirely bared of leaves and branches in the foreground; the suggestion of a fourth tree at the far right; and, finally, a second house enveloped in vegetation to its immediate left. These fragmentary, elusive details establish the scene's lone spatial and narrative coordinates. Inness seems to challenge even their authority by obviating the foreground and distance at the far right edge of the scene, which he has unified in a single field of speckled green and brown paint. Complementing this heightened aura of suggestiveness are Inness's activated brushstrokes, notably those in the foreground. Again, although the phylogenic identities of these grasses and flowers will remain unknown, their representation in paint signals Inness's artistic presence. Here, again, the "living motion" of nature and the "inner life" of the artist function on parallel tracks and serve as the painting's authentic subjects.

In Inness's worldview, divine influx fueled not only the "living motion" of nature but also artistic inspiration. Inness alluded to this identity when he explained, "The greatness of art is not in the display of knowledge, or in material accuracy, but in the distinctness with which it conveys the impressions of a personal vital force, that acts spontaneously, without fear or hesitation."[52] For Swedenborg, each person's "vital force" stems from spiritual influx. Inness's belief in the presence of an invisible "living motion" in nature and a "vital force" in the individual helps to explain why we rarely see narrative, mythological, or even meticulously represented scenes from Inness's hand. It helps to explain the anonymity of such views as *Christmas Eve* and *Winter, Close of Day,* scenes devoid of identifiable landmarks. By contrast, representations of known, familiar scenes—for example, the Rocky Mountains, frequently painted by Inness's Hudson River School colleagues—generally valued the role of *place* more than the *engagement* of the artist with his subject. For Inness, they failed to acknowledge the artist's possession of a "vital force," perhaps even his role as conduit for divine influx—divine inspiration.

> Gradually, year after year, I discovered one truth after another until I had a scientific formula of the subjective of nature. My whole aim for twelve or fifteen years has been to apply this. —George Inness in 1884[53]

> . . . all thinkers are apt to become dogmatic, and every dogma fails because it does not give you the other side. The same is true of all things, art, religion and everything else. You must find a third, as your standpoint of reason. That is how I came to work in the science of geometry, which is the only abstract truth. —George Inness in 1894[54]

Born in Newburgh, New York, Inness lived and worked primarily in New York City until he moved, with his wife and children, to Medfield, Massachusetts, in 1860. From 1864–67, he lived and taught art at the utopian socialist community of Eagleswood, in Perth Amboy, New Jersey. It was during his third trip to Europe—to Italy in 1870–74—that Inness effected another highly influential change in his landscape paintings. He began to structure spaces and forms in nature around geometric shapes and mathematical principles. From this point forward, many of his landscape paintings would exhibit a somewhat heightened—indeed, somewhat unnatural—sense of order and arrangement. This change may also have been motivated by Inness's study of Swedenborgian doctrine, specifically by Swedenborg's Doctrine of Forms, which affiliated spiritual and psychological properties with the most complex of nature's forms.[55]

We discern early evidence of this tendency in *Lake Nemi* (1872; Plate 15), a work that Inness, in a rare expression of self-gratification, deemed "one of my very best."[56] Here, a lone Capuchin monk, staff in hand, perambulates the grounds of a monastery on the border of the lake. Sunlight emerging through a bank of trees in the middle distance silhouettes his form.[57] More striking is the way in which Inness has constructed the entire composition around the geometric shape of the triangle. The foreground contains at least three distinct triangular spaces, one nested within the other. The first is a small triangle at the lower edge, its apex marked by a patch of white at the top of the monk's path. The second comprises this triangle but extends, by means of the patch of sunlit grass at the right of the monk, to the right edge of the composition. The third contains both of these smaller triangles but extends their hypotenuse to the edge

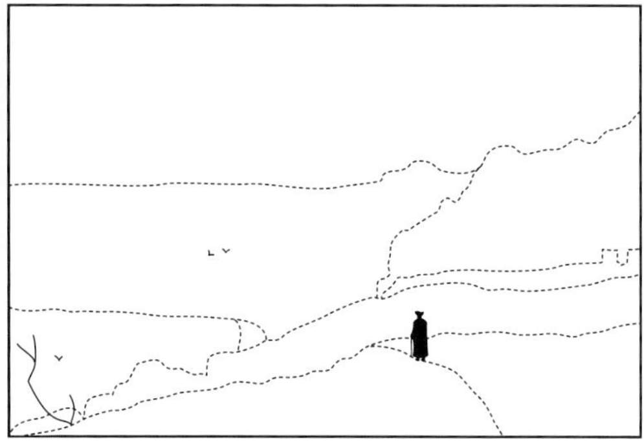

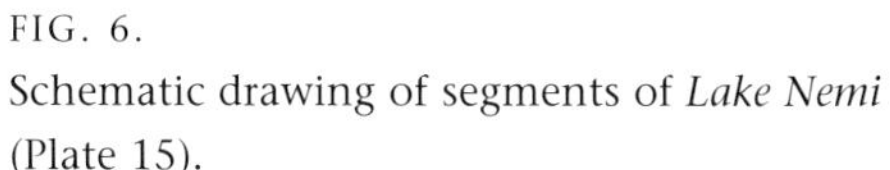

FIG. 6.
Schematic drawing of segments of *Lake Nemi* (Plate 15).

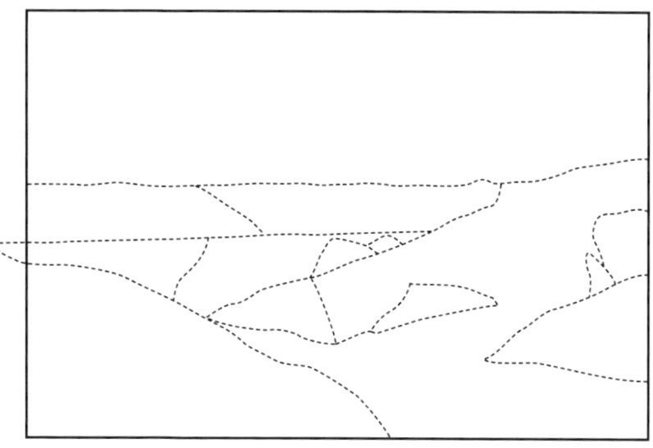

FIG. 7.
Schematic drawing of segments of *Castel Gandolfo* (Plate 17).

of the hill, the base of the wall demarcating the boundary of the monastery's grounds. There is, also, the triangular shape of the bank of backlit trees behind the wall and the triangular form of the lake itself. Still other triangular segments of form and space may be identified (fig. 6).

Inness extends his investigation of the evocative power of compositional order in *The Monk* (1873; Plate 16), one of his most haunting works and among the finest paintings of the nineteenth century. The setting for this extraordinary landscape is thought to be a particularly secluded corner of the grounds of the Villa Barberini, near Castel Gandolfo, a summer residence of the pope located some fifteen miles south of Rome.[58] As in *Lake Nemi,* Inness pictures a solitary, cowled monk, a staff in his hand, strolling the grounds of an enclosed garden. He is dwarfed, first, by a tall stone wall behind him and again by a bank of extremely tall, slender Italian pines in the middle distance. Although Italian pines are common features around Rome and the Marches, and although Inness had painted the Villa Barberini on many occasions, only in *The Monk* does he set the dark shapes of the pine arbors so effectively against a glowing yellow-ocher sky. By using unified brushmarks to diminish—nearly to eliminate—details within these arbors, Inness devised these natural forms as abstract patterns of interconnected ensiform shapes. He must have been particularly delighted by the way in which they create, at their upper edge, a lissome, serpentine line of vivid beauty, one made even more dramatic when offset by the strong vertical lines of the tree trunks below. (The silhouetted bank of trees in *Christmas Eve,* of 1866, anticipated the abstract rendering of these tall pine arbors.)

Inness produced a similar physical incarnation, although one without quite the same dramatic impact, in *Stone Pines* (1874; Virginia Museum of Fine Arts), where the central cluster of pine trees creates a line of dark brown that ascends steeply from the lower left to upper right corner of the painting, an abstract form once more set against an incandescent yellow sky.

Inness returned to this setting when painting *Castel Gandolfo* (1876; Plate 17). As in *Lake Nemi,* he envisioned the bucolic setting as a somewhat esoteric system of interlocking geometric shapes. Lake Albano, at the middle left, appears as an inverted triangular-shaped body of water. A partially leafless tree that projects from the left-hand hill subdivides the lake into a smaller triangular form on its left. Meeting at the apex of the lake are two similarly triangular-shaped sections of the foreground coulisse. In the middle distance, filtered sunlight falls along the hill bordering the lake to divide this patch of land into sections of two (modified) mirror-image rhomboids. Again, as in *Lake Nemi*, additional geometric forms may be identified (fig. 7).

These geometric subdivisions of space—of which I have pointed out only a few of the most evident examples—lend a heightened aura of constructed stability, of well-reasoned organization and harmony to Inness's landscapes. To be sure, *Castel Gandolfo* possesses more naturalistic detail than *Lake Nemi*. In the former, Inness clearly intended to elucidate the physical appearance of the leafless tree jutting from the coulisse at the right, the sharp division of light and shade on the Castello at the far right, and the distinct shapes of animals grazing in the landscape. Still, he seems to unify compositional spaces more than he distinguishes characteristics of the physical elements within them. Furthermore, by suffusing large regions of the landscape in shadow, Inness expunges details that might detract from the systematic organization of those regions into a unified whole.

Inness's delight in the suggestive power of geometric forms emerged with even greater force after 1878, when he regularly raised horizon lines to the middle of his landscapes in order to bisect compositional space. In this way, he transformed the traditional proportions of landscape painting from one-third land and two-thirds sky to equal parts of land and sky. Moreover, he often vertically subdivided the section of sky into one-half trees and one-half sky, thereby producing a new ratio of one-quarter sky to three-quarters vegetation. We see initial evidence of this spatial construction in the modest pastoral *Landscape with Cattle* (c. 1877; Plate 18). It emerges, with still greater force, in such brilliant late landscape paintings as *Early Moonrise, Tarpon Springs* (1892; Plate 19) and *Indian Summer* (1894; Plate 33). Inness presented somewhat more discrete expressions of this geometric ordering of space and form in three masterful late paintings: *Summer, Montclair (New Jersey Landscape)* (1891; Plate 24), *October Noon* (1891; Plate 25), and *Hazy Morning, Montclair* (1893; Plate 39).

To underscore this architectonic division of space, Inness often included a tree, devoid of horizontal branches, at or very close to the center of the painting. We see versions of this tree in *Sunset at Montclair* (1892; Plate 12), *The Trout Brook* (1891; Plate 14), in *Summer, Montclair (New Jersey Landscape)* (1891; Plate 24), *Indian Summer* (1894; Plate 33), *Sunset Glow* (1883; Plate 35), *Sunrise* (1887; Plate 37), *Near the Village, October* (1892; Plate 38), and *Hazy Morning, Montclair* (1893; Plate 39). This median tree tends to block our wandering gaze, to stymie our access into the represented recesses of pictorial space. It challenges the long-standing identity of pictorial space as a mirror of observed reality. Although Inness is frequently identified as a Tonalist artist, I would suggest that this geometric organization of compositional space distinguishes his work from that of his Tonalist contemporaries, such as John Francis Murphy and Dwight William Tryon. In their landscapes, enigmatic spaces and forms remain relatively unconstrained by the somewhat occult presence of compositional order.

INNESS AND LUMINISM: AFFINITIES AND DISTINCTIONS

Closer in style and ideology to Inness's work is the refined, pictorial style that came to be known, a century later, as Luminism. A frequent participant in exhibitions and auctions that represented the works of Fitz Hugh Lane, Martin Johnson Heade, John Frederick Kensett, and Sanford R. Gifford, Inness was unquestionably familiar with the works of Luminist artists.[59] Like Inness, Luminists often alluded to the presence of a dominant, controlling force in nature by building their landscapes around regular, nearly mathematical principles and quasi-geometric shapes. What prevented Inness, then, from turning to the works of *these* artists, instead of to Swedenborg, for inspiration in constructing his own landscapes?

To a certain extent, works such as Inness's *Lake Nemi, The Monk,* and *Castel Gandolfo* reflect the artistic ideals of Luminism. Here, Inness engaged the Luminist passion for economical, refined design. His representation of light in *Lake Nemi,* a warm, diffused light that bathes the setting with an incandescent glow, effectively embodies the Luminist aesthetic. It finds its counterpart in the light of Gifford's own luminous representation of

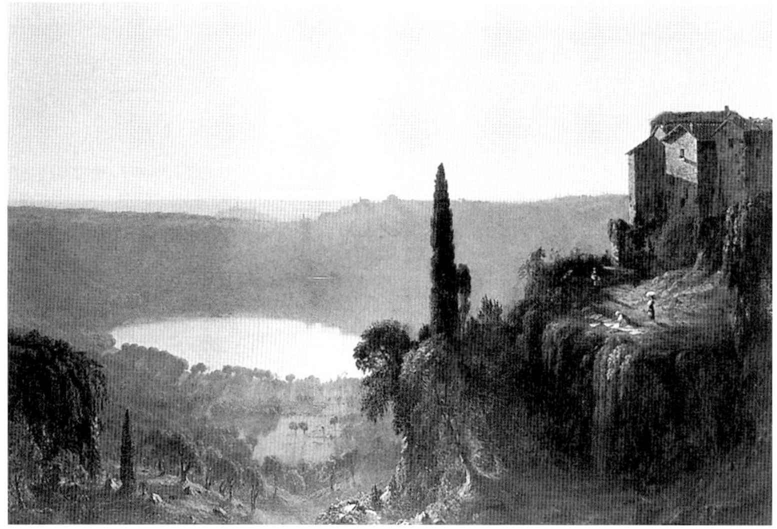

FIG. 8.
Sanford R. Gifford (1823–1880), *Lake Nemi*, 1856–57, oil on canvas, 39⅝ x 60⅜", Toledo Museum of Art, Ohio. Purchased with funds from the Florence Scott Libbey Bequest in Memory of her Father, Maurice A. Scott.

Lake Nemi (1856–57; fig. 8). In both cases, light dissolves and erases naturalistic details in the distant hillsides, leaving only silhouetted, marginally differentiated blocks of terrain.

And yet, notable differences remain. Light in the distance of Gifford's *Lake Nemi* may represent the light of dissolution, but in the foreground it changes to the light of elucidation. Here, light clarifies minute physical details in nature. In the form of stark, orange-yellow beams, light radiates from the sky, infiltrating each crevice and each craggy edge of the hillside. On the landing at the right of the scene, light brings to our attention the forms and actions of three figures. It catches the upper edges of the sleeve and the bundle carried on the head of the woman at the right. It illuminates five sheets of white cloth that the woman at the center carefully arranges on the ground. It highlights her white kerchief and the white sleeve of her blouse. It glances off the right sleeve and the right-hand edge of the red skirt of the third figure standing in the distance. On the edges of the rocky terrain that supports the figures, light filters through individual bushes and branches to illuminate their vascular structure. Light allows us to identify each plant and even to sense the texture of each furrow in the ground, each crumbling brick in the building at the right edge of the scene.

For all the occasions in which Luminist light seems to dissolve the ontological identities of some objects in nature, it elucidates others with equal fervor. The light in the foreground of Gifford's *Lake Nemi* is this light of infiltration, investigation, and elucidation. It is a far more aggressive and revealing light than the light of Inness's

Lake Nemi, which seems content to leave large portions of the landscape hazy and obscure. Even in Kensett's final, most abstracted compositions—in *Eaton's Neck, Long Island* (1872; The Metropolitan Museum of Art, New York), for example—the Luminist artist cannot resist using light to clarify the presence of tiny ripples on the surface of the water. He cannot resist revealing the presence of tiny boats at the edge of the horizon. Steadied by his capacity for self-control, the Luminist confronted the substances of nature with a measuring stick, confident in his ability to divulge their identity as reflections of an authority greater than himself.

The control that the Luminist brushstroke exhibits helps to identify artistic restraint as a leading feature of the Luminist aesthetic. Search as we may, we rarely find a stroke of paint out of place in these compositions. Every detail appears to have been seamlessly and effortlessly integrated into the unified whole. The mystery of the Luminist landscape originates from this sense of compositional control. With little sign of an artistic presence, of a mortal architect originating and engineering the representation, we begin to attribute the Luminist's fixation on order and structure not to the artist's own unique, potentially capricious temperament but rather to the implied presence of a more powerful organizing force operating above and through the artist, operating through and in concert with nature herself. In the project of landscape representation, the Luminist artist becomes something of an impartial conduit through which supernatural forces design and construct their vision. For this reason, Luminism has been aligned with Emersonian Transcendentalism, a philosophy in which communion with divinely created nature resulted in the mystical surrender of the self, an act epitomized by Emerson's own self-identification as a "transparent eyeball" before nature.[60]

Herein lie distinctions between Luminist landscapes and Inness's paintings, even his most geometrically structured works of the early and mid-1870s. For despite all of their constructed elements, Inness's paintings remain, in many areas, enigmatically produced. They are, in short, filled with capricious features. In addition to the near absence of detail in the pine bowers of *The Monk,* we add the inscrutable foregrounds of many of Inness's most ordered compositions. In *Lake Nemi, The Monk, October Noon, The Home of the Heron, The Lone Farm,* and *Hazy Morning, Montclair,* for example, Inness's rapidly executed brushmarks telegraph the presence, without ever representing the identities, of organic forms. More often than not, they appear to rest on the surface of the canvas, wholly unaffiliated to other features of the composition. It may be said that they correspond to divine influx, to its force and to its incarnation as artistic inspiration, rather than serve the exigencies of illusionistic representation. In the end, these brushstrokes deny the Luminist's and the Transcendentalist's submission of the self and, conversely, assert the presence of the artist in the correspondential relationship between nature and the divine.[61]

THE RHYTHM OF THE WORKING HAND

> In all his painting [Inness] was dependent on emotion—the victim of moods. Thus, he saw Niagara many times apparently without considering it as a subject for a picture until suddenly one morning at an inexcusable hour he routed a local painter out of bed, demanding the loan of colors, brushes and canvas—"Quick, Selsted, I must paint."
>
> —George Chambers Calvert[62]

> Aren't we all seeking intensity of thought rather than tranquility of touch?
>
> —Vincent van Gogh[63]

The role of the brushstroke, with all of its theological and metaphysical implications, gained greater influence in Inness's approach to painting after his return, in 1875, from this third trip to Europe. From the late 1870s on, Inness shaped his landscape paintings around its expressive power. He also refined a characteristic feature that I have come to identify as the synoptic form, a pictorial form of *multum in parvo* that conveys the greatest amount of information by means of the fewest marks of the brush.[64]

The motivations for this development were probably not commercial; according to his son, Inness was, by the mid-1870s, receiving a sufficient income through sales of his work through Williams & Everett, his Boston dealers. Furthermore, for the first time in Inness's career, exhibition reviews regularly sounded a laudatory note. It seems, instead, that Inness needed to explore an aspect of his work that he had, in large part, suppressed while painting in Italy.

The pictorial theme through which Inness formulated his exploration of the character and uses of the brushstroke and the power of the synoptic form was the storm scene.[65] Although not all of Inness's paintings of the late 1870s reflect this preoccupation—for example, *The Homestead* (c. 1877; Haggin Museum, Stockton, California) remains one of the artist's most lyrically placid and traditional compositions—most represent convulsive natural phenomena whose unpredictable forces threaten to overwhelm and, ultimately, promise to remake the appearance of an otherwise peaceful setting. The intensified temporal and atmospheric suggestiveness featured in such well-known works as *Kearsarge Village* (1875; Museum of Fine Arts, Boston), *Saco Ford: Conway Meadows* (1876; Plate 28), *A Gray, Lowery Day* (c. 1877; Davis Museum and Cultural Center, Wellesley College, Massachusetts), and *The Coming Storm* (1878; Plate 29), and maintained in *Homeward* (1881; Plate 32) and *The Storm* (1885; Reynolda House, Museum of American Art, Winston-Salem, North Carolina), endows each landscape with an inviting aura of restless agitation, with the promise of transformation. Inness's dynamic brushstrokes ideally suited the tenor of these compositions.

Saco Ford: Conway Meadows (1876; Plate 28) remains an especially impressive outcome of the artist's trip to the White Mountains of New Hampshire during the summer of 1875. Clouds are just beginning to sweep above and through the darkening hills. The few glimpses of narrative—the gesticulating figure in black on the foreground coulisse, small clusters of grazing cattle that seem nearly indistinguishable from bales of hay—are compositionally and symbolically overwhelmed by the character and variety of brushstrokes used to suggest the impact of the impending storm on the landscape. The long streaks of yellow ocher, kelly green, and olive green that compose the open fields capture the prolonged effect of wind coursing through the terrain, while short daubs of olive green and brownish-green from the tips of Inness's bristles mimic the blustery vibrations of wind rustling among masses of fragile leaves. A drop of white paint, daubed and gently smeared, capped by an even smaller daub of yellow and infiltrated by a tiny daub of brown mysteriously conveys the presence of a seated woman, sporting a hat and a scarf, near the figure of the man in black. Here, Inness demonstrates his extraordinary facility with the synoptic form.

(I have based my descriptions of the brushes and colors Inness may have used on the appearance of the brushstrokes on the paintings. Although we cannot know precisely which brushes Inness used in each painting, examples of the types described here remained in Inness's studio at the time of his death. I refer to the palette and brushes in the Montclair Art Museum, Montclair, New Jersey [figs. 9a-c]. The absence of round brushes, which are traditionally used for touching in small areas of detail, corresponds with the absence of refined details in Inness's paintings. On Inness's final palette, colors are both neatly organized, according to the traditional arrangement from darks to lights, and highly smeared, reflecting a great deal of blending and jabbing with brushes.)[66]

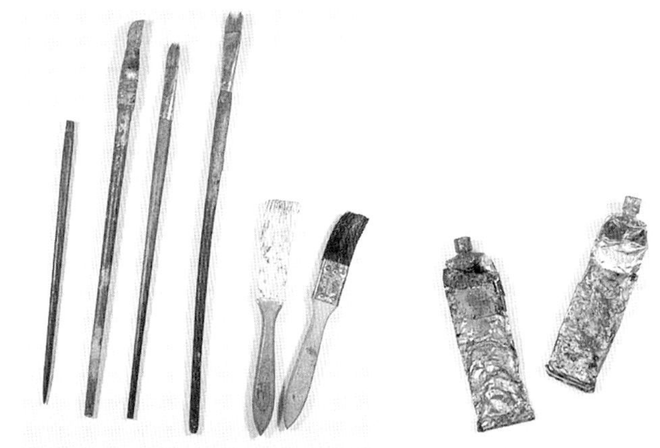

FIGS. 9A–B.
Inness's brushes and paint tubes, Montclair Art Museum, Montclair, New Jersey. Gift of Mrs. F. H. Hooper, 36.209A–C.

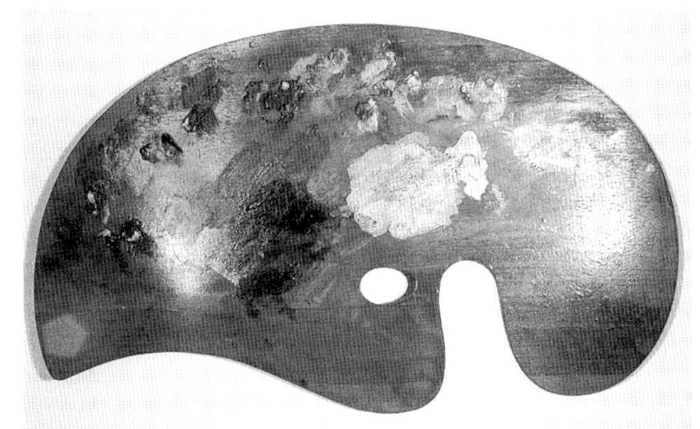

FIG. 9C.
Inness's palette, Montclair Art Museum, Montclair, New Jersey. 88.135.

The Coming Storm (1878; Plate 29) embodies all of the richness and variety of Inness's brushstroke technique and his use of synoptic forms during the transformative period of the late 1870s. Dark gray rain clouds permeating the sky emerge in the final marks of what must have been a long history of repeated, rotating brushstrokes loaded with viscous oil paint. Using a second type of brush, probably a miniature liner brush, Inness briefly interrupted the illusion of rain clouds with four or five flecks of ivory-black, mixed with a few daubs of white, to produce two small black birds trapped in the tumult. Using a fan brush, Inness swirled golden yellow-ocher into the bank of trees, now past their summer prime, that stretch along a wide pasture below the clouds. In creating these trees, Inness reduced the speed and energy of his brushstrokes. He used tempered flecks of color on the trees at the left and whirling strokes for the trees in the middle distance. This subtle distinction not only generates the illusion of space between the two banks of trees, it suggests that wind is coursing more forcefully through the trees in the distance, that the trees to the left have not yet received the full gale force of the wind.

Inness uses a fourth type of brushstroke, perhaps created with the side of a Filbert brush, to simulate the illusion of wind streaming above the fields: striated lines of virtually undiluted lemon-chrome on top of a green-and-brown undercoating. In the lower right foreground, on a small hillside, short daubs, flecks, and swirls of white, orange, brown, green, black, and gray paint telegraph the presence of grasses, rocks, and fallen twigs without representing their characteristic physical features. Here, again, are the synoptic forms on the order of the three-daubed woman from *Saco Ford: Conway Meadows*. Inness suggests identities for these forms through an ontological alignment of fragile brushstrokes with delicate objects in nature. In other words, he conveys the identities of the grasses, rocks, and fallen twigs without fulfilling traditional obligations to reproduce them according to their conventional, mimetic appearance. This alignment of brushstroke with object creates a gap between artistic intention and artistic tradition that the viewer, engaging his or her imagination, instinctively fills.

Furthermore, by means of the judicious placement of key landscape details, Inness structures our primary visual path to reproduce, more or less, the circular motion of vortexical wind formations. He draws our gaze counterclockwise, from the highlighted rocky coulisse in the right foreground, up to the tip of the trembling birch tree, across the streak of grayish-white clouds, and over to the two dark, fragile birds hovering in the rain-soaked sky. He settles it on a tiny, vaguely defined but unmistakable house on the hill at the far left edge of the scenery. The deeply shadowed trees below this house carry us from the horizon line to the ground, where we stop, temporarily, at the shadowy image of a farmer with two cows. After we cross the chasm of nebulous space to the right of this figural grouping and alight on the flecks and dashes of white paint that demarcate the lower left edge of the sloping coulisse, we wind our way up the coulisse, now ready to repeat the visual journey. When we focus our attention on the painting's few narrative details, we see with a kind of circuitous vision that mirrors the swirling motion of the approaching storm, the implied subject of Inness's painting.

In both *Saco Ford: Conway Meadows* and *The Coming Storm,* the range and variety of Inness's brushstrokes, and the uncanny precision with which he uses them, persuasively embody the dynamism and unpredictability of oncoming storms. Here, Inness's brushstrokes serve two causes. They construct narrative information that will generate complex illusions of turbulent scenes in nature. At the same time, they generate the many subtle and distinct moods and sensations associated with those climatic events. Inness persuades his viewers of the legitimacy of his illusion not only through the presence of the narrative forms familiar to storm scenes but also, and still more effectively, by the *technical* means through which he has represented those elements and conveyed those sensations. Indeed, the synoptic nature of some of those elements—the three daubs of paint to construct the figure of the woman in *Saco Ford: Conway Meadows* and the flecks of paint to convey the illusion of rocks and branches in *The Coming Storm*—elevates technical means above the power of narration.

TO "AWAKEN AN EMOTION"

In my earlier discussion of Inness's *Christmas Eve* and *Winter, Close of Day,* I described these two extraordinary middle-period paintings as embodiments of Inness's interpretation of nature's "living motion," rather than the "outer fact" of her exterior appearance. I suggested that Inness obtained an understanding of this "living motion" through repeated observations of nature; he then amalgamated the essence of his observations into a single, representative interpretation. I further suggested that, as a student of Swedenborgian doctrine, Inness may have aligned the idea of the "living motion" with the principle of spiritual influx, the divine source of all life. Finally, he aligned spiritual influx with divine inspiration; this affiliation distinguished his work from that of his Luminist colleagues, who avoided the potentially haphazard effects of the capricious force of inspiration.

Building on these ideas, I would now like to suggest that Inness extended his interpretation of artistic inspiration to the inspiration that he hoped *his viewers* would feel when in contact with his paintings. He expressed this desire in the course of one of his many definitions of the purposes of art. According to Inness,

> A work of art does not appeal to the intellect. It does not appeal to the moral sense. Its aim is not to instruct, not to edify, but to awaken an emotion. That emotion may be one of love, of pity, of veneration, of hate, of pleasure, or of pain; but it must be a single emotion, if the work has unity, as every such work should have, and the true beauty of the work consists in the beauty of the sentiment or emotion which it inspires.[67]

Again, a successful work of art should not originate in didactic, hermeneutic vehicles, such as myths and morality tales. Nor should it "instruct" by adhering too closely to data received through physical sight. Instead, for Inness, art achieves its true purpose when it activates, within the viewer, a single, powerful emotional response, when it "awakens an emotion." Given that all art maintained a theological identity for Inness—that he aspired to 'resolve' theology into the "scientific form" of landscape painting—it is likely that Inness viewed the capacity of art to "awaken an emotion" as akin to a spiritual awakening.

During the late 1880s, Inness explored this theme in depth. He engaged his viewers more effectively than ever by generating complex illusions of forms in nature through an admixture of virtuosic brushstrokes. *The Old Barn* (c. 1888; Plate 30) offers a particularly fine example of this achievement. It is likely that, as Michael Quick has suggested, the setting is Inness's property in Montclair, New Jersey.[68] Inness's familiarity with the scene may have motivated him to paint it with a heightened sense of immediacy. Here, Inness presents every type of brushstroke and method of applying pigment. Bright swirls of green paint build the illusion of wind rustling through a spring lawn. Highlights on the central tree trunk emerge through rapid strokes of light yellow paint. Streaks from dry brushes capture a gentle rustling of arbors. Scratches from the tip of his brush handle reveal contrasting darkness below the swatches of yellow-orange on the barn.

Appealing to our primitive attraction to the material and sensual qualities of paint, Inness left many objects thickly impasted in unadulterated colors: the splash of red on the wheelbarrow pusher's head—a tribute, perhaps, to Inness's admiration for the works of the Barbizon painter Corot—provides a striking complement to the globules of pure white that generate highlights on his shirt. Equally undiluted are the rough patches of bright turquoise between black streaks that together construct the woman's dress. Particularly striking is the wheelbarrow behind the barn. The dozen (or so) strokes that crystallize this complex form bear the hallmarks of the finest examples of Zen calligraphy: the aura of intensity, the balance of control and freedom, and the call to read the negative spaces as meaningful factors. Like the Zen masters, Inness laid bare, in a single form, an entrenched knowledge of the essence of an object. What that object or objects may be, in the case of the splotches of black and white-orange paint on the lawn, or where the bowers end and the barn begins in the upper right corner of the painting, Inness leaves entirely to his viewer's imagination.

A fragment of a conversation with Inness underscores this intention. Reginald Coxe, a friend of the artist's, recorded an exchange between Inness and a man who once asked him about one of his paintings in which there was a barn—a work resembling *The Old Barn*:

> "Mr. Inness, what is that spot there alongside the barn?" the gentleman inquired.
> "What do you think it looks like?" Inness asked.
> "Well, I should say it was a wheelbarrow," the gentleman responded.
> "Good, that's just what I thought it was, too," Inness concluded.[69]

Had the inquisitive gentleman suggested that the "spot there alongside the barn" appeared to be a pile of branches or part of a broken fence, Inness may well have concurred. Underlying this exchange was the pleasure Inness appears to have taken in exchanging roles with the viewer, in this case, the anonymous "gentleman," and in requiring him to determine the meaning of the work for himself. That the "spot" *could be* a wheelbarrow meant that Inness's brushstrokes provided the viewer with just enough information to elicit a *suggestion* about the identity of the form while also remaining vague enough to require the viewer to *bring meaning,* through his imagination, to the brushstrokes. The double-barreled force of "that spot there alongside the barn"—its robust suggestiveness and its capacity to stimulate the interpretive powers of the viewer—served Inness's most deeply felt aspiration: to "awaken an emotion" in his viewers.

A FEW MARVELOUS SWEEPS

Saco Ford: Conway Meadows; The Coming Storm; and *The Old Barn* bear witness to the painting practices that would confer near mythic status on Inness during his lifetime. Put simply, painting for Inness appears to have been, in equal parts, a physical, psychological, and spiritual activity. Infrared and visual examinations, which provide information on the history of paintings and on their final incarnation, suggest that Inness engaged all of his energies in the activity. They suggest, further, that he viewed the act of painting as a process without a fixed, predetermined goal.

First-hand accounts of this process, recorded by Inness's friends and colleagues, corroborate this visual information. While living in Montclair, New Jersey, the town to which Inness moved permanently early in 1885, Inness befriended S. C. G. Watkins, who became the artist's dentist.[70] Watkins frequently observed the artist at work; his recollections provide insight into Inness's perspective on the act—and art—of painting. About Inness, Watkins recalled,

> His enthusiasm knew no bounds. That was wherein he excelled. When he worked, his mind was concentrated on what he was doing. The outside world meant nothing to him. His whole being was in that painting.... His whole being, body and soul, was so wrapped up in the intensity of his work that it could be truly said it was his soul's work, and his canvases were different from others from that fact.[71]

The artist Elliott Daingerfield, a friend of Inness's and an habitual observer of his work, provided a kindred description of the intensity of Inness's working methods. Of Inness, Daingerfield recollected,

> What a delight it was to watch him paint when in one of those impetuous moods which so often possessed him. The colors were almost never mixed;—he had his blue theories, black, umber, and in earlier days bitumen: he even had an orange-chrome phase. With a great mass of color he attacked the canvas, spreading it with incredible swiftness, marking in the great masses with a skill and method all his own, and impossible to imitate; here, there, all over the canvas, rub, rub, dig, scratch, until the very brushes seemed to rebel, spreading their bristles as fiercely as they did in the days of yore along the spine of their porcine possessor.[72]

In another account, we learn of a young painter who invited Inness to his studio to critique his work. As expected, several of the artist's friends were in attendance when Inness arrived. Frederick Stymetz Lamb recounted the events:

> All of the young men were anxious to understand Inness' method of painting. The eventful day arrived, a Sunday, when Inness could spare the time.... When Inness arrived he rushed at once to the studies and started to give his theories of painting.... He spoke of color combinations, showed methods of brush work and finally set aside both brush and palette. Taking his thumb he drew the color together with a few

> marvelous sweeps—as was often his habit—then excitedly seizing his friend by the lapel of his coat, he explained the reason at the same time leaving beautiful color combinations on the Sunday coat![73]

Arthur Turnbull Hill, the son of the painter George Waldo Hill, one of Inness's colleagues, reiterated the impression of Inness as entirely enveloped in his work. Hill described Inness as "a most remarkable man—his manner of working was entirely different from that of any painter I have ever seen." Furthermore, Hill added,

> The energy of his attack upon a canvas (in this case it was literally an attack), the rapidity and accuracy of his drawing and brushwork and the amount of space he would cover in a few moments, was simply marvelous to watch. At such times his eyes fairly glowed and snapped and he would often talk while he worked, in this rapid way, expressing his thoughts and giving his reasons, scientific and artistic, for what he was doing at the moment.

Arthur Hill recalled how Inness once visited his father's studio and, finding the father absent, took the liberty—and quite a liberty it must have been—of reworking one of the paintings on view. After Inness "plunked" down a whole tube of white paint on a palette, he transferred the "entire lot of white" to the "middle of the sky." According to the son,

> Then began that rapid brushwork—that scrubbing, rubbing, spreading of the paint across the canvas without seeming to lift the brush from its surface which I have never seen anyone else do in anything like the same way. The whole thing was done without, so to speak, stopping to take breath; other colors, black, blue, orange, had followed in quick succession after the while, and in a few moments the color scheme of the picture was completely changed. It was very wonderful to me—whether my father agreed with what Inness had done or not.[74]

Following a long tradition of artists—Leonardo, Titian, Turner, and others—who abandoned the intermediary of the brush altogether in order to paint with their fingers,[75] Inness left finger prints embedded in the impasto of several of his late landscape paintings.[76] Watkins (the dentist) alluded to this technique when he recalled that Inness would "receive suggestions [for his paintings] from anyone." He described the following encounter with the artist:

> I once said to him in looking at a picture, a sunset, "Isn't that sun a little peculiar in color? Would it not be better if it had a little more orange in it?" Instantly he grabbed the tube of orange, put a little on his thumb and rubbed it into the sun—jumped back a couple of feet, looked at it and said, "That does help it; that does help it; that is an improvement."[77]

The increasing authority that Inness gave to his brushstroke, and then his abandonment of the brush in favor of his fingers, suggest that Inness's pictorial marks appeal less to our sense of sight than they do to our more primitive sense of touch. If we look again at *The Coming Storm,* we notice how Inness's great rotating swirls of paint generate the balmy intensity of storm clouds coursing through the sky, while sharper flecks of paint from the tips of his brush conjure the chaotic pulses of wind through desiccated fall leaves. We read coursing movement into swirls and erratic movement into flecks. We read fragility into staccato dashes and corporeality into thick, viscous daubs of paint. The character of these marks—made with Inness's brush, a rag, a stick, or his fingers—transfers meaning and character, without didactically providing identities, to their subjects. If we return to *The Old Barn,* we see how Inness's sinuous streaks of turquoise paint, edged in black, capture the dynamism, without scrupulously describing the activity, of the woman in the middle distance. By exploiting the signifying capacity of pictorial marks in this way, Inness activates our prelinguistic power to associate feelings with forms, to know nature—ultimately, to develop a sense of our own identity—through the sensory system of touch.[78]

"NO GREAT ARTIST EVER FINISHED A PICTURE OR A STATUE": INNESS ON ART IN PROGRESS

> Who ever thinks about Michael Angelo's work being finished? No great artist ever finished a picture or a statue. It is mercantile work that is finished, and finish is what the picture dealers cry for. Instead of covering the walls of his mansion with works of character, or, what is better, with

> those works of inspiration which allure the mind to the regions of the unknown, he is apt to cover them with the sleek polish of lackadaisical sentiment, or the puerilities of impossible conditions.
>
> —George Inness[79]

> I have a horror of something finished. Death is final. A revolver shot finishes off. The not completely achieved is life. —Pablo Picasso[80]

For George Inness, the immanent expressive capacity of the brushstroke and the evocative power of the synoptic form found their logical counterpart in the appeal of the unfinished painting. Inness's son described this attraction succinctly when he recalled that, for his father, "After a picture was completed, it lost all value for him. He had no more interest in it. . . . He would take a canvas before the paint was really dry, and, being seized with another inspiration, would paint over it." Inness, Jr., a regular visitor to his father's studio, described what can now only be seen through infrared reflectography: "I have known him to paint as many as half a dozen or more pictures on one canvas, in fact, as many as the canvas would hold."[81] The art critic George Sheldon, who often visited Inness's studio, corroborated the son's account when he described how he would find Inness working simultaneously on an even greater number of paintings. Sheldon observed, "On the dozen or more canvases in his studio he worked as the humor seized him, going from one to another with palette and maul-stick. . . . "[82]

In his profile on Inness in 1896, the art critic A. T. Van Laer described Inness's seemingly obsessive need to repaint canvases as follows: "As long as a canvas was within easy reach it was liable to repainting. . . . Upon one canvas he painted twenty-five pictures—the first was painted some years ago, the last was exhibited at the recent sale." Van Laer reproduced one such landscape with the following, slightly facetious caption: "The twenty-fourth picture painted on canvas by Inness. The twenty-fifth was the same subject slightly changed."[83] Addressing the reasons for this seemingly counterproductive behavior, Inness, Jr., identified his father's lack of "interest" in completing paintings, while Alfred Trumble, who wrote the catalogue for the executor's sale of Inness's works, cited Inness's inability to derive a feeling of satisfaction from them. "[W]hile [Inness's] method of execution was rapid at the starting of a picture," Trumble recalled, "his speed would diminish as he advanced, and as the difficulty of realizing the result he aimed at grew upon him, canvas after canvas would be set aside and another subject commenced."[84] In an extended tribute to Inness written three decades after the artist's death, the art critic George Chambers Calvert, who seems to have observed the artist at work, described the dramatic physical changes that some compositions would undergo as the artist superimposed images. Calvert recalled how Inness

> was continually changing [paintings] on which he was working; and what began as a spring morning in a meadow might be transformed into a marine and finish as a snow scene. So, too, if the mood to paint seized him and no other canvas was at hand he had no hesitancy about painting a new picture over an old one.[85]

The artist and art critic Arthur Hoeber confirms the frequency of such transformations and described the threat of ruin that comes with overpainting:

> Yet in point of fact no man worked harder than did Inness to achieve his end, for while it frequently happened that at a single sitting he would dash off a masterpiece—thus it is said he did his *Gray, Lowery Day* [c. 1877; Davis Museum and Cultural Center, Wellesley College] within the twenty-four hours—the amount of work he destroyed was appalling. He was just as likely, at a second painting, to completely change the scheme of a beautiful start and, finally, in despair, to scrape out all he had done. It not infrequently happened that patrons would bring him their pictures for some little repainting and return to find their prized possessions quite unrecognizable.[86]

To be sure, Inness's early and middle-period paintings confirm that he closely studied nature to know her forms and to refine proper painting techniques. However, as in the late paintings of Titian, Turner, Cézanne, and Picasso, Inness's late paintings resonate with the artist's interpretation of painting as a process rather than a goal, with his need to extend the life of each painting as long as humanly possible.

FINISH: HISTORICAL PRECEDENTS AND PROSPECTS

The dominant theme of repainting raises the ubiquitous problem of determining whether or not Inness's late landscape paintings are finished.[87] Famous paintings in this debate include *The Lone Farm, Nantucket; The Home of the Heron;* and *Hazy Morning, Montclair.* Several issues may perhaps assist us as we consider this question.

First, Inness expressed admiration for famously unfinished works of art. It is likely that he saw and studied Michelangelo's many unfinished sculptures in Florence during both his first (1851–52) and third (1870–75) trips to Europe. Reflecting on the history of this expressive mode, Inness posed the rhetorical question, "Who ever thinks about Michael Angelo's work being finished?" His own reply silenced debate: "No great artist ever finished a picture or a statue." It is therefore likely that Inness derived support for his decision to leave paintings unfinished from his admiration for Michelangelo's unfinished *Slaves* in the Galleria dell'Accademia and allegorical figures for the Medici Chapel at San Lorenzo in Florence. He joined the ranks of those who had long allied excessive pictorial finish with commercialism when he added, "It is mercantile work that is finished, and finish is what the picture dealers cry for."[88] For Inness, the unfinished painting possessed an inherent value recognized by the old masters. Furthermore, it functioned as a political statement, a stance against the undertow of commercialism.

Second, Inness exploited the power of the unfinished through the ability of the synoptic form to stimulate the imagination. While still maintaining the basic component parts of land, sky, and trees in *Indian Summer* (1894; Plate 33), Inness nearly dissolved alliances between brushstrokes and naturalistic referents. The daub of greenish-yellow paint on the horizon is as much a pure pictorial mark as the illusion of a tangible tree. Horizontal streaks of gray paint at the left edge of the scene attempt, with only minimal success, to provide form to a small shed. Finally, and perhaps most dramatically, a single dash of vibrant yellow-white just below the center of the painting struggles to evoke a human being. By leaving these areas unrefined, Inness actively and deliberately engages us in his visionary scheme. We scan our memories for forms to match Inness's synoptic daubs of paint. We attempt to complete what the artist has omitted from his painting.

The theme of omission is important because the viewer's distinct, private attempts at pictorial completion, acts performed in the mind, stimulate his or her attention and imagination. The less information the artist presents, the greater is our active role as participants in the artist's project. At the beginning of this text, I identified Inness's late landscape paintings as visionary for their prescience, for the way in which they tend to anticipate some of the hallmarks of modern painting. Inness's work warrants this identification through its exploitation of the evocative power of pictorial absence. We recall, by means of comparison, the case of Henri Matisse. For *The Swimming Pool* (1952; The Museum of Modern Art, New York; fig. 10), Matisse

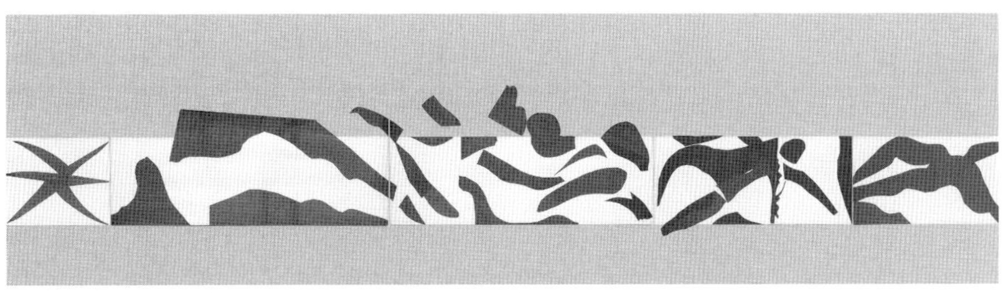

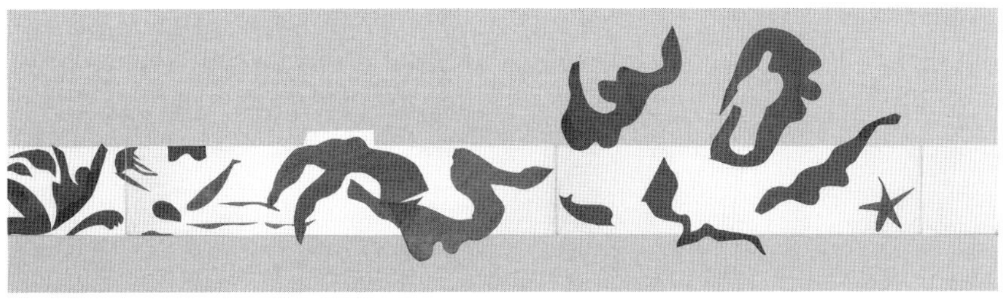

FIG. 10.
Henri Matisse (1869–1954), *The Swimming Pool*, 1952, Nine-panel mural in two parts: gouache on paper, cut and pasted, on white painted paper mounted on burlap, a–e, 7' 6⅝" x 27' 9½"; f–i, 7' 6⅝" x 26' 1½", The Museum of Modern Art, New York. Mrs. Bernard F. Gimbel Fund.

formulated two elutriated sequences of vibrant blue shapes on a striated white-and-burlap background. These forms telegraph shifting semiotic signs of bodily movement through an aquatic medium. Here, in Matisse's succinct phrase, is "a form filtered to its essentials."[89] Inness summarized his grasp of the power of omission and the corresponding authority omission donates to extant, koanic forms. Upon confronting one of his own landscapes, he observed, "I paint in all these details in order that I may know how to paint them out."[90]

Third, the question of finish maintained a proprietary value for Inness. Like his compatriot James McNeill Whistler, Inness insisted on determining when—and if—his paintings were finished.[91] For Inness, his paintings always remained his property, regardless of whether or not he received money for them through sales. Again, George Inness, Jr., provides further insight into his father's position on the matter:

> My father had the idea firmly established in his mind that a work of art from his brush always remained his property, and that he had the right to paint it over or change it at will, no matter where he found it or who had bought it, or what money he may have received for it. Wherever he found

> his pictures after they had left his studio he criticized, and would in most violent language declare the thing was "rot," that the sky was false or the distance out of key, and in a very matter of fact way would say "Just send it around to the studio to-morrow and I'll put it into shape."[92]

Inness, Jr., recorded another occasion in which the owner of an Inness painting tried to prevent the artist from reworking it by simply declaring his preference for the work in its existing condition. Inness apparently retorted, "It makes no difference what you like; I say the thing is false. . . . And I want you to understand, sir, that I claim the right to go into any house and change a work of mine when I am not satisfied with it, and see where I can improve it." Inness then posed the key—and astringently rhetorical—question: "Do you think," he inquired, "because you have paid money for a picture of mine, that it belongs to *you*?"[93] The critic Montgomery Schuyler, who counted himself among Inness's friends, reiterated the artist's position: "So long as a picture remained in the studio it was not finished to the painter's mind nor safe from his hand. At any time he might take a fresh dash at it and render it unrecognizable."[94] Thomas B. Clarke, Inness's chief patron during his later years, was known to cart off Inness's paintings from the artist's studio while the paint was still wet on the canvas.[95] Alluding to conduct like Clarke's, Schuyler added, "So well was this habit understood among the habitual buyers of Innesses, that they would lie in wait for the 'state' in which a canvas satisfied them, and artfully convey it out of the reach of the painter's study of perfection. Sometimes, however, the new picture bore no relation whatever to the old."[96]

Fourth, Inness identified *himself* with all of the implicit potential of the unfinished work of art. In a letter of March 1884 to the art critic Ripley Hitchcock, Inness described himself as follows: "I have changed from the time I commenced" painting. "I had never completed my art and as I do not care about being a cake I shall remain dough subject to any impression which I am satisfied comes from the region of truth."[97] Inness's self-identification as "dough" recalls Gaston Bachelard's description of our ongoing desire to construct and inhabit a "dream house"—a house that is "better built, lighter and larger than all the houses of the past." Bachelard illuminates the pitfalls of such a dwelling:

> . . . a house that was final, one that stood in symmetrical relation to the house we were born in, would lead to thoughts—serious, sad thoughts—and not to dreams.

"It is better," Bachelard concludes, "to live in a state of impermanence than in one of finality."[98] In this "dough"-like condition, this paradoxically permanent state of impermanence, Inness, like Bachelard's house-dreamer, could remain open to all possibilities, receptive to all sources of inspiration.

Finally, as with all issues concerning Inness and his landscapes, the forces of art and theology again united in determining the identity and scope of the unfinished painting. To be sure, Inness recognized in this art form the potential to stimulate the viewer's imagination; more than this, however, it could create a new form of consciousness. Combating what he described as the desire on the part of "the intellect . . . to define everything," Inness admitted that "the paramount difficulty with the artist is to bring his intellect to submit to the fact that there is such a thing as the undefinable [*sic*]," which he further identified, alluding to the power of touch, as "that which hides itself that we may feel after it."[99] Reasserting the alliance between art and theology in his worldview, Inness explained, "God is always hidden, and beauty depends upon the unseen—the visible upon the invisible."[100]

As we explore Inness's many late landscape paintings, it is worth considering the possibility that their unfinished condition did not maintain the pejorative connotations of "unfulfilled" or "deficient" that traditionally accompany the term *unfinished*. It was not, I would suggest, that they required *more work* or *more consideration* on the part of the artist to realize their potential. Seen in the context of Inness's theological preoccupations, the late, seemingly unfinished landscapes suggest that Inness deliberately and knowingly used "marvelous sweeps" of color and synoptic marks, that he continuously reworked paintings and left others "unfinished," in order to persuade the viewer's intellect to "submit to the fact of the undefinable," in short, to know the divine.

THE JAMESIAN STREAM OF THOUGHT

In his late landscape paintings, Inness used brushstrokes in ways that resonate deeply with William James's innovative description of consciousness as a "stream of thought" or "stream of subjective life" (fig. 11). During the 1870s and 1880s—concurrently, that is, with the creation of Inness's visionary paintings—James, then a professor of psychology at Harvard University, developed this idea in several professional journal articles. Opposing the prevailing theory that thought entails purely cognitive judgments—that is, "judgments that things do, as a matter of fact, exist"[101]—James

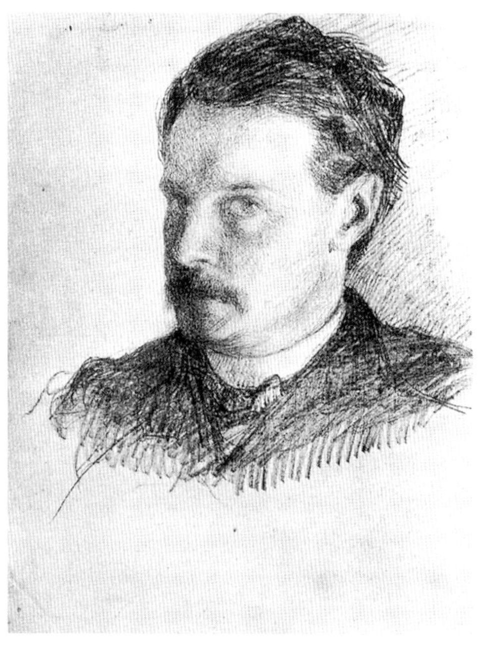

FIG. 11.
William James (1842–1910), *Self-Portrait*, c. 1866, pencil on paper, William James Papers, bMS Am 1092.2, Houghton Library, Harvard University, Cambridge, Massachusetts. Courtesy of Houghton Library and Alexander R. James.

argued that subjective factors (emotional states, errors, prejudices, habits, and the like) all help to shape what we know and how we learn. James criticized the tendency to ignore those subjective psychic states and conditions for which we have no real name. He gave as an example of an intense but ultimately evanescent mental condition the peculiar feeling of trying, to no avail, to remember a specific word, or a person's name. James illuminated "signs of direction" in human thought, such as the tone of language, or pauses before the expression of an idea. These "signs of direction" provide a "value" to an idea *before* we can readily describe or define what that value is. (Speed and hesitation condition responses to a given question in very different ways.) James described the mental quality that binds both types of thought—identifiable *substantive* forms of thought and vague *transitive* states—as "a stream" for two reasons. First, transitive and substantive states flow seamlessly into one another; even when rising from a deep sleep, for example, the transition to consciousness, to the waking state, seems entirely familiar, seems, in James's words, "warm and intimate."[102] Second, even when conscious transitive states feel ruptured—when a forgotten word is suddenly revealed to consciousness—thought *feels* continuous. Changes from transitive to substantive states (and visa versa) are, therefore, never absolutely abrupt.[103]

James's theory of the "stream of thought" was widely accepted into the most advanced fields of psychological research. Not only did it play a formative role in shaping the character of modern psychology, it exerted a potent influence on the arts as well. For example, Gertrude Stein, a psychology and philosophy student of James's at Harvard Annex (later Radcliffe College) during the late 1890s, derived considerable inspiration from her teacher for the development of her own distinct, free-flowing literary style.

Inness's characteristic and innovative use of the brushstroke served as an artistic counterpart to the Jamesian stream. From the late 1870s on, Inness mirrored the identities of transitive and substantive states of consciousness by balancing loose, unconstricted brushstrokes with sharper, representational ones in his landscapes. In *Sunset Glow* (1883; Plate 35), for example, daubs of bright orange paint at the horizon effectively represent the luminous setting sun (a "substantive" form). By contrast, sharp jabs of brownish-green paint from the tips of Inness's brushes generate the roughly hewn forms of the central bank of trees; these bristly marks of paint merge with nearly identical strokes on the grassy terrain below. In this way, Inness's unified brushstrokes blend ontologically distinct forms and the spaces they inhabit into a single, vague, natural ("transitive") entity. His activated brushstroke technique, which mimics the very character of the alliance of substantive and transitive states, invites the viewer to ponder these enigmatic, melded identities.[104]

One may argue that, during the last third of the nineteenth century, American painting in general became more suggestive, more resonant with the Jamesian idea of consciousness as a "stream." Tonalist artists such as Thomas Wilmer Dewing, Henry Ward Ranger, and James McNeill Whistler all created paintings in tonal hues and kindred compositional brushstrokes to evoke moments of temporal transition and other poetic moods. Yet Inness's work, especially his late landscape paintings, remains distinct from Tonalist painting in its complete absence of decorative qualities. It remains distinct, too, for its seemingly esoteric mathematical and geometric structures, which we have seen so brilliantly executed in *Lake Nemi, The Monk,* and *Castel Gandolfo,* and which reemerge, after a hiatus during the late 1870s, in such masterful late landscape paintings as *October Noon* and *The Home of the Heron*. In these works, the covert, underlying presence of structure alludes, as it does in Luminist landscapes, to the authority of an omniscient, organizing force within nature, a force that may well be described as divine.

How, then, did Inness accommodate both the allusion to the divine in nature—a form of philosophical and theological absolutism—and the suggestion, made through his idiosyncratic, synoptic brushmarks, that the individual and his sense of free will donate meaning to the landscape representation, a form of philosophical pragmatism, or pluralism?

Inness and James accomplished this seemingly paradoxical goal in similar ways through different media. Both asserted the presence of the individual within the visionary religious experience and both suggested that free will plays a role in the relationship between nature and the divine. We may best understand this double-edged evocation through a comparison of Inness's most effective late landscape paintings and William James's findings on the varieties of religious experience.

> We may be in the universe as dogs and cats are in our libraries, seeing the books and hearing the conversation, but having no inkling of the meaning of it all. —William James[105]

From the mid-1880s until his death in 1910, James extended his study of transitive psychological states first into the region of pathological states of mind and, later, into religious states, all of which he described as existing "on the margins of consciousness." His work in this field represented the apex of a vast effort, on the part of many prominent late-nineteenth-century psychologists, to understand the mystical religious experience from a rigorously scientific perspective. In 1896, James delivered a series of eight lectures at the Lowell Institute in Boston on these psychopathological and religious conditions: on Dreams and Hypnotism, Hysteria, Automatisms, Multiple Personality, Demonical Possession, Witchcraft, Degeneration, and Genius.[106] Fighting the prevailing prejudice in the field of physiological psychology against psychical research, James explored psycho-religious states because he felt it was unscientific, even unjust, to ignore the testimonies of individuals who had experienced them. He took the pragmatic approach—formulated on the belief that one must follow "either logic or the senses . . . to count the humblest and most personal experiences"—that conditioned all of his scientific and philosophical explorations. To this end, James studied numerous historical records of experiences in which individuals became aware of a visionary quality greater than, *distinct from*, but potentially continuous with their own selves.[107] "There are . . . possibilities," James explained,

> that take our breath away, [possibilities] of another kind of happiness and power, based on giving up our own will and letting something higher work for us, and these seem to show a world wider than either physics or philistine ethics can imagine.[108]

James later described how such visionary experiences often arrive unexpectedly, that our natural, or waking experiences represent only "a fragment of real human experience." Employing a pictorial analogy that nearly conjures one of Inness's late landscape paintings, James described how visionary experiences "soften nature's outlines and open out the strangest possibilities and perspectives."[109] He pinpoints what Margaret Miles later described as the ability of the religious image to "boggle" and 'dizzy' the mind, to take the breath of the viewer. [110] In this way, the religious image may situate the viewer within the limbic, or "threshold" space. Through his work as an artist, Inness searched for this state in the divinely inspired "freshness" of the artist's "first perception" of nature.

Perhaps the finest pictorial counterpart to James's evocative description of the limbic visionary experience is Inness's *Summer, Montclair (New Jersey Landscape)* (1891; Plate 24). In a scene of supreme tranquility, we sustain allegiances both to the known and the unknown. A modest pastoral setting of verdant grasses and trees, a subdued but effective sun, and a fragmentary pool of water combine to anchor our sense of physical location. Nearly every other feature—indeed, the absence of physical features—attempts to disengage that anchor. Inness's reduced palette, a nuanced range of olive and lemony greens, pale blues, warm browns, and warm ochers, employed in concert with the delicately structured organization of forms—the raised horizon line, the subdivision of the upper half of the composition, the striated patches of land, the mirroring of sky and water—assert a somewhat unnatural sense of order. In this way, color and form enigmatically minimize ties to the natural realm. Here is the systematic structure of Inness's great Italian paintings of the early 1870s; here, too, is the virtuosity of the storm scenes of the late 1870s and the pastoral landscapes of the 1880s. Through this seamless intersection of form and freedom, Inness alludes both to the omniscience of the divine in nature *and* to the artist's sense of self, to the immutable power of his free will. Through its masterful construction and subtle allocation of hues, *Summer, Montclair* may effectively guide our responses to those metaphysical questions posed at the beginning of this essay: What do we see and what do we know? How is our world constructed? What relationships might it maintain to other, unseen realms?

THE ANONYMOUS FIGURE, FOR INNESS AND JAMES

> The adjective "mystical" is technically applied, most often, to states [of mind] that are of brief duration. . . . Unpicturable beings are realized, and realized with an intensity almost like that of an hallucination.
>
> —William James[111]

Inness used a final pictorial device in his drive to 'resolve' theology into "a scientific form" of landscape painting and to shift the frame of mind in which his viewers engaged with his work. That device was the representation of a single human figure in the landscape. The gender, character, and identity of this figure often remain ambiguous; in certain cases, particularly in Inness's late landscape paintings, only the head-and-body combination signifies the figure's anthropomorphism. Depicted with the same vivid brushstrokes that Inness used for the rest of his landscapes, the figure can be difficult to discern, especially in reproductions. It rarely crosses the horizon line, remaining, instead, deeply embedded within the texture of nature. It often assumes the identity of what Roland Barthes described as "the punctum," or point of particular interest (as opposed to the subject), of the work of art.[112] Elliott Daingerfield addressed this distinction when he recalled that, for Inness, the figure "must not reach above the horizon, else it becomes subject matter and therefore a figure picture."[113]

Inness's "anonymous figures," as I have termed them, rarely act. They are, in this way, quite different from the figures in the artist's landscapes whose actions confer on them known identities, such as the shepherds in *A Bit of the Roman Aqueduct* (1852; Plate 1), the fishermen in *Landscape* (1860; Plate 3) and *Clearing Up* (1860; Plate 6), the fisherwoman on the right side of *The Trout Brook* (1891; Plate 14), the waving man in black in *Saco Ford: Conway Meadows* (1876; Plate 28), the two laborers in *The Old Barn* (c. 1888; Plate 30), the woman in *Woman with Calf* (1886; Plate 31), and all of the figures—the woman waving and the two figures in the rowboat—in *Shades of Evening* (c. 1877; Plate 34). These active figures fulfill the traditional pictorial identity of *staffage,* or accessories to the scene. They participate in and corroborate the illusion of the representation. There is little need to question the nature of their activities, much less their core humanistic identities.

By assuming a wholly contemplative demeanor, Inness's "anonymous figures" nearly disengage from the pictorial representations in which they exist. They tend, therefore, to stimulate the viewer's attention even more effectively. Early examples of this type include the two figures in the foreground of *Sunset* (c. 1860–65; Plate 8) and the hunched, silhouetted figure in *Christmas Eve (Winter Moonlight)* (1866; Plate 9). (In *Lake Nemi* [1872; Plate 15] and *The Monk* [1873; Plate 16], Inness manifests the contemplative identities of the anonymous figures through their religious garb.) In *October Noon* (1891; Plate 25), *Sunrise* (1887; Plate 37), and *Near the Village, October* (1892; Plate 38), the anonymous figure shrinks dramatically in size, emerging, in some cases, through no more than a virtuosic fleck or two of paint. In *Home at Montclair* (1892; Plate 21), *Summer, Montclair (New Jersey Landscape)* (1891; Plate 24), *The Lone Farm, Nantucket* (1892; Plate 26), and *Hazy Morning, Montclair* (1893; Plate

39), the figure is so summarily depicted that its very existence seems to depend on the interpretation of each viewer.

It is tempting simply to identify Inness's "anonymous figures," figures on the verge of corporeal dissolution, as phantasmagoric beings of the type Swedenborg tells us he encountered and derived insight from in the spiritual realm. Given that, according to Inness, the purpose of art was "not to instruct, not to edify, but to awaken an emotion," it is unlikely that the artist would have condoned such a literal interpretation. Indeed, these anonymous, nearly ephemeral creatures correlate more closely to the elusive *character* of the visionary experience than to the region of the descriptive, even when the subject of the descriptive is the spiritual realm.

In this visionary role, Inness's "anonymous figures" engage in an important trope of nineteenth-century American (and some European) paintings and photographs: the image of the contemplative figure in the landscape. In Asher B. Durand's *Early Morning at Cold Spring, New York* (1850; Montclair Art Museum, Montclair, New Jersey) and Jasper Francis Cropsey's *Starrucca Viaduct, Pennsylvania* (1865; Toledo Museum of Art, Toledo, Ohio), for example, this figure stands with his back to the viewer as he gazes into the distant landscape. In this pose, he adopts our own position and renders us increasingly aware of our identity as contemplative beings. Barbara Novak has described how, in nineteenth-century American literature, the act of looking at nature became a form of religious devotion.[114] For Emerson especially, communion with divinely created nature resulted, as noted earlier, in the mystical surrender of the self and his self-identification as a "transparent eyeball" before nature. Martin Johnson Heade's *The Stranded Boat* (1863; Museum of Fine Arts, Boston; fig. 12), with its minuscule figure standing at the edge of the rocky cove, serves as the definitive pictorial counterpart to Emerson's transcendent act.

Like Heade's figure, Inness's anonymous figure gazes deeply into the landscape; it appears "to commune with a nature of which it has just become aware."[115] Yet Inness's pictorial technique distinguishes his figures from their Luminist counterparts. Created by the same, succinct daubs of paint that produced the rest of Inness's scenes, these anonymous figures quite literally embody Inness's most primal actions. The evocation of these actions renders us increasingly aware not only of the artist's generative role as inventor but also of our own role as interpreter of the pictorial forms and field. Adopting distinctly introspective poses, Inness's anonymous figures do indeed call to mind visionary activities. Unlike contemplative Luminist figures, however, they *accentuate* the implied presence of the artist and the viewer—of the self—before divinely imbued nature.

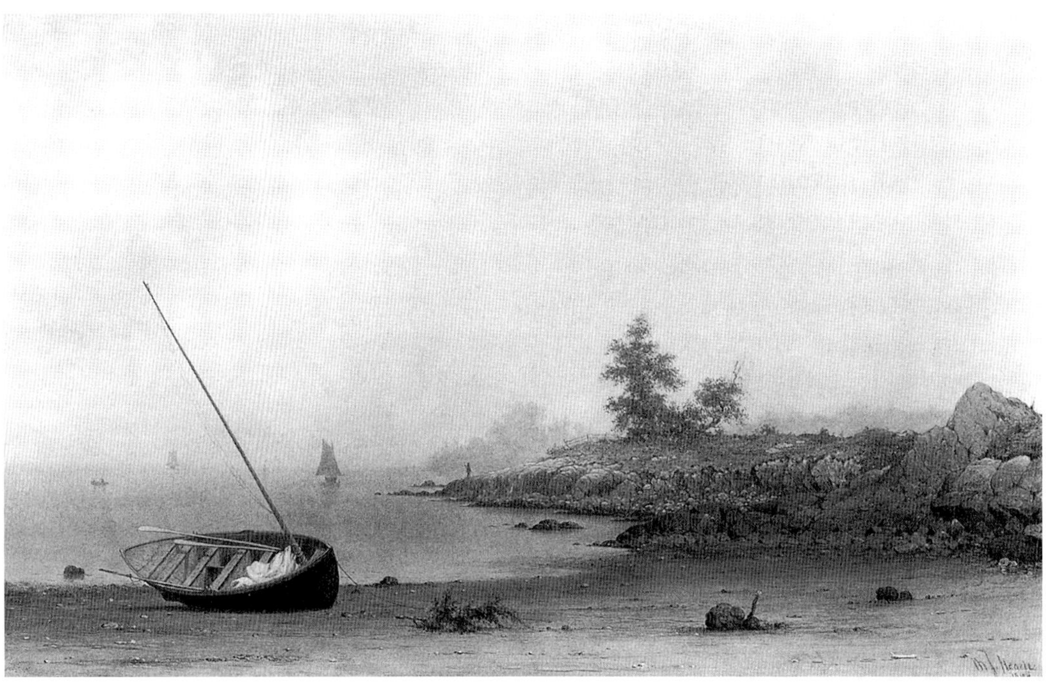

FIG. 12.
Martin Johnson Heade (1819–1904), *The Stranded Boat*, 1863, oil on canvas, 22¾ x 36½", M. and M. Karolik Collection, Museum of Fine Arts, Boston.

For this reason, Inness's anonymous figures find their philosophical counterpart not in the idealism of Transcendentalism but in William James's pragmatic research into psychical states of consciousness. They appear in Inness's paintings concurrently with James's full engagement in the field of psychical research. In 1884, James became a member of the British-based Society for Psychical Research and a founding member of the American branch of the society.[116] The following year, he participated in séances and met the trance medium Leonora Piper, who provided him with evidence of mental telepathy and veridical hallucinations (fig. 13).[117] James culminated his work in this field in his Gifford Lectures on Natural Religion at the University of Edinburgh in the spring of 1901, which were published the following year as *The Varieties of Religious Experience*.

The Varieties of Religious Experience remains one of our most valuable and influential modern studies on the psychology of religion. It served as a forum for James's critically important questions on how religious experiences are constituted and how they are experienced within the human mind. Through his explorations of, for example, "the reality of the unseen," "the divided self," "conversion," "saintliness," and "mysticism," James came to the conclusion that religious experiences are pervasive, they are experienced in every culture and every historical period, and they relate to a field of human nature with unusually close ties to subliminal states of consciousness. These states are not, as previously determined, aberrant states; for James, they may even represent "superior points of view, windows through which the mind looks out upon a more extensive and inclusive world."[118] They must be tested, James argued, along the lines of other psychological conditions to see if they function in harmony with our other needs and to see if they enrich our understanding of the world.

In his analysis of *The Varieties of Religious Experience*, William Joseph Gavin parallels the affinities between James's earlier desire, as expressed in *The Principles of Psychology* (1890), to incorporate the ephemeral transitive psychological states into his more inclusive definition of human consciousness with his later investigation of religious experiences in which the individual becomes conscious of a larger world, an "unseen order."[119] For Gavin, *The Varieties of Religious Experience* reflects James's metaphysical position that, given the existence of this unseen order, we must accept the fact that uncertainty and vagueness are pervasive; the study accords, therefore, with James's "pluralistic, contextual, and multidimensional" worldview.[120] According to Eugene Fontinell, the desire to "reinstate the vague to its proper place in our mental life,"

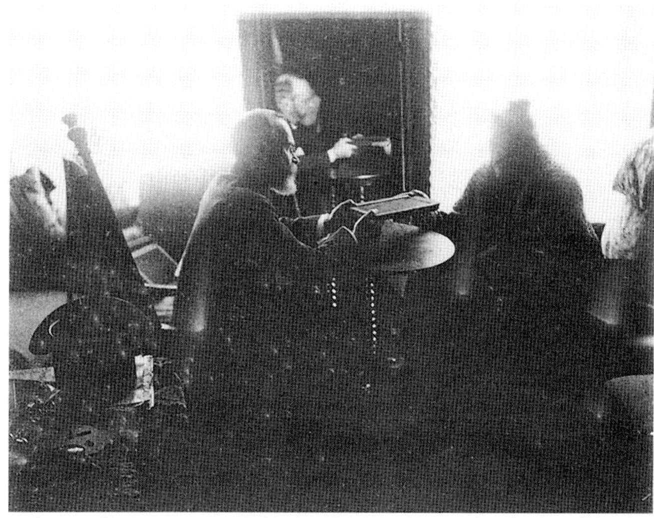

FIG. 13.
William James Participating in a Séance, c. 1880s, photograph, William James Papers, bMS Am 1092.2, Houghton Library, Harvard University, Cambridge, Massachusetts. Courtesy of Houghton Library and Alexander R. James.

which James describes as one of his primary goals, is not "a defense of obfuscation or romantic cloudiness. Paradoxically, it is an effort to describe our experiences as rigorously as possible and to avoid any procrustean cutting of experience so as to fit neatly into what can be named or conceptualized."[121] In other words, for James, religious experiences, lucid or vague as they may be, reflect the richness, expansiveness, and uncertainties of both human thought and human life.

WILLIAM JAMES'S SWEDENBORGIAN SOURCE

James rejected the lack of diversity in the idealist's (including the Transcendentalist's) interpretation of the religious experience. He rejected the idea of God as an all-controlling magistrate who suppressed the individual's free will and posited notions of truth for all eternity. For James, experience, including religious experience, is a profoundly human activity. It represents the vast, continuous process of life, a process of "things in the making," indeed, of reality. "Reality . . . *mounts* in living its own undivided life," James explained, "it buds and bourgeons, changes and creates."[122] James studied enlightening religious experiences, such as conversions, providential leadings, and sudden mental healings, and decided that he "firmly believe[d] that most of these phenomena are rooted in reality."[123] He likened the feeling of enlightenment, of communion with the "MORE . . . in the universe" outside, of budding and burgeoning life, to Swedenborg's concept of "influx." For James, "the word 'influx,' used in Swedenborgian circles, well describes this impression of new insight, or new willingness, sweeping over us like a tide."[124] By assimilating this notion of influx into his modern pragmatic metaphysics, James effected an important step in overturning the traditional antitheological basis of empiricism and in expanding the search for God beyond the external senses. Furthermore, in his own way, James found a viable, scientific context for Swedenborgian spirituality in the modern age.

James's decision to explore the authenticity of the mystical religious experience, and in all likelihood his introduction to Swedenborg, stemmed from the presence in his life of his father, the philosopher Henry James, Sr.[125] The author of numerous books and articles on Swedenborgian theology, the elder James became one of the leading spokesmen for Swedenborgianism in mid-nineteenth-century America.[126] Henry James, Sr.'s commitment to independent thinking and his validation of Swedenborgian metaphysics tell us that religion did not simply play an integral role in William James's childhood. Rather, all five James children were raised in a household in which the ideas of Swedenborg—a man who renounced a distinguished career in the sciences to prepare exegetical treatises on the basis of spirit communications—were regarded as not only legitimate, not only worthy of extended scholarly investigation, but as capable of providing a new and inspiring worldview based on the central role of the spiritual in nature.[127]

William James, like George Inness, confronted the rift between science and religion generated by Darwin's severance of God from the process of evolution. As a scientist, James needed as many empirical proofs as he could find for the existence of God. He came closest to proof in his Hibbert Lectures on Immortality (1908–09). Referring to the corpus of his work on religious experiences, James admitted that he found "in some of these abnormal or supernormal facts the strongest suggestions in favor of a superior consciousness being possible."[128] He had treated such evidence empirically, validating its existence on the basis of both his own research and the experience of historical figures. He overturned the assumptions of orthodox, absolutist religions by proposing that "empiricism once again be associated with religion, as hitherto, through some strange misunderstanding, it has been associated with irreligion. . . ." Responding to the Darwinian gauntlet, James resolved that, with this affiliation in place, "a new era of religion as well as of philosophy will be ready to begin."[129]

The question of whether or not Inness read James's pre-1894 articles on consciousness or even his landmark textbook, *The Principles of Psychology* (1890), remains unknown; Inness's library, which may have contained such texts or letters about them, was destroyed with the rest of the artist's personal effects.[130] We do know, however, that James and Inness met on at least one occasion. In June 1863, James joined Inness on a sketching trip to Mount Desert in Maine. Accompanying them was James (Steele) MacKaye, who would soon become a friend and pupil of Inness's at Eagleswood, the social reform community in Perth Amboy, New Jersey, where Inness spent the years 1864–67.[131]

It is possible that the Mount Desert sketching trip was not the first occasion on which Inness and William James met one another. Inness may have come into contact with the James family, perhaps with Henry James, Sr., in the mid-1850s, when the two men counted Samuel Gray Ward (1817–1907) as a mutual friend. A patron of the arts and letters, Ward began purchasing Inness's paintings and corresponding with the artist as early as January 1852.[132] He corresponded with the elder James on Swedenborgian matters in 1854.[133] Given Ward's interest in Swedenborgian doctrine in the early 1850s and given the likelihood that Inness gained his initial exposure to this subject through William Page in Florence in 1851–52, it is possible that Ward made Inness aware of the elder James's work, perhaps even facilitated their acquaintance.[134] The prospect of Inness's early introduction to the James family sets in a reasonable context the meeting of William James and Inness in 1863.[135]

IN SEARCH OF THE SELF

> I am seventy years of age, and the whole study of my life has been to find out what it is that is in myself; what is this thing we call life, and how does it operate.
>
> —George Inness in 1894[136]

Inness's final, most metaphysical statement was published on 12 August 1894. Nine days earlier, Inness, who had traveled to Scotland to improve his failing health, died while viewing a particularly beautiful sunset. According to the son's theatrical rendition (one rather well suited to his father, who, two decades earlier, had incarnated Hamlet), Inness saw the "big red ball" as it went below the horizon, "threw up his hands into the air and exclaimed, 'My God! oh, how beautiful!,'" and then fell to the ground.[137] A few minutes later, Inness died in the arms of his wife. His body was returned to New York where it lay in state at the National Academy of Design. There, Inness was honored with a full-scale funeral, complete with silver casket, violet ribbons, palm leaves, wreathes of white roses, ivy, and lilies of the valley. Surrounding the casket and Jonathan Scott Hartley's bronze bust of his father-in-law (fig. 14) was a collection of Inness's finest paintings. The Swedenborgian minister John Curtis Ager presided. The funeral was, by all accounts, the most lavish produced for any of Inness's colleagues. In the months that would follow, Inness's life and art would be celebrated in numerous obituaries and biographical profiles.

Although Inness was the subject of few exhibitions and few scholarly studies until the mid-1960s, he enjoyed somewhat greater and more regular attention than the majority of his Hudson River School colleagues. One reason for the artist's enduring interest may have been the unmistakable engagement of his sense of self in all of his artistic endeavors, an engagement that resonated deeply with the most progressive artists of his generation. Like Théodore Rousseau, Inness bypassed the traditions of narrative and mythology in landscape painting to probe nature's finest details for "the echoes they have placed in our soul." Like the mystic Albert Pinkham Ryder, Inness was "trying to find something out there beyond the place on which" he had a footing. Both Inness and Ryder presciently recognized that the synoptic, Zen-like mark, when successfully executed, could transport greater meaning to the canvas than any carefully studied representational line or brushstroke. As we recall the boldly brushed woman of turquoise and black in *The Old Barn* and the sinuous pine bowers of *The Monk,* as we reflect on the humanistic daub of white at the center of *Indian Summer* and the carefully striated bands of color at the horizon of *Summer, Montclair (New Jersey Landscape),* we are reminded of the richly communicative power of the graceful line and the flawlessly executed pictorial mark. Meyer Schapiro best characterized this achievement when expressing his admiration for Eugène Fromentin's analysis of the works of Peter-Paul Rubens. According to Schapiro, "The interest in Fromentin lies in his power to make us see that the highest human values are involved in a patch of color, the bend of a line."[138]

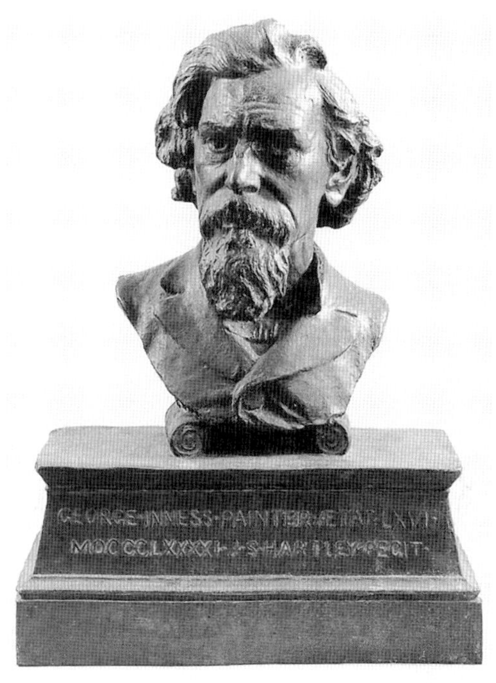

FIG. 14.
Jonathan Scott Hartley (1845–1912), *George Inness,* 1891, bronze, 14½ x 10¾ x 5½", National Academy of Design, New York, Gift of the artist, 1891.

Moreover, Inness's work presaged many of the ideas and efforts of twentieth-century American and European artists. Anticipating Picasso, Inness maintained "a horror of something finished." Inness's art *was* his life; to terminate the former was, in a sense, to block a potential path on his quest for self-knowledge. No amount of persuading by clients or exigencies of commerce would change his mind. If Inness found in Swedenborg's writings a sense of the visionary experience that he could translate through pictorial techniques into a new vocabulary for landscape painting, he may have explored that vocabulary, early in his career, in the amorphous spaces, reduced color palette, and lone, silhouetted figure of *Christmas Eve*, a work that, like van Gogh's *Crows over the Wheat Fields* (1890; National Museum Vincent van Gogh, Amsterdam), reflects both the inscrutability and idiosyncrasy of the personal religious experience. The legacy of *Hazy Morning, Montclair,* a manifestation of Inness's later, vibrant brushstrokes and their unmistakable ability to convey a profound sense of the artist's deep engagement with his work, may reside in the opulent, communicative rivulets of paint from Willem de Kooning's and Jackson Pollock's brushes. Here, too, are pictorial manifestations of James's revolutionary concept of consciousness as a "stream of thought."

By contrast, the structured organization of features in *Lake Nemi* and *October Noon* (among many other works), which conjure allusions to Platonic forms and which cohabitate with Inness's erratic, highly personal brushmarks, together produce a seamless sense of unity, a 'resolution' of "theology" into "a scientific form" akin to Piet Mondrian's resolution of his Theosophical beliefs, through architectonic forms and colors in space, in his paintings of the 1930s. We might extend this legacy to Mark Rothko's expression of "the human drama" in his hazy, floating blocks of color, or Barnett Newman's evocation of Kabbalistic themes in his "zip" paintings of the late 1940s and 1950s.

Inness's "anonymous figures"—as seen in such alluring paintings as *The Lone Farm, Nantucket; October Noon;* and *Hazy Morning, Montclair*—fuse the mysterious with the revealing. Often incarnated with only two or three rapid brushstrokes, these figures lure us into a deeper engagement with the landscape so that, over time, we may potentially discern reflections of our own humanity in Inness's visionary spaces. Broadly brushed and often barely visible, they depend, for their very existence, on our desire and ability to conceive them, to incarnate them within our imagination. Our search for their identity activates our most intense, most contemplative powers; in this way it engenders a form of reverie. Now, in this liminal place, we may begin our authentic search, Hamlet's search, for that "something . . . that is more than natural." Here, on the Jamesian "margins of consciousness," we may, perhaps, gain insight into James's notion of our unity with "some form of superhuman life with which we may, unknown to ourselves, be co-conscious."[139] In this place, we may begin to address those metaphysical questions that Inness posed, that inspired him throughout his life, and that engendered his most provocative visionary paintings: "what is this thing we call life, and how does it operate"?

PAINTINGS AND COMMENTARIES

The wisest and best way to know George Inness is to sit before his works, to search them to their depths, to study each item of composition, its bearing upon the great mass, to find, if one may, the law by which he constructed his proportions and placements, to discover the reasons for color or tone choice, or that deeper significance, the impulse, artistic and religious, which created it.

—Elliott Daingerfield

Inness's Artistic Self-Education

GEORGE INNESS'S first great artistic epiphany may have come about 1843, when he was studying with the French itinerant landscape painter Régis-François Gignoux. Feeling frustrated with his work one day, Inness went for a walk and noticed an engraving after an old-master painting in the window of a print shop. "I could not then analyze that which attracted me to it, but it fascinated me," he later recalled. He asked the print-seller to show him others. "There was a power of motive, a bigness of grasp in them. They were nature rendered grand instead of being belittled by trifling detail and puny execution. I began to take them out with me to compare them with nature as she really appeared; and the light began to dawn."[1] Inness reflected the grandeur of these old-master paintings in *A Bit of the Roman Aqueduct* (1852; Plate 1), although, as noted earlier, he diminished the significance of the eponymous subject, the Roman aqueduct. For Inness, the artist's interpretative powers would always supplant any inherent value to known sites or narrative skeins.

During trips to Paris in 1852 and in 1853–54, Inness visited the Salon and studied works by Barbizon painters. Although Inness's pictorial practices were already somewhat freer than those of his American colleagues, his exposure to the School of Fontainebleau—especially its appreciation of the brushstroke as an expressive tool—spurred his incipient desire to challenge the more conservative artistic traditions of his native country. *Hackensack Meadows, Sunset* (1859; Plate 2) and *Landscape* (1860; Plate 3) reflect the new direction of Inness's work and his admiration for many of Barbizon's essential features: the informal setting (*paysage intime*), the exploration of subtle tonal harmonies, the "liquid freedom" (to use Robert L. Herbert's eloquent description) of Théodore Rousseau's brushstrokes,[2] and, perhaps most important, a deep concern for humanistic ideals, for the plight of the individual.

In Paris, Inness may also have been exposed to the ideas of Thomas Couture who, in his art classes, encouraged his students to break from the academy, from its dependence on historical narratives and other such compositional formats. Although Couture insisted on never re-touching a work (a principle that ran counter to all that Inness did), he did teach his students to penetrate and capture the inception of the creative act, the "*première pensée*." We sense Inness's appreciation of this idea in works created after his move to Medfield, Massachusetts, in June 1860. Inness masterfully captures Barbizon's freshness in the cool blue and lilac shadows of *Winter Evening, Medfield* (c. 1860; Plate 5); the bold daubs of dusky yellows, pinks, and lavenders that represent billowing clouds in *Clearing Up* (1860; Plate 6); and in *Evening Landscape* (1862; Plate 7), with its feathery streaks of brown leaves against a radiant yellow-orange sun. In *The Huntsman* (1859; Plate 4), Inness translates the freshness of the *ébauche*—a sketch, a vehicle for the spontaneous expression of the first perception—into a finished painting, an arena for a lively, ongoing dialogue between man and nature.

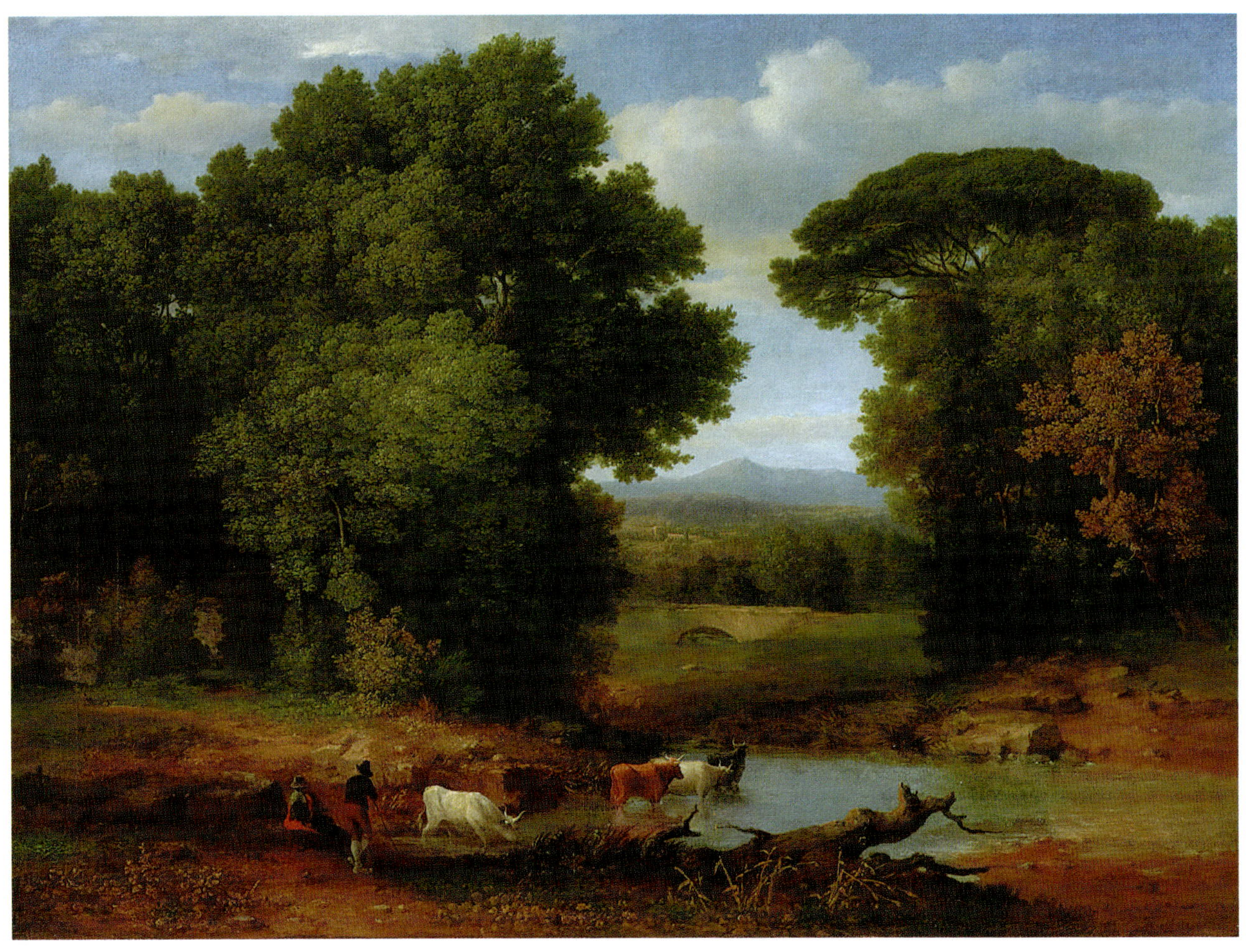

1

1. A BIT OF THE ROMAN AQUEDUCT

1852, oil on canvas, 39 x 53 9/16"
High Museum of Art, Atlanta
Purchased with funds from the Members Guild and through exchange, 69.42

Following pages:

2. HACKENSACK MEADOWS, SUNSET

1859, oil on canvas, 18 1/4 x 26"
The New-York Historical Society, on permanent loan from The New York Public Library, Stuart Collection 22

3. LANDSCAPE

1860, oil on paper, 16 1/4 x 24"
National Academy of Design, New York

4. THE HUNTSMAN

1859, oil on canvas, 30 x 25"
Collection of Robert K. Fitzgerel

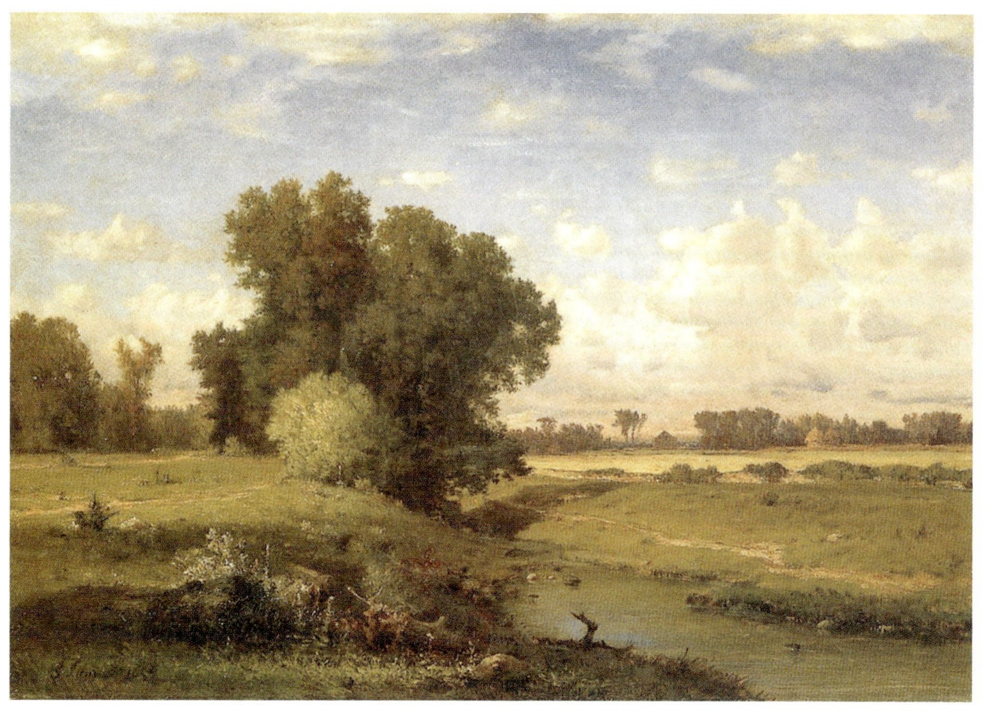

2

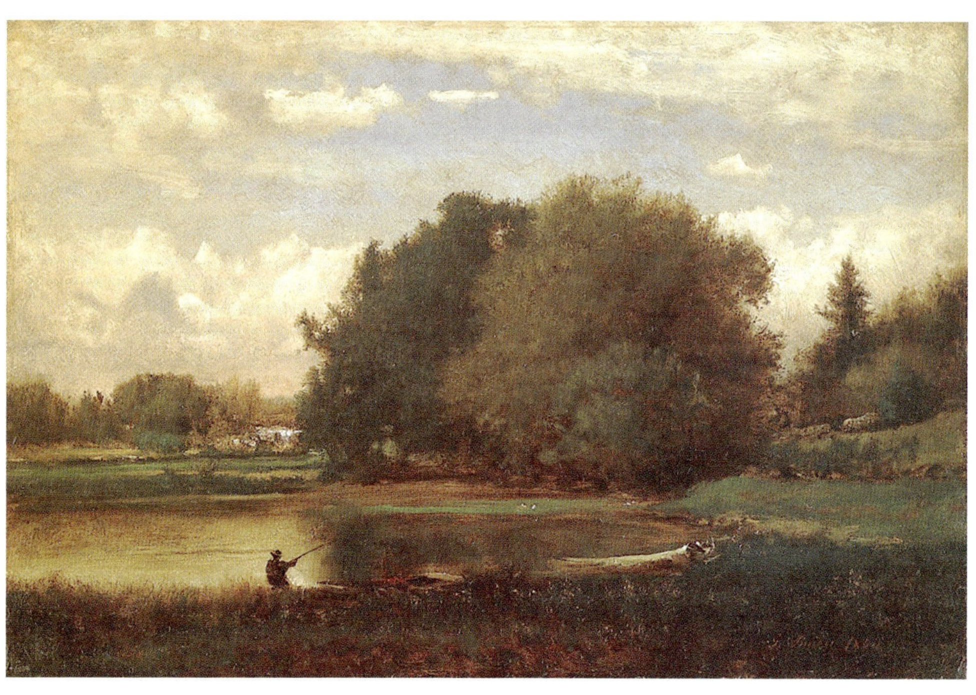

3

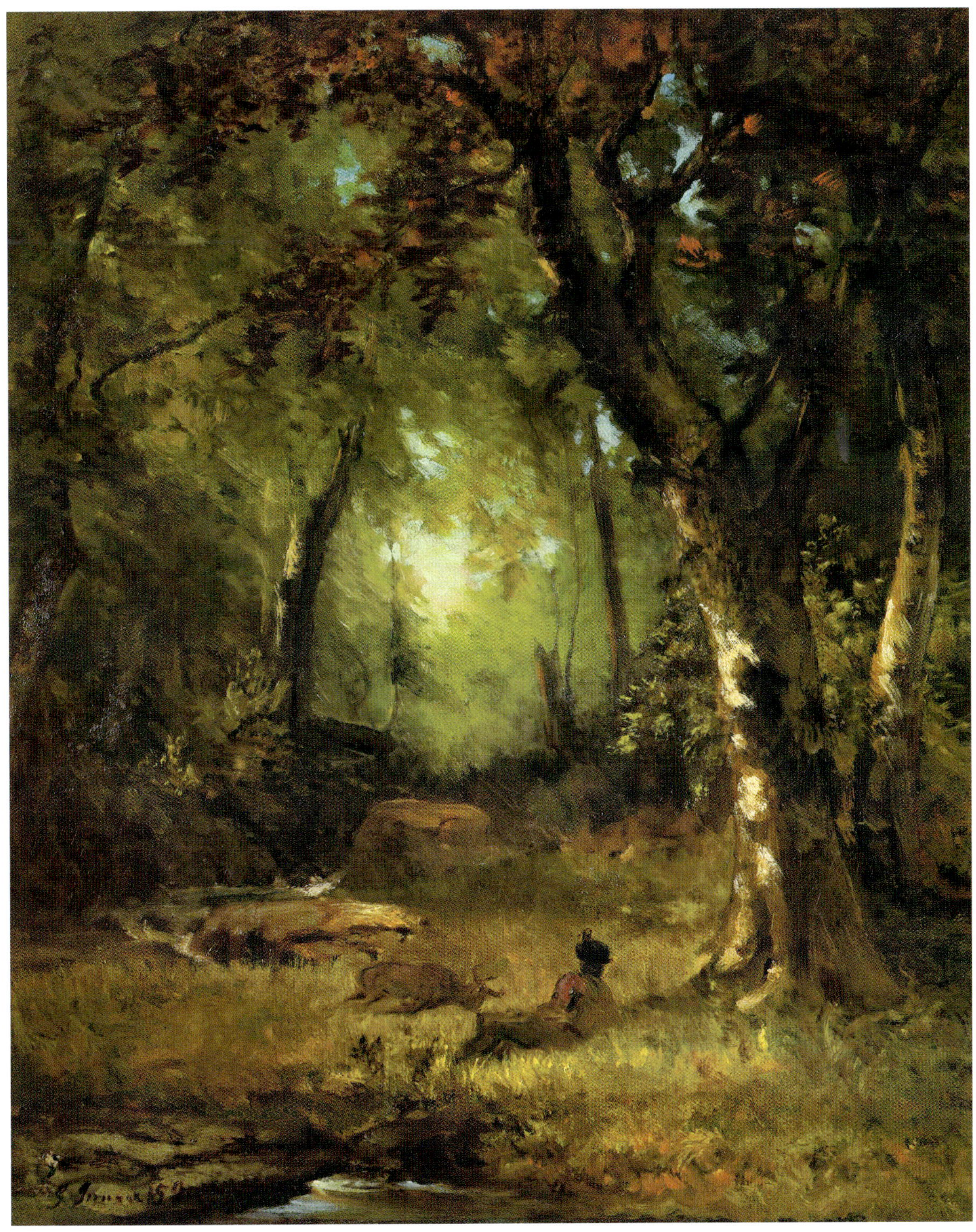

4

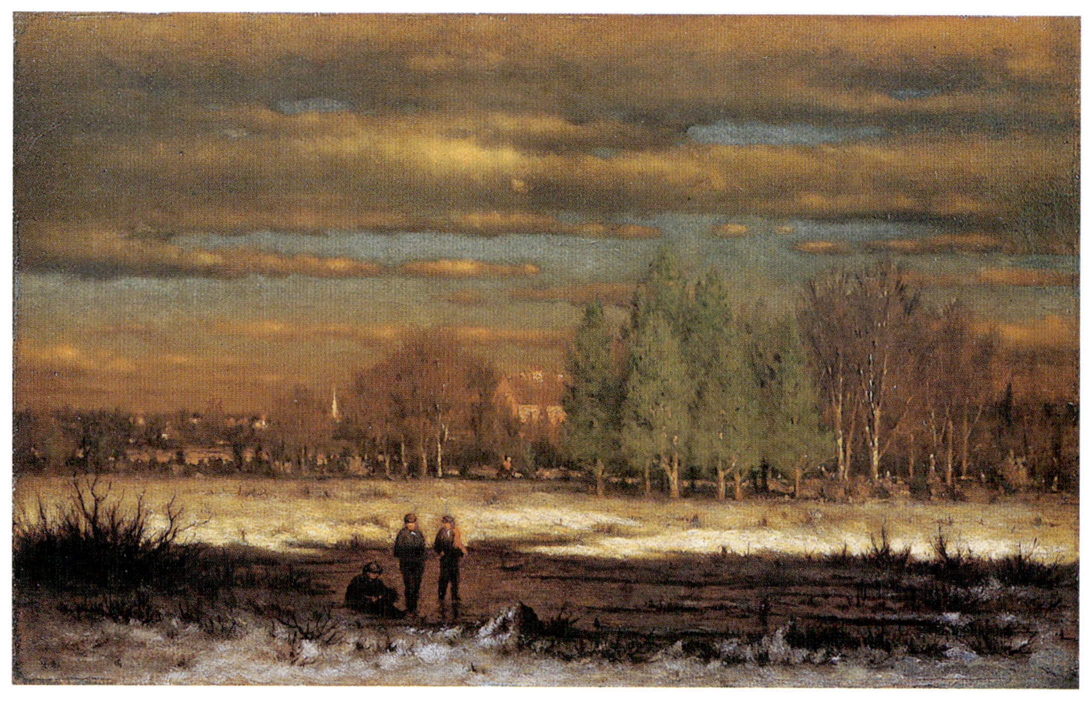

5

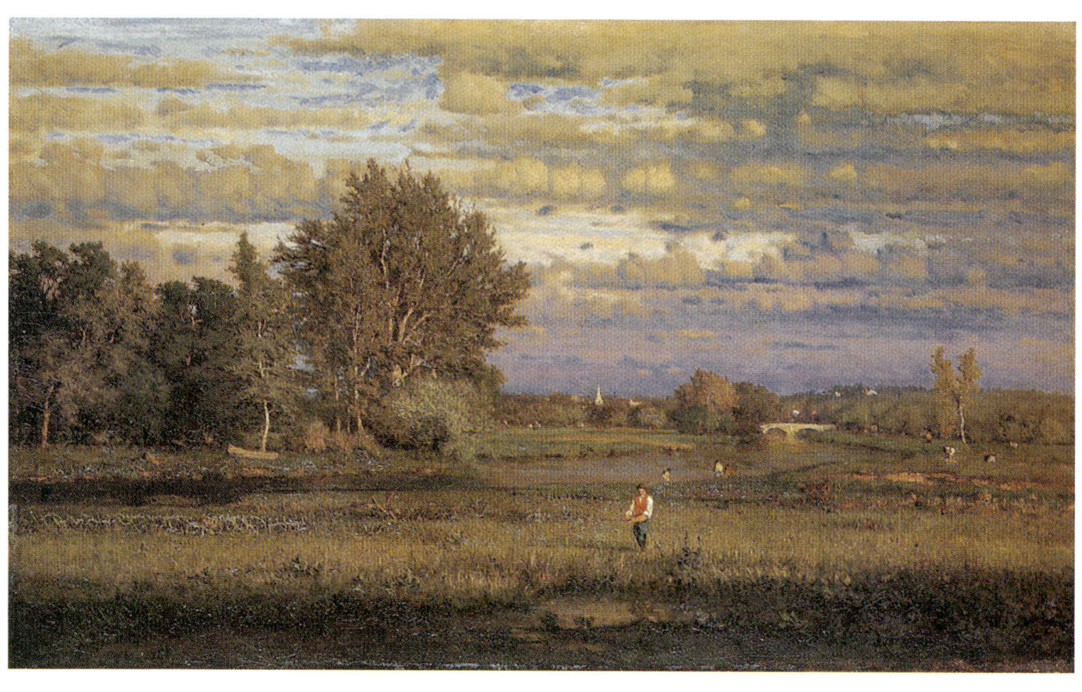

6

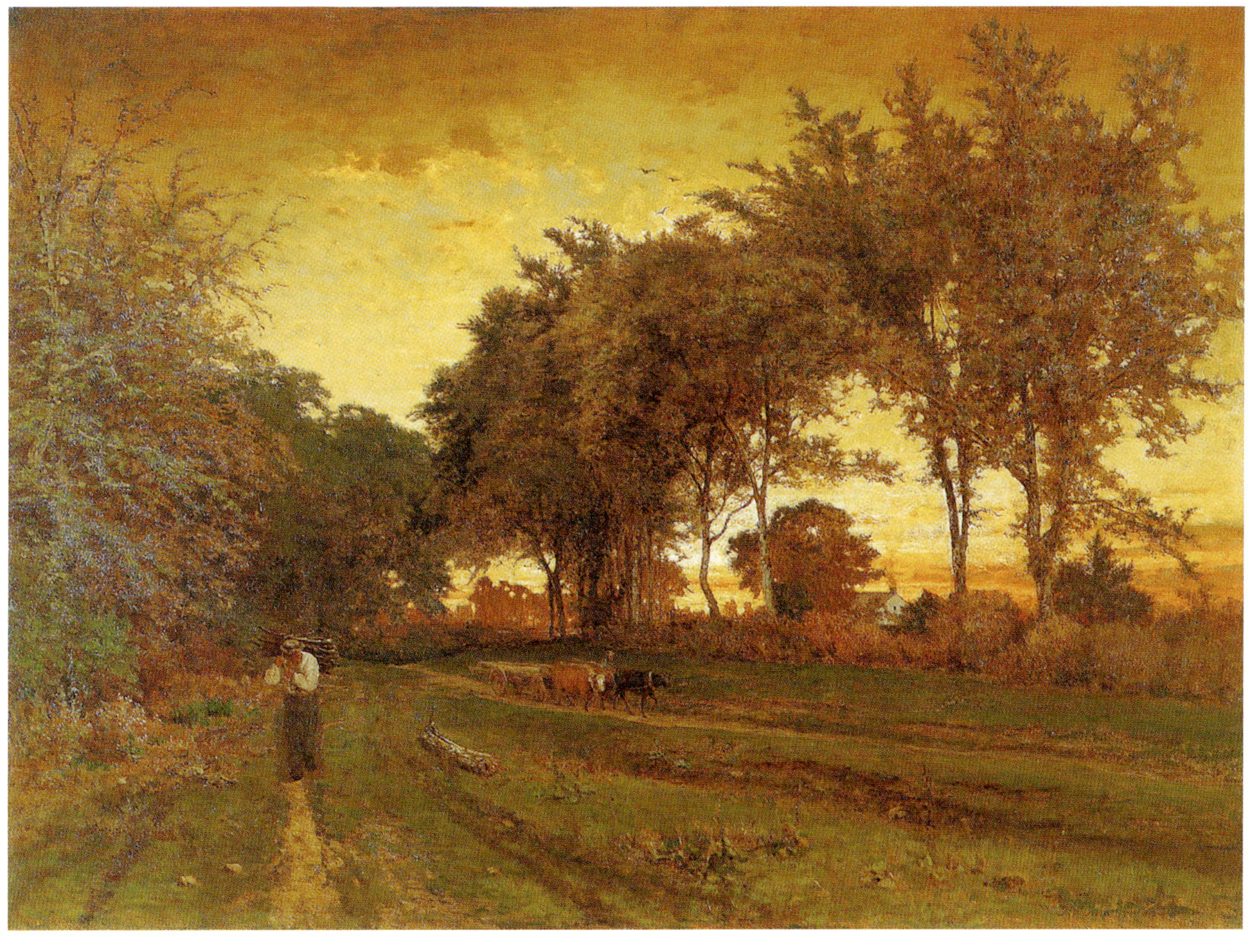

5. WINTER EVENING, MEDFIELD

c. 1860, oil on canvas, 10 x 16"
Private collection, New England,
courtesy of Thomas Colville Fine Art

6. CLEARING UP

1860, oil on canvas, 15 x 25"
George Walter Vincent Smith Art Museum, Springfield,
Massachusetts, George Walter Vincent Smith Collection
Photography by David Stansbury

7. EVENING LANDSCAPE

1862, oil on canvas, 48¼ x 66¼"
Permanent Collection, Museum of Art,
Washington State University, Pullman

Art and Poetry: Inness and Swedenborg on Spiritual Space

> All journeys in the spiritual world occur by means of changes of the state of more inward things, to the point that journeys are simply changes of state. This is how I have been brought into the heavens by the Lord. . . . My spirit has been brought, while my body stayed in one place. This is how all angels travel. So they do not have any spatial intervals, and without spatial intervals, there are no spaces. . . . When anyone travels from one place to another—be it within his community, within his own grounds, in his gardens, or to others outside his community—he gets there more quickly if he is willing and more slowly if he is unwilling. . . . I have often witnessed this, and marveled at it.
>
> —Emanuel Swedenborg[1]

ACCORDING TO SWEDENBORG'S STRIKING DESCRIPTION, spiritual space possesses a paradoxical character. It is both organic, in that it contains features recognizable to humans (gardens, roads, and fields) but nonspatial, in that distances cannot be measured according to established spatial standards (units of distance such as miles and furlongs, even high, wide, long, and deep). Although travel in the spiritual realm signifies a change from one place to another, it is not conducted by physical activity but, as Swedenborg mystically explains, by thought. The greater the desire to travel, the faster the mission is accomplished.

The idea, fundamental to Swedenborgian theology, that spiritual space is both organic and nonspatial—that objects and individuals appear as they do on earth but that spaces are conceived of completely differently, that space and time are byproducts of thought—intrigued artists and poets of Inness's generation. Elizabeth Barrett Browning (1806–1861) had been introduced to Swedenborgian doctrine in 1851; by 1857, she described herself as a "Swedenborgian."[2] In all likelihood, she nourished her interest in the doctrines after she and her husband, the poet Robert Browning (1812–1889), moved in November 1853 into an apartment on the Boca di Leone in Rome directly above that of the Swedenborgian William Page. Page and the Brownings soon developed a friendship and each of the Brownings subsequently sat for portraits by the artist.[3] Robert Browning became especially interested in Page's analysis of the Swedenborgian affiliation of numbers with the proportions of the human body; it is, therefore, likely that Page discussed other aspects of Swedenborg's writings with Mrs. Browning. In "Aurora Leigh," she alluded to the mystical character of spiritual space in her portrayal of the dual physical/spiritual identity of nature:

See the earth,
The body of our body, the green earth,
Indubitably human like this flesh
And these articulated veins through which
Our heart drives blood! there's not a flower
of spring
That dies ere June, but vaunts itself allied
By issue and symbol, by significance
And correspondence, to that spirit-world
Outside the limits of our space and time,
Whereto we are bound.[4]

Writing in the midst of a great outpouring of interest in spiritualism and spiritualist mediums, at a time when trance writing and trance lecturing were commonplace and widely attended activities, Walt Whitman frequently referred in his poems to immortality—to the extension of life after bodily death. In the first edition of *Leaves of Grass,* Whitman asks, "What do you think has become of the young and old men? // And what do you think has become of the women and children?" "They are alive and well somewhere," he replied. "The smallest sprout shows there is really no death." And later: "All goes onward and outward. . . . and nothing collapses, // And to die is different from what anyone supposed, and luckier."[5]

As a young journalist, Whitman revealed his particular interest in Swedenborg. He attended New Church meetings in 1858 and, the same year, published a profile on Swedenborg in the *Daily Times,* of Brooklyn, New York. Whitman seems to have been especially impressed by the matter-of-fact tone of Swedenborg's writings: "he never faints, or goes into literary or any other hysterics," Whitman acknowledged. For this reason, Whitman asserted that we "never think of Swedenborg as an impostor; his life, and all about him, when studied, forbid such an inference." The coherence of Swedenborg's ideas—his descriptions of conversations with angels and the like—allowed Whitman to acknowledge Swedenborg's influence and relevance not only for "his followers, among whom are some of the leading minds of our nation," but also for "American thought, theology, and literature" in general.[6]

In his revised edition of *Leaves of Grass* of 1891–92, Walt Whitman absorbed the paradoxical identity of spiritual space and the Swedenborgian notion of influx into his conception of his own world. In a stream-of-thought style that itself conjures the idea of Swedenborgian influx, Whitman wrote,

I know I am solid and sound,
To me the converging objects of the universe perpetually flow,
All are written to me, and I must get what the writing means.

I know I am deathless,
I know this orbit of mind cannot be swept by a carpenter's compass,
I know I shall not pass like a child's carlacue cut with a burnt stick at night.[7]

Although not known today as a poet, George Inness wrote several poems that allude to immortality and to the Swedenborgian notion of the organic but nonspatial space of the spiritual realm. In "Exaltation," Inness implores his readers to

Sing joyfully!
Earth-bound no more,
We rise.
Creation speaks anew
In brighter tones.
Life now enthrones
Its image forms,
Winged with a joy that
Ne'er from nature grew. . . .

Sing joyfully!
A real world we see.
Earth's meadows and its hills
Within thy heart
Their joys impart
To us as well as thee.
Sing joyfully!
God all space fills.[8]

Beginning in the mid-1860s, Inness developed a conception of pictorial space that calls to mind Swedenborg's descriptions of spiritual space and forms. In this unusual incarnation, forms appear both recognizable and wholly enigmatic. For example, the huddled figure walking down a snowy path in *Christmas Eve (Winter Moonlight)* (1866; Plate 9) is clearly human, but his mission and even identity cannot be discerned. His body casts more than one shadow, and these shadows seem as corporeal (or as spiritual) as he is. Furthermore, his silhouetted form visually aligns with the silhouetted bank of trees in the distance; the two narrative elements compress the illusion of three-dimensional, naturalistic space. Space, in this sense, appears to be organic but nonspatial.

Inness enacts a likeminded disorientation of space and forms in *Sunset at Montclair* (1892; Plate 12), one of his most captivating and successful late landscape paintings. Here, a thick web of intersecting greenish-brown brushstrokes extends from the upper right to the lower right edge of the painting. It resists identification as an extended leafy bower and remains essentially unaffiliated with any single naturalistic form. It seems, quite simply, to remain a web of intermingled brushstrokes on the surface of the canvas. By obviating the illusion of foreground, middle ground, and distance, this web erases coordinates of extent and scale, of light and shade, of form and function, all of which might permit us to establish a three-dimensional interpretation of the landscape's setting. Along the same lines, the reflection of the glowing orange sun in the lower right edge of the painting—perhaps on a small body of water—visually aligns two seemingly distant physical coordinates. Again, Inness alludes to the identities of naturalistic forms and yet renounces the illusion of naturalistic, three-dimensional space.

In *Edge of the Woods* (c. 1890; Plate 13), Inness extends the unifying structure of *Sunset at Montclair* by reducing the segment of lavender-blue sky to a small section of the left-hand side of the painting. He overlays the lower half, the right side, and a small section of the left side with an amorphous network of daubed green brush marks. Although these marks clearly refer to trees, the relationships of the individual bowers are wholly uncertain. In the midst of this uncertainty, a slight patch of red at the right edge and a few, tiny daubs of white at the left provide hazy indications of houses. The identities of these forms, while marginally known, vacillate between the physical and the ephemeral, the seen and the unseen, the known and the mysterious. Inness's extraordinarily inventive pictorial technique tempts viewers with allusions to the familiar while invalidating their expectations of representational legibility. In Whitman's memorable phrase, they are forms and spaces that "cannot be swept by a carpenter's compass."

8. SUNSET

c. 1860–65, oil on board, 10¼ x 14½"
Private collection, courtesy of
Berry-Hill Galleries, Inc.

9. CHRISTMAS EVE (WINTER MOONLIGHT)

1866, oil on canvas, 22 x 30"
Montclair Art Museum, Montclair, New Jersey, Museum
Purchase; Florence O. R. Lang Acquisition Fund, 1948.29

BY THE LATE 1850s AND EARLY 1860s, Inness was probably reading texts by Swedenborg in which the author inscrutably described spiritual space as "organic but non-spatial." It is also likely that Inness's preoccupation with the concept of the unknowable or "unseen"—which he expressed in his manuscripts, in interviews of the late 1870s, and through his late landscape paintings—took root during this early phase of his artistic career.

Two paintings that presciently embody Inness's preoccupation with "organic but non-spatial space" are *Sunset* (c. 1860–65; Plate 8) and *Christmas Eve (Winter Moonlight)* (1866; Plate 9). It is likely that Inness's point of departure for *Sunset* was the Delaware Water Gap. We note its trademark indentation in the hills at the center of the composition. The subject was eminently familiar to Inness, who had painted it, in far more representational incarnations, in several works of the late 1850s (see, for example, the version of 1857 in the Montclair Art Museum, Montclair, New Jersey). Here, by contrast, the subject may as well be unknown. Inness focuses our attention not on the site itself but at the epicenter of the painting, where he has embedded signs of his directorial presence within the thick yellow-orange impasto of the sun. Light from this sun illuminates spaces that possess no clear geographical coordinates. Trees are without phyto- graphic details, and the two figures, which gaze at the sun from their foreground outpost, are seen only in silhouette.

In *Christmas Eve,* Inness reverses climatic conditions but uses a similar compositional structure to conjure an equally enigmatic aura. Snow has fallen on a desolate terrain; again, we see the central figure only in silhouette. A precursor to the "anonymous figure" of Inness's late landscape paintings, this figure simultaneously absorbs and rejects any number of identities that we might impose on him: the artist's or viewer's double; the lonely pilgrim on a long "spiritual journey" or path to transcendence; oneiric character shadowed by what Carl Gustav Jung later will identify as signs of the unconscious or aspects of his personality accessible only in dreams. No matter, for our interest in him lies in the multiplicity, the expansiveness, of his identities. In the end, while ruminating on *Sunset* and *Christmas Eve,* we aspire not to transcend Inness's "organic but non-spatial" spaces but, instead, to inhabit them ourselves.

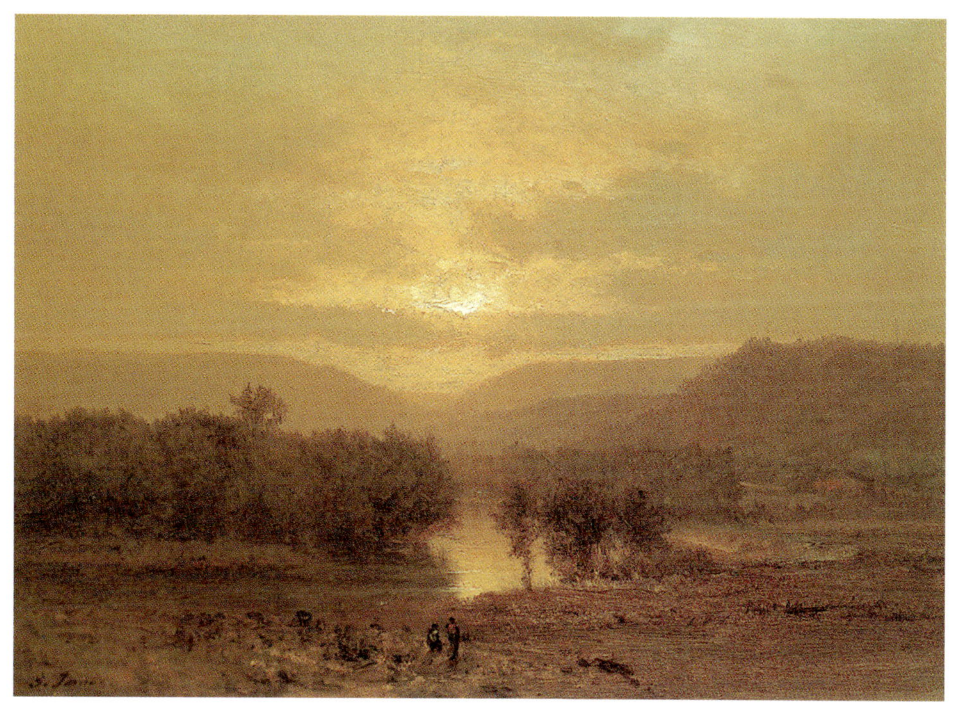

8

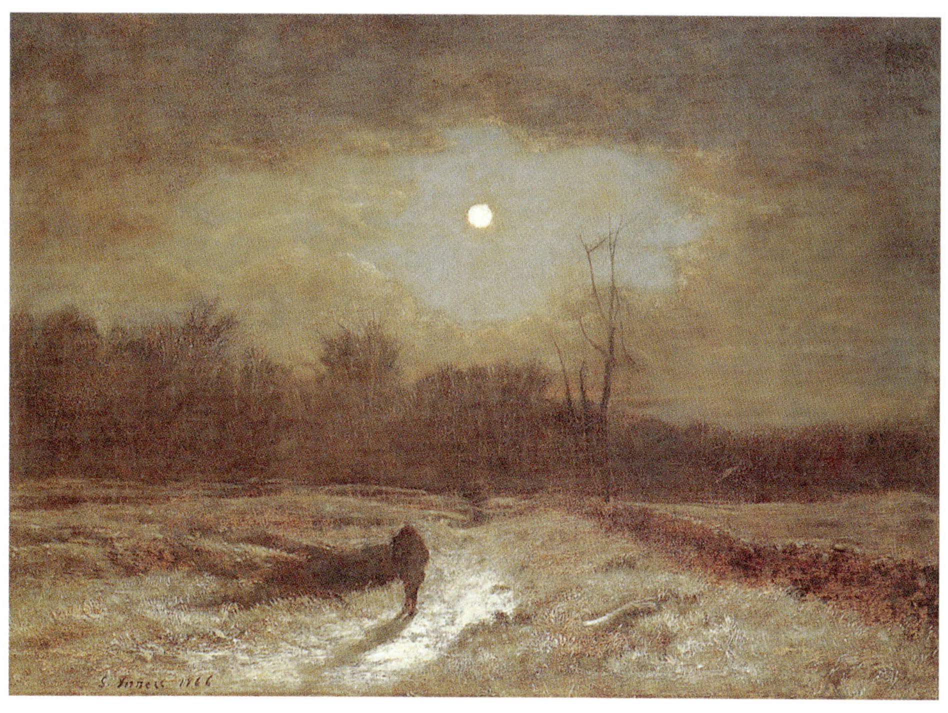

9

10. WINTER, CLOSE OF DAY (A WINTER SKY)

1866, oil on canvas, 22 x 30½"
The Cleveland Museum of Art
The Charles W. Harkness Gift, 1927.388

IN 1865, THE REVEREND HENRY WARD BEECHER (1813–1887) delivered a lecture in which he elucidated the essential artistic qualities in landscape painting.[1] As a well-known author of essays on art and as an enthusiastic collector of paintings and sculpture, including at least eight landscapes by Inness, Beecher was recognized as a valuable commentator on the subject.[2] In keeping with his long-standing trust in the ability of human emotion to galvanize communion with the divine, Beecher censured any image that "awakens in the beholder any *physical* ideas," meaning, he said, colors and forms that are pleasing for their own sake.[3] Beecher admitted that the pleasure derived in sensing "harmony & variety, in physical things, addressed to the physical sense" grants "a vivid gratification, worthy to be satisfied." Still, he asserted, "If a man sees no more & feels no more, in the presence of an exquisite scenery, than any other or ordinary man . . . he does only well." For Beecher, such paintings represented "the anatomical landscape"; they were works of a "useful copyist." What, Beecher asked, "is more?"

Beecher believed that artists, in general, were capable of eliciting the "heart & imagination" of the viewer. The superior demonstration of this ability, according to Beecher, "makes Geo. Inness the first of American landscape painters." Beecher permitted himself an exuberant description of Inness's work:

> His real pictures are steeped & saturated with feeling. His heart is as fitful as an Eolian harp, but every wind swells it with wild music. His pictures are almost a journal & confession. This one is ragged, craggy & fierce in its hateful clouds, its sky is chilly, its rocks & trees are weird and ugly. You would think that a crew of devils damned had just danced there & nothing had been cleared up after them.

Not all of Inness's work required such tempestuous descriptions. Evoking a title he had given to one of Inness's paintings ("The Light Triumphant"), Beecher described another work by the artist as "tender & harmonious, so radiant with light triumphant over storm, that you will, any time you look upon it, feel new courage to fight despondency with." Of a "sad, evening scene" by Inness, Beecher proclaimed, "Now & then he has a picture of perfect peace. The heavens & the earth & he that look upon them are at deep rest. It tranquilizes the soul even to look upon it." Inness's landscape paintings called to Beecher's mind certain profound religious qualities: tranquility, contemplation, even absolution.

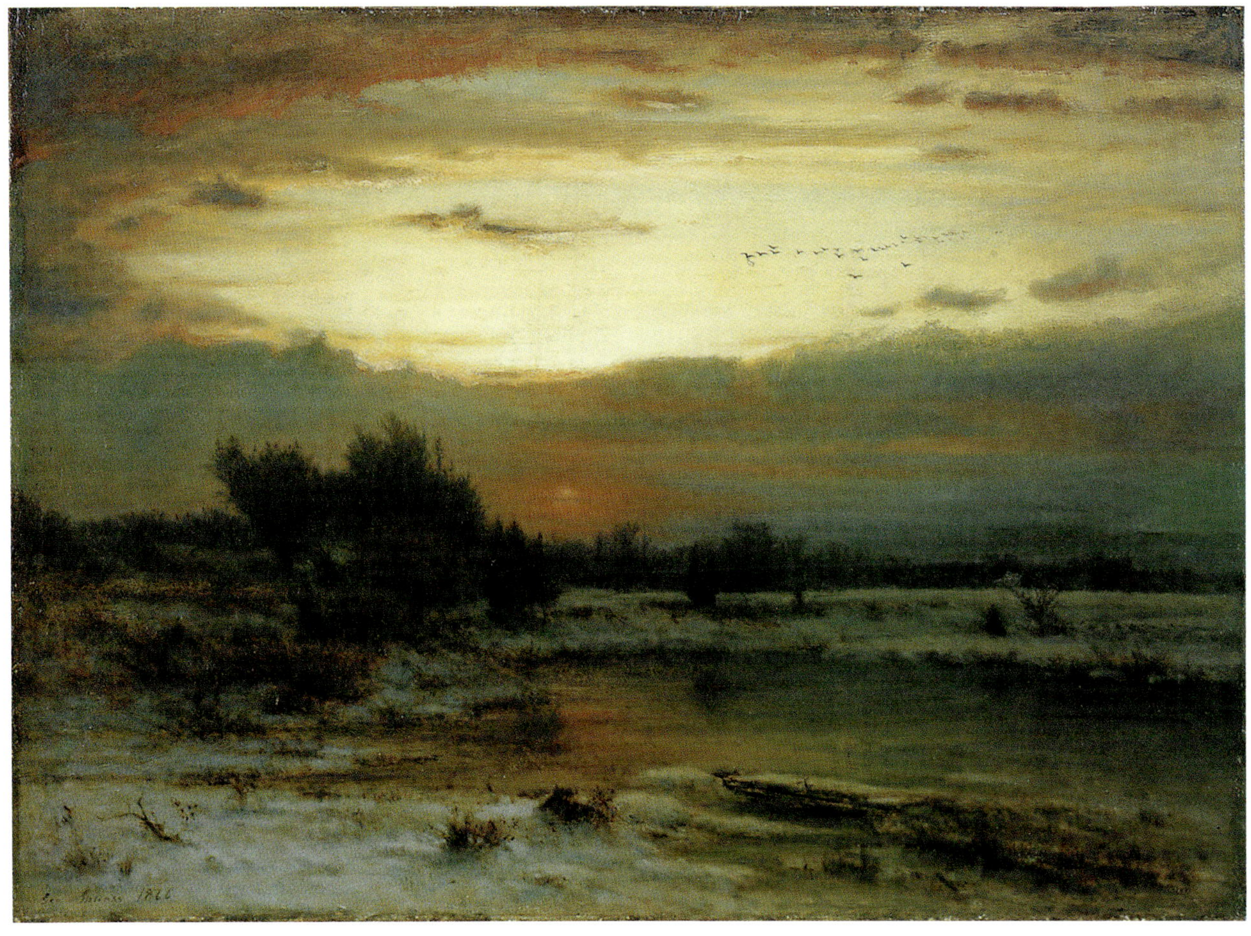

10

Winter, Close of Day (A Winter Sky) embodies Beecher's description of Inness's finest landscape paintings. In this scene of near-Paleolithic dislocation, Inness eliminated all distracting features to focus on the way in which sunlight gradually resurrects a petrified terrain. A faint reflection of the setting sun—an echo in tenuous streaks of persimmon—warms a small patch of the frozen pond. At both edges of the forest, faint silhouettes of houses emerge from the scumbled brown fusion of trees. During an era in which Inness's Hudson River School colleagues gladly celebrated the physical beauty of popular, recognizable settings, Inness offered pure topographical anonymity. Rather than attempt to "awaken in the beholder any *physical* ideas," Inness desired to "awaken an emotion" in his viewers. Inspired, in all likelihood, by his prolific reading of Swedenborgian literature during the 1860s, Inness captured, in this quietly impressive painting, the fundamentally and profoundly enigmatic character of the religious experience.

11. THE VALLEY OF THE SHADOW OF DEATH

1867, oil on canvas, 45⅝ x 72⅞"
The Frances Lehman Loeb Art Center, Vassar College, Poughkeepsie, New York
Gift of Charles M. Pratt, 1917.1.6

THE VALLEY OF THE SHADOW OF DEATH (Plate 11) represents both an atypical and fitting work within the context of this interpretation of Inness's paintings and metaphysical ideas. It is atypical in having derived from narrative texts—a rare occurrence in Inness's body of work and unique in this presentation of his paintings. It is entirely fitting, though, in that the narratives relate to Swedenborgian doctrine, the theme of much of this study. An impressive work on the scale of the "great pictures" of Frederic E. Church and Albert Bierstadt, it nevertheless repudiates the Hudson River School artist's devotion to illustrating nature's myriad physical beauties. The subject of extensive press attention when first exhibited in May 1867, *The Valley of the Shadow of Death* was probably viewed by more people than any other Inness painting to date.[1] For these reasons and others, it remains central to most investigations of Inness's pictorial intentions and achievements.

The Valley of the Shadow of Death appears to be the only intact surviving painting from a three-part series on the theme of The Triumph of the Cross.[2] According to Inness's son, "a syndicate of gentlemen, Fletcher Harper, Chauncey Depew, Clarke Bell, and others" were so impressed by Inness's ideas on Swedenborgian doctrine that they pledged $10,000 for the artist to use during the course of a year as he painted a series on a Swedenborgian theme. The theme of The Triumph of the Cross relates to Swedenborgian doctrine in that, in *The Last Judgment (and Babylon Destroyed)* (1758), Swedenborg describes the Last Judgment, as foretold in the Book of Revelation, as an historical event that he had already witnessed. It consisted of the end of the "old" Christian church, the Lord's Second Coming, and the establishment of a new church, or "New Jerusalem," in the spiritual world. This new church intended to "counter the dogmatism of traditional Christianity" and embody new freedoms of thought in spiritual matters.[3]

Loosely following the Swedenborgian theme, Inness painted, as the second and third works in this series, *The Vision of Faith* and *The New Jerusalem*. In a circular that accompanied the exhibition of the paintings, he described the progression of events represented. He endeavored, in *The Valley of the Shadow of Death*,

> to convey to the mind of the beholder an impression of the state into which the soul comes when it begins to advance toward a spiritual life, or toward any more perfected state in its journey, until it arrives to its Sabbath or rest. Here the pilgrim is leaving the natural light, whose warm

> rays still faintly illumine the foreground of the scene. Before him all is uncertainty. His light hereafter must be that of faith alone. This I have represented by the cross, giving it the place of the moon, which is the natural emblem of faith, reflecting light upon the sun, its source, assuring us, that although the origin of life is no longer visible, it still exists; but here, clouds may at any moment obscure even the light of faith, and the soul, left in ignorance of what may be its ultimate condition, can only lift its eyes in despair of Him who alone can save, and lead it out of disorder and confusion.[4]

In *The Vision of Faith,* Inness derived inspiration from John Bunyan's *Pilgrim's Progress.* Here, the pilgrim (Christian) is "lifted from out the Dark Valley [and] is ministered to by angels." Surrounded by sheep and by the Delectable Mountains in a pastoral landscape, he holds up a "glass" to examine the Holy City before him, the goal of his journey. In *The New Jerusalem,* the pilgrim rests in a "landscape where no part is left uncultivated, but all is made subservient to the pleasure and happiness of its residents." According to Inness, faith becomes "the love of the purified heart, and the perfect understanding, now always acting from its true source of life. [It] acknowledges nothing as the effect of human intelligence, but that all things come from God."[5]

According to Inness's descriptions, *The Valley of the Shadow of Death* appears to be the least overtly narrative of the three grand paintings. The luminous cross in the sky and the pilgrim represent the scene's only recognizable symbols. They form dual focal points in, as Inness wrote, a wholly 'uncertain' setting, a cavernous construction where rocks and striated clouds open into an ocular space in the middle of the scene. (The shape of this space is presaged by the ovoid patch of blue sky in *Christmas Eve [Winter Moonlight]* [1866; Plate 9] and is echoed in the numinous face that emerges through the arching clouds.) Inness does not invite us to peruse this 'uncertain' setting; here, we find none of the designated pathways—commonplace in Hudson River School paintings—that seem to extend from the represented landscape into the viewer's space. (There is little indication, even, of how the pilgrim navigated the treacherous terrain.) The highly reduced palette of muted browns, deep blues, and dusky yellows disassociates the scene from the realm of naturalism.

And yet, spaces and forms are not obscured, as they will be in Inness's late landscape paintings. They may be 'uncertain,' but they are presented lucidly, with all of the restrained brushwork of Inness's landscapes of the early 1850s.[6] Our challenge, therefore, is not to *perceive* Inness's visionary scene but to *comprehend* it. In this sense, *The Valley of the Shadow of Death* resonates with Swedenborgian doctrine through both its narrative theme and its conception of organic forms in the nonspatial spaces of the spiritual realm. In all likelihood, the exquisite clarity of this visionary scene, the clarity that arrives through one's visionary consciousness, inspired Walt Whitman when, in 1889, he composed a poem to accompany a photomechanical reproduction of the painting in *Harper's Weekly*. In his final years, Whitman probably recalled his illuminating visits to wounded Civil War soldiers in makeshift hospitals in Washington. Remembering these visits and inspired by Inness's painting, he would compose "Death's Valley":

> Nay, do not dream, designer dark,
> Thou hast portray'd or hit thy theme entire:
> I, hoverer of late by this dark valley, by its confines, having glimpses of it,
> Here enter lists with thee, claiming my right to make a symbol too.
> For I have seen many wounded soldiers die,
> After dread suffering—have seen their lives pass off with smiles;
> And I have watch'd the death-hours of the old; and seen the infant die;
> The rich, with all his nurses and his doctors;
> And then the poor, in meagerness and poverty;
> And I myself for long, O Death, have breath'd my every breath
> Amid the nearness and the silent thought of thee.
> And out of these and thee,
> I make a scene, a song (not fear of thee,
> Nor gloom's ravines, nor bleak, nor dark—for I do not fear thee,
> Nor celebrate the struggle, or contortion, or hard-tied knot),
> Of the broad blessed light and perfect air, with meadows, rippling tides, and
> trees and flowers and grass,
> And the low hum, of living breeze—and in the midst God's beautiful eternal right hand,
> Thee, holiest minister of Heaven—thee, envoy, usherer, guide at last of all,
> Rich, florid, loosener of the stricture-knot call'd life,
> Sweet, peaceful, welcome Death.[7]

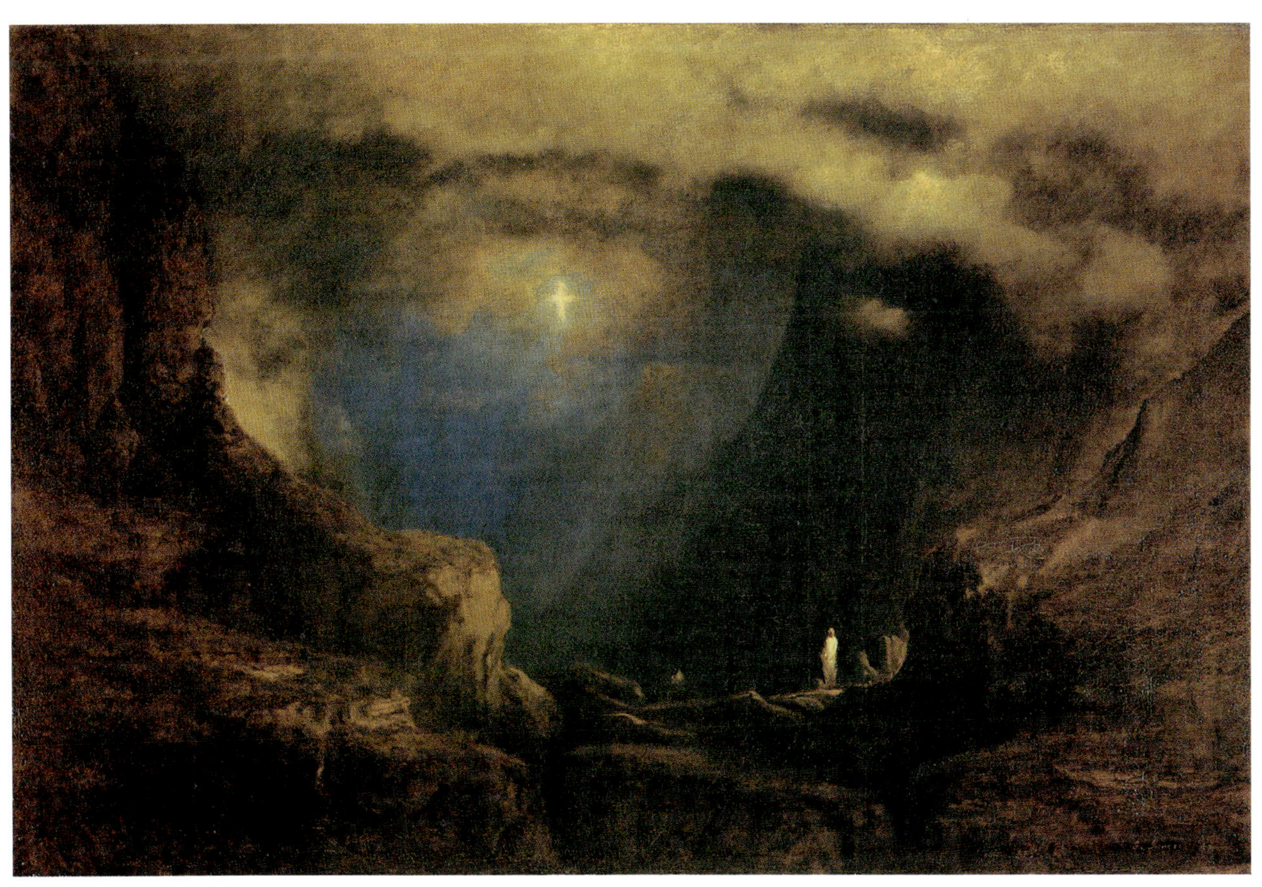

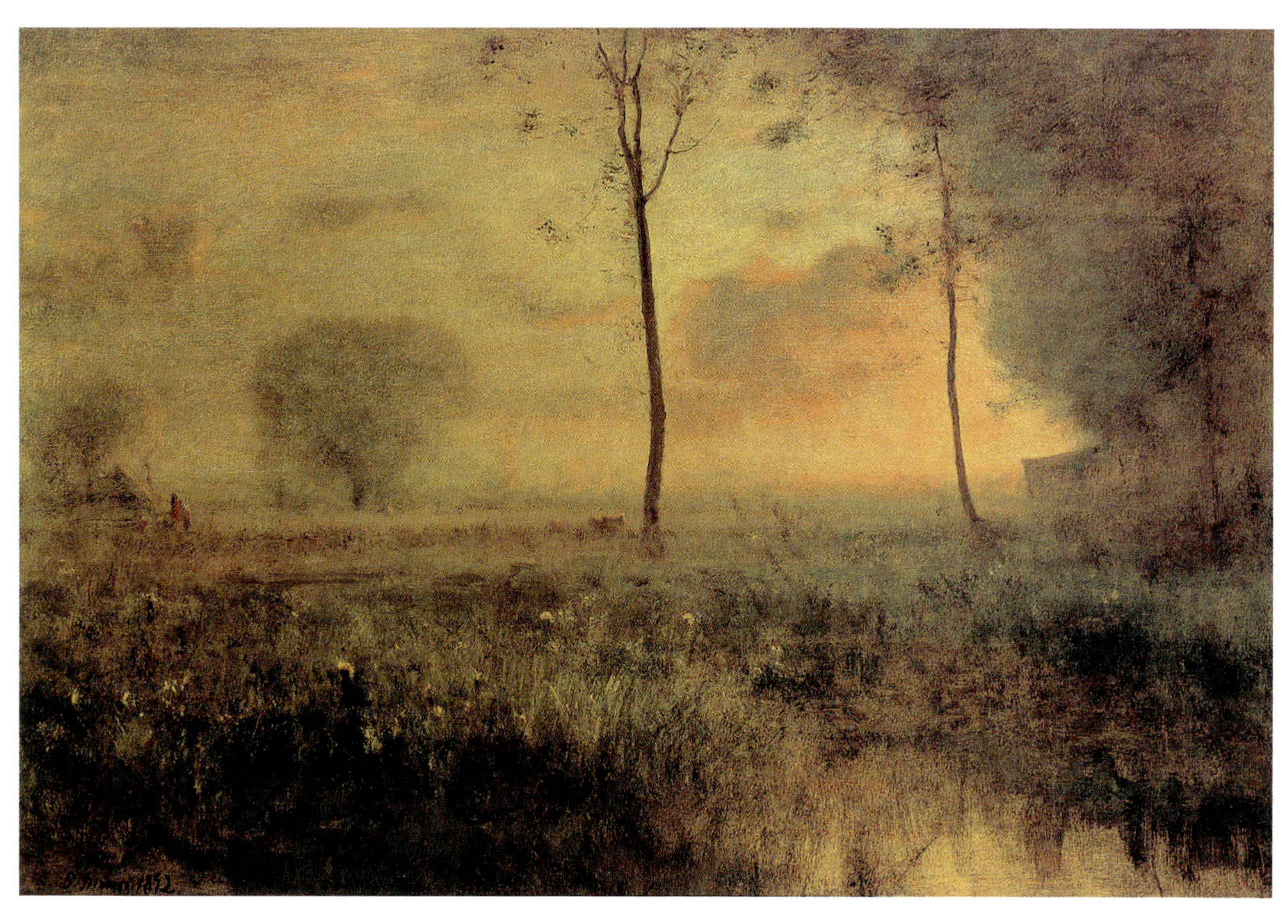

12

12. SUNSET AT MONTCLAIR

1892, oil on canvas, 30 x 45"
Private collection, courtesy of Berry-Hill Galleries, Inc.

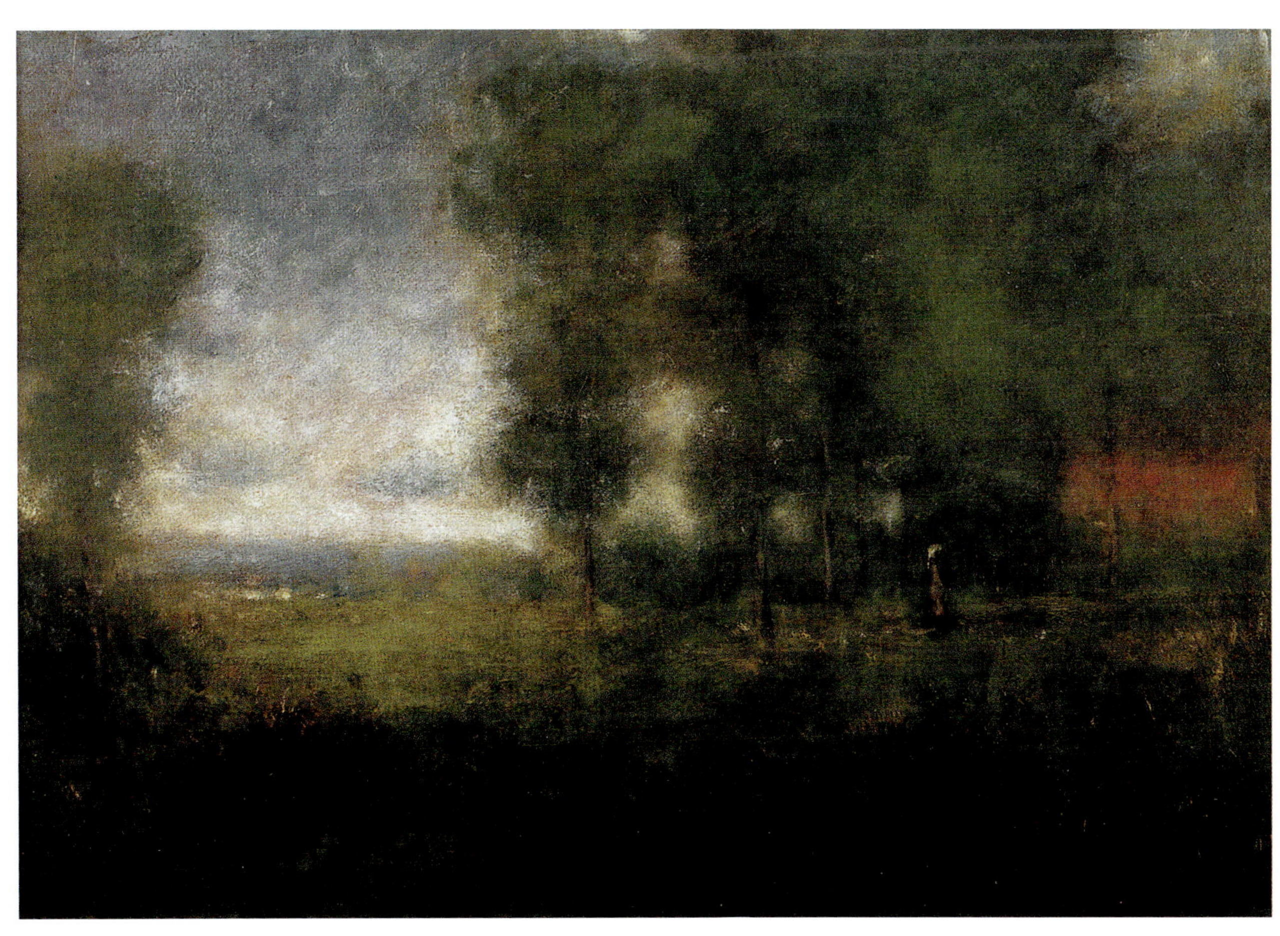

13. EDGE OF THE WOODS

n.d. (c. 1890), oil on canvas, 22 x 32"
National Academy of Design, New York
Gift of Liza and Michael Moses, 2000

14. THE TROUT BROOK

1891, oil on canvas, 30¼ x 45¼"
The Collection of The Newark Museum, New Jersey
Purchase 1965, The Members' Fund

> I heard these sounds again, the very identical sounds themselves, although situated so far back in the past. . . . I was startled at the thought that it was, indeed, this bell which was still tinkling within me and that I could in no wise change its sharp janglings, since, having forgotten just how they died away, to recapture it and hear it distinctly, I was forced to close my ears to the sound of the conversations the masks were carrying on around me. To endeavor to listen to it from nearby, I had to descend again into my own consciousness . . . [T]his distant moment still clung to me and I could recapture it, go back to it, merely by descending more deeply within myself. It was this conception of time as incarnate, of past years as still close held within us, which I was now determined to bring out into such bold relief in my book. —Marcel Proust[1]

> Regardless of the fact that everything in heaven happens in sequence and progresses the way things do in the world, still angels have no concept of time or space. . . . [T]here are no years or days in heaven, but changes of state. —Swedenborg[2]

IN MANY OF HIS LATE LANDSCAPE PAINTINGS, notably *The Trout Brook* (Plate 14), Inness uses forms and brushmarks to embody different levels of temporal awareness. The large, centrally located tree—the painting's most prominent feature—blocks our immediate visual entry into the space of the represented landscape. It seems, in this way, to arrest the flow of time. Feathery streaks of warm browns and yellows to the left and right of the top half of the central tree obfuscate the middle zone and distance of the scene. We penetrate part, but not all, of the space; time, as interpreted through these marks, seems to have been only temporarily suspended. Counteracting both of these interpretations is the freshness of the green, lemony yellow, and yellow-ocher strokes that Inness has used to represent foreground grasses and the reflection of the sun in the pond. These activated brushstrokes lend an aura of immediacy and liveliness, of uninterrupted time, to the landscape.

It is this uncanny combination of conceptions of time that likens Inness's *The Trout Brook* and many paintings of this period to the conception of time experienced by Marcel Proust's narrator as he struggles, in a Jamesian stream-of-thought style, to remember the sound of a jingling bell. Time starts and stops with his powers of self-reflection. It defies the laws of Newtonian time by failing to adhere to any absolute or objective standard. For Inness as for Proust, time is a

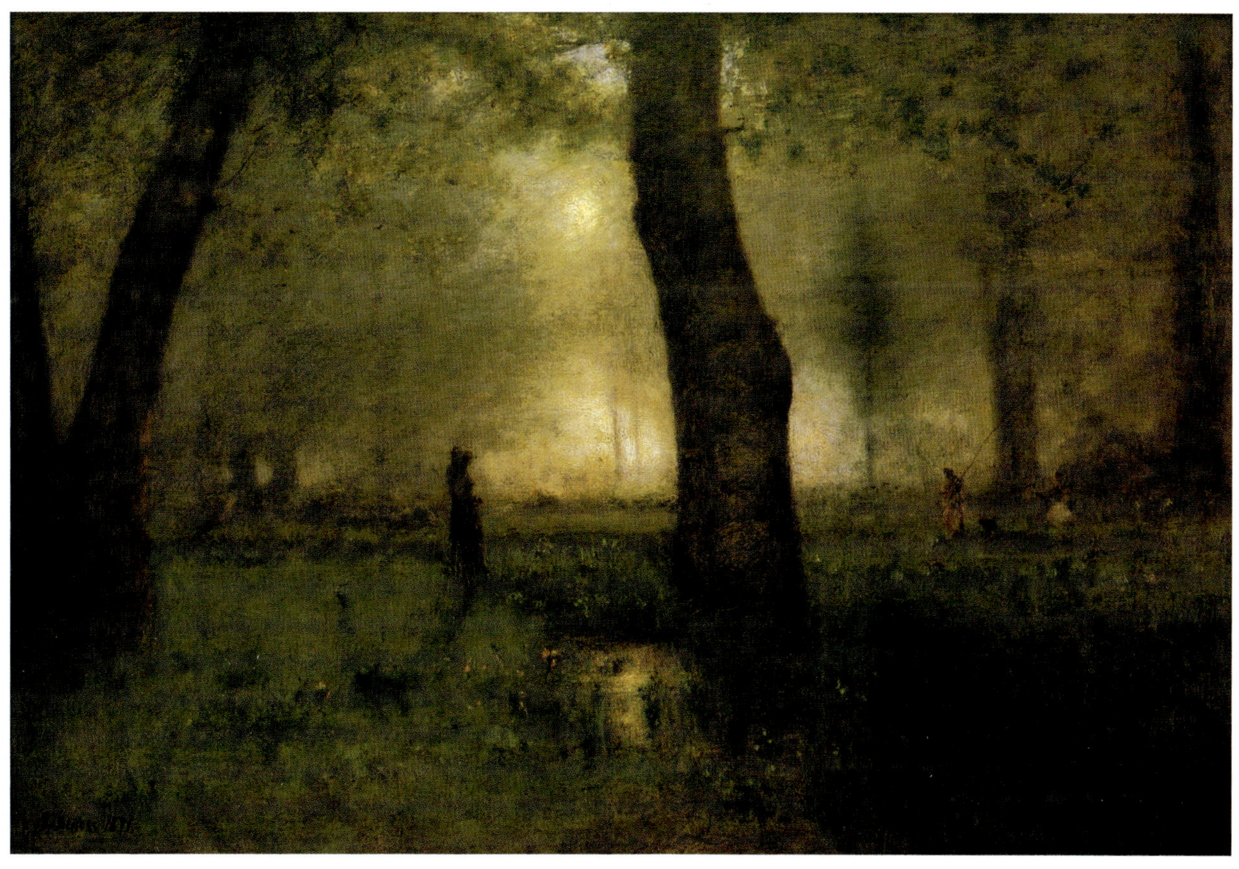

14

servant of consciousness; if so desired, the past can possess all of the immediacy of the present.

The multifaceted notion of time suggested by the physical construction of Inness's *The Trout Brook* and explored by Proust resonates with Swedenborg's description of time in the spiritual realm. According to the Swedish visionary, spiritual time, like spiritual space, cannot be measured by natural standards, by our commonly held notion of duration. Rather, time is measured according to our psychological state. For Swedenborg, the corresponding idea, in the natural realm, is the sense of time passing slowly when waiting but passing quickly when one is enjoying oneself. Swedenborg argued that our use of regular, fixed intervals of duration (minutes, hours, days, and so on) is, therefore, fundamentally false, that it misrepresents reality. For Proust, time is measured by a pluralistic consciousness; for Swedenborg, it is measured in one's spiritual consciousness. Inness may have derived inspiration from Swedenborg's sense of spiritual time as he invented such visionary paintings as *The Trout Brook,* or he may have anticipated Proust's nonsequential description of time. Perhaps, he did both.

Science, Art, and the Visionary in Italy

SINCE THE 1760s, when Benjamin West was the first American painter to travel there, artists and writers have flocked to Italy for inspiration. The palpable presence of her ancient past, her bucolic countryside, her encyclopedic array of architectural styles, the glories of her art—these features provided, and continue to provide, endless subjects for paintings and ideas for poems and novels. Moreover, scenes of Italian landmarks could be counted on to attract clients. A painting of the Roman Campagna represented more than a souvenir from the grand tour; it reflected the knowledge and sophistication of its owner. Although Inness rarely painted landmarks in America, he was persuaded by Williams & Everett, his Boston dealers, to try his hand at more "salable" works in Italy. In April 1870, Inness and his family began a four-year stay in Rome, with summer trips to Venice, Perugia, Pieve di Cadore (the birthplace of Titian), and Albano.

The commercial motivations of Inness's Italian sojourn belie the originality of the works he produced there, for during the early 1870s Inness created some of the most innovative, evocative paintings of his career. When we compare *Lake Nemi* (1872; Plate 15), whose frequently painted subject lies fifteen miles south of Rome, to *Catskill Mountains* (1870; Plate 15a), which represents an equally popular tourist site in upstate New York, we see how, in only two years' time, Inness refined spaces and forms within similar compositional structures. In *Lake Nemi*, Inness presented the segments of land, water, and vegetation as roughly triangular forms. He eliminated the houses, freestanding trees, and groups of figures that we see in *Catskill Mountains*, as they detract from the unity of his composition. Instead, we see only a lone Cappucin monk perambulating the hillside and the Palazzo Cesarini, one of the summer residences of the pope, which emerges in outline through a thick, obscuring sunlight. Here, the paucity of familiar details—the absence that becomes a presence in Inness's work—alludes to what George Inness, Jr., would later describe as the "mathematical exactness" that gave his father's paintings a "perfect harmony of vision."[1]

This "perfect harmony" may allude to Swedenborg's affiliation of spiritual identities with natural and celestial forms and to his belief that the contemplation of those forms may activate unchartered realms of human consciousness. It also evokes the sense of unity that, having devoted himself to the study of various religious and exceptional psychological conditions, William James knew existed between the individual and "the unseen or mystical world." Whether or not one identified this realm with God was at the discretion of the individual; for James, it represented "a wider self through which saving experiences come. . . ," a dimension of existence with which we are, in fact, more intimate than with the "sensible and merely 'understandable' world."[2]

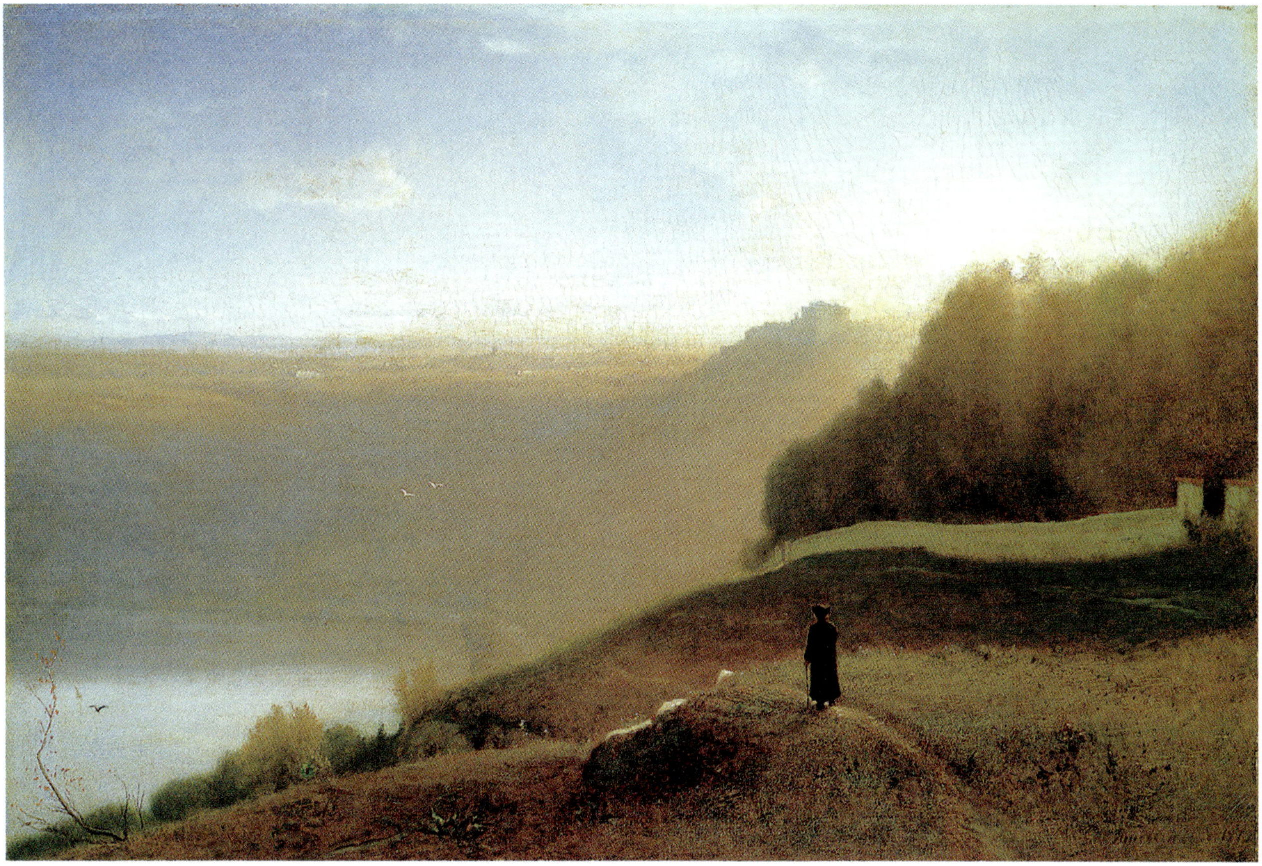

15

15. LAKE NEMI

1872, oil on canvas, 30 x 45"
Museum of Fine Arts, Boston
Gift of the Misses Hersey, 1949; 49.412

15A. CATSKILL MOUNTAINS

1870, oil on canvas, 48¼ x 72¼"
The Art Institute of Chicago,
Edward B. Butler Collection

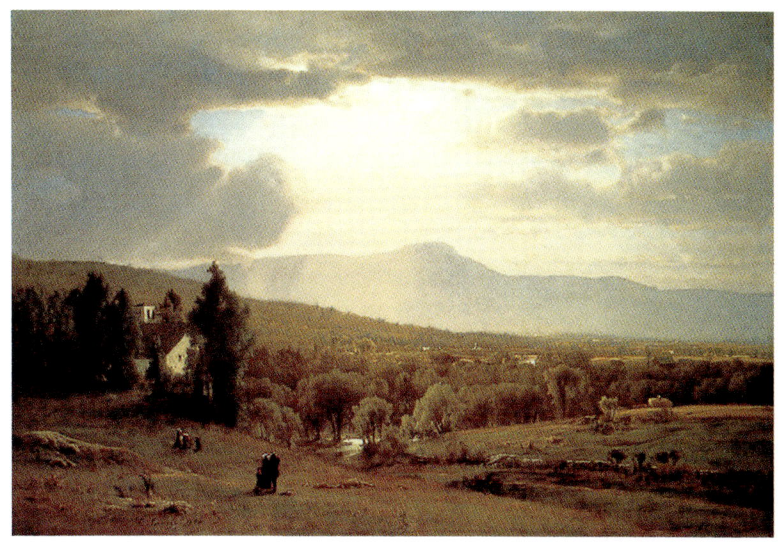

15A

16. THE MONK

1873, oil on canvas, 38 9/16 x 64 1/8"
Addison Gallery of American Art,
Phillips Academy, Andover, Massachusetts
Gift of Stephen C. Clark, Esq., in recognition of the 25th Anniversary of the Addison Gallery

THOUGHT TO HAVE BEEN SET in a particularly secluded corner of the grounds of the Villa Barberini, near Albano, Italy, *The Monk* achieves much of its dramatic impact from its articulate formalism—its reduced spatial planes, dramatically silhouetted Italian pine bowers, and sharp, amplified contrasts of warm yellow-orange and deep brown tonalities.[1] The full realization of such formalism by 1873, in the midst of Inness's Italian sojourn of 1870-74, alerts us to one of the artist's finest, and most unprecedented, achievements. As suggested earlier, it may be that Inness derived inspiration for such formalism from his engagement with Swedenborgian doctrine, notably Swedenborg's affiliation of spiritual and psychological properties with what he believed to have been increasingly complex forms in nature and the heavens. If so, we may concede that, in *The Monk*, Inness may well have realized one of his longstanding goals: to 'resolve' this theology into "a scientific form."

By engaging the power of line to allude to spiritual principles, Inness may also have derived inspiration from his American colleague Elihu Vedder. Although Regina Soria has suggested that it was Inness who nourished Vedder's "spiritual and artistic development" in Italy during the summer of 1871, the reverse may have been true as well, as Vedder was already painting in a highly visionary style.[2] The upper edge of the thick bank of clouds from which a ghostly face emerges in Vedder's *Memory* (1870; Los Angeles County Museum of Art) anticipates the sinuous upper edge of the bowers in *The Monk*. Later, Symbolists such as Edvard Munch and Frank (Frantisek) Kupka would extend into the twentieth century—to great expressive effect—this same capacity in their own visionary paintings.

Unforgettable, too, in *The Monk* is the solitary, cowled subject of the painting. The absence of facial features on this individual suggests that his personal, worldly identity has been subsumed—erased—by his spiritual one. It is a striking omission that accords with the paucity of details in the unified bank of pine bowers and the seamless transitions from one ensiform shape to another. The preternaturally harmonious arrangement of these forms complements, and fortifies, the monk's spiritual identity, his singular position on one side of an immutable boundary between the city and the monastery, the ephemeral and the eternal, the profane and the sacred.

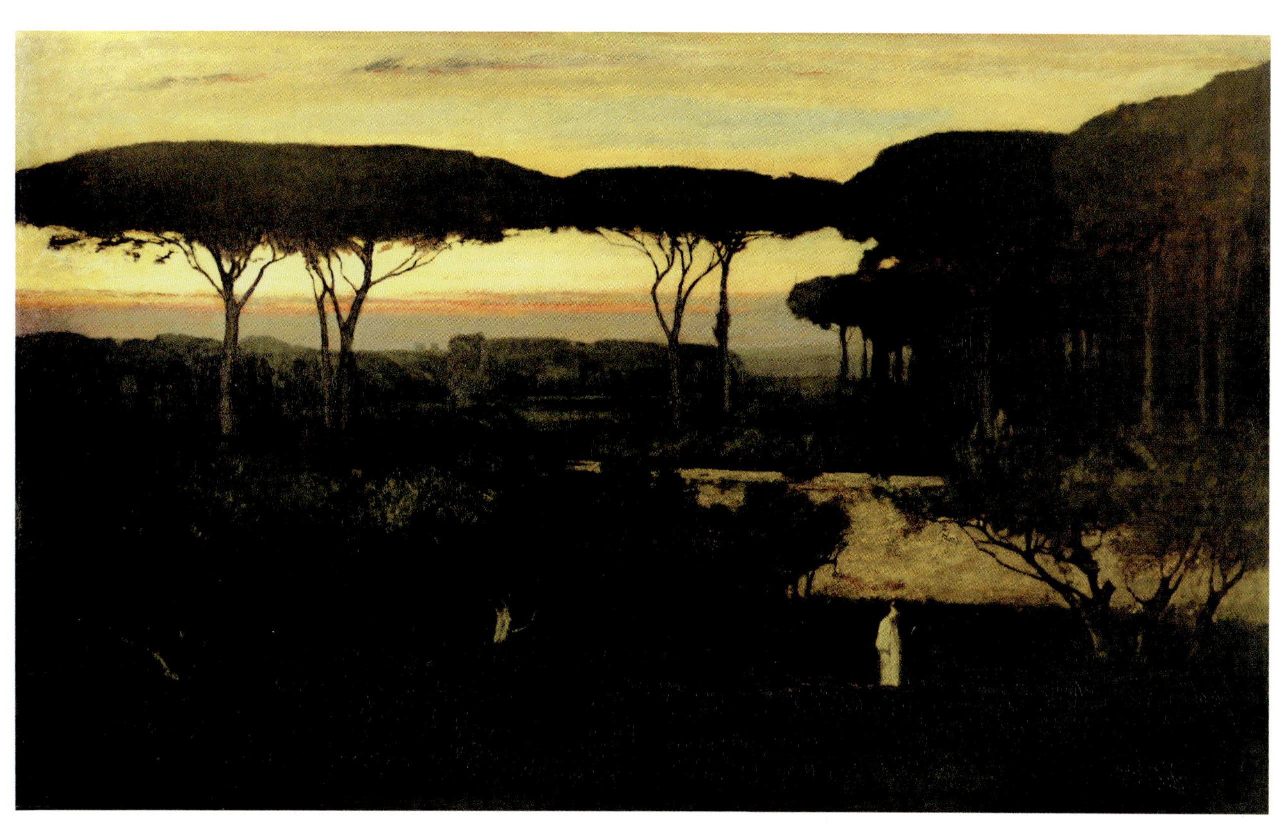

16

17. CASTEL GANDOLFO

1876, oil on canvas, 20⅛ x 30⅛"
Portland Art Museum, Oregon
Helen Thurston Ayer Fund

THE EXQUISITELY CONSTRUCTED LANDSCAPE of *Castel Gandolfo* (Plate 17) features Lake Albano, the larger of the two most famous lakes to the south of Rome in the Alban Hills (the other is Lake Nemi), and, in the upper right corner, the papal palace of Castel Gandolfo, surrounded by a tall, conspicuously shadowed stone wall.[1] As in *Lake Nemi* (Plate 15), Inness constructed a vantage point from which the lake and surrounding hillsides appear as interlocked geometric segments of nature. The triangular portions of the foreground hills overlap; the lake, an inverted obtuse triangle, conjoins with them on two sides and, on its third, with a hillside segmented by a single oblique shadow into two mirror-image, albeit somewhat modified, rhomboids. Inness augments the precision of these alliances with the quiet elegance of the arching shadow at the lower right, the curved outline of the foreground rock, and the delicately silhouetted ram. Seen as a whole, *Castel Gandolfo* illuminates Inness's extraordinary ability to reveal hidden formal unities within nature. It captures his desire to create a new pictorial expression of nature's divine order.

Pervading *Castel Gandolfo* is a sense of the effortlessness of Inness's choice and arrangement of forms and colors. An anonymous critic highlighted precisely this quality while reviewing an exhibition of Inness's Italian paintings for the *Boston Daily Globe* in the summer of 1875. Inness's "color and effects seem to be in great measure the result of instinct; they produce themselves instead of being sought after. They come as naturally as a beautiful thought is born of a poet."[2] Jorge Luis Borges (1899–1986) would later highlight this sense of inevitability when elucidating his own working methods. Borges said that, when writing, he had the feeling that his words had already been chosen; his task was, somehow, to reveal them. He described this phenomenon as "the aesthetic event," an experience "as evident, as immediate, as indefinable as . . . the taste of fruit, of water."[3] Crowned by a sliver of the moon and a few scattered clouds, *Castel Gandolfo* intimates that for Inness, at times, the artistic process meant not the production but the revelation of the most suitable, most expressive artistic forms.

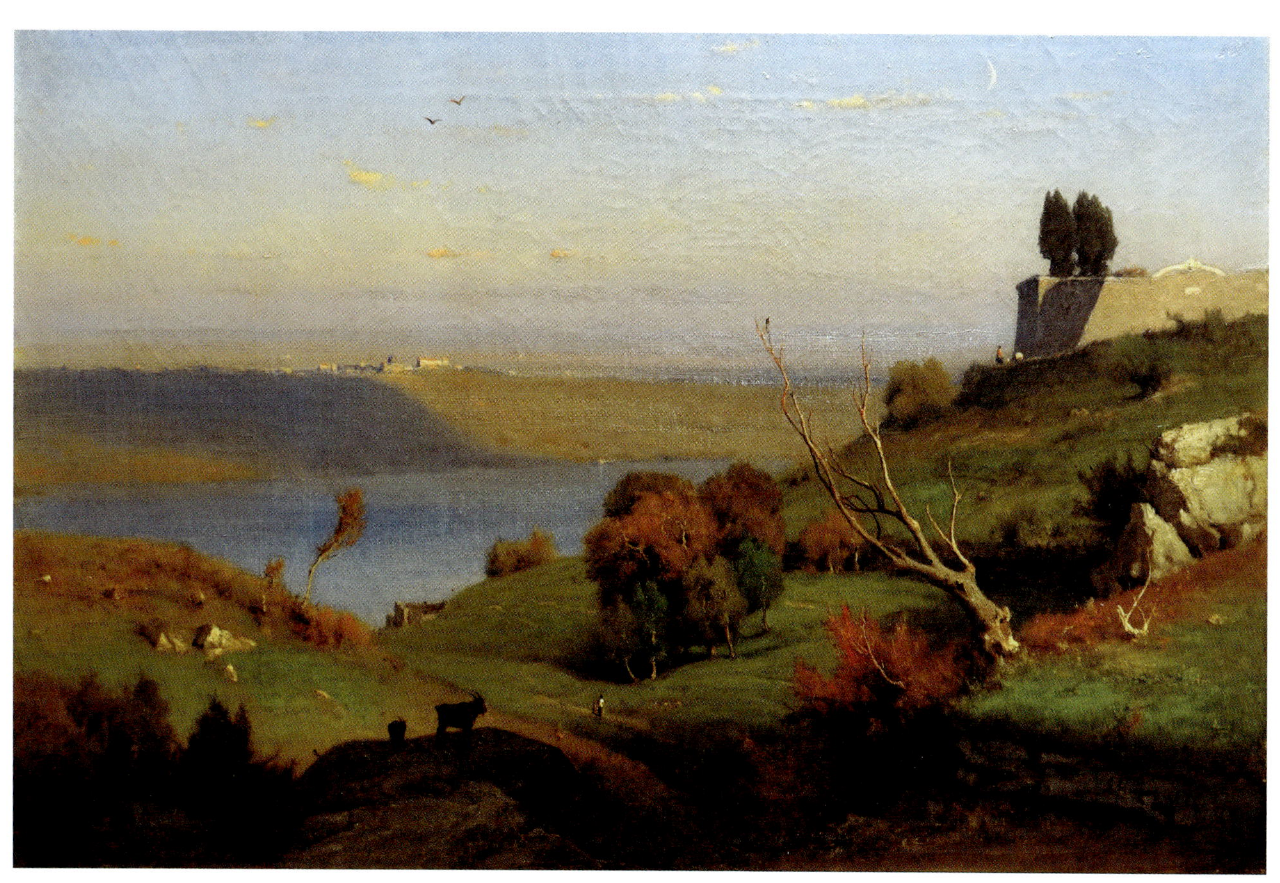

18. LANDSCAPE WITH CATTLE

c. 1877, oil on canvas, 12 x 18⅛"
Private collection

19. EARLY MOONRISE, TARPON SPRINGS

1892, oil on canvas, 32 x 42"
Collection of Fayez Sarofim

BETWEEN 1877 AND 1879, Inness gave three interviews that revealed his blend of conservative and progressive ideals.[1] In "Strong Talk on Art," he bristled at what he felt to be the National Academy of Design's valuation of political clout over artistic merit when designating artists as Academicians. However, in "Mr. Inness on Art-Matters," he exposed his own conservatism when praising Titian's *Sacred and Profane Love* (c. 1516; oil on canvas, Galleria Borghese, Rome) for its absence of "improper intent"—veiled approbation for Titian's refined depiction of the nearly nude Venus. He exhibited a provincial aversion to Dutch painting but a highly progressive desire for art to convey "the impressions of a personal vital force, that acts spontaneously, without fear or hesitation," an attitude that forecasted the approaches of Willem de Kooning, Franz Klein, and Jackson Pollock, among others.

The strengths and conflicts of these perspectives also emerge in Inness's paintings of the 1870s. He followed the spare, refined compositions of *Lake Nemi* (Plate 15), *The Monk* (Plate 16), and *Castel Gandolfo* (Plate 17) with more conventional—although no less pleasing—scenes in *The Old Homestead, Medfield, Massachusetts* (1877; Vose Galleries, Inc.) and *Landscape with Cattle* (c. 1877; Plate 18).

Still, *Landscape with Cattle* possesses a somewhat prescient compositional structure. Here, Inness segmented space into one-quarter sky (in the upper right) and three-quarters vegetation (land and trees). This proportion would become the basis for such late landscape paintings as *Early Moonrise, Tarpon Springs* (1892; Plate 19). In the latter (as in *The Monk*), Inness silhouettes the outer edges of trees against a neutral sky; he allows those edges to form a supple, cadenced line of great drama and beauty. He harmonizes the refinement of this line with the distinctly triangular segment of the stream, crossed by a fragile bridge, and with staccato bars of trees at the left. These are the tall, nearly branchless trees of Tarpon Springs, a city on the west-central coast of Florida where Inness spent the last several winters of his life. They also inspired such magnificent paintings as *Early Morning, Tarpon Springs* (1892; The Art Institute of Chicago) and *The Home of the Heron* (1893; Plate 40).[2]

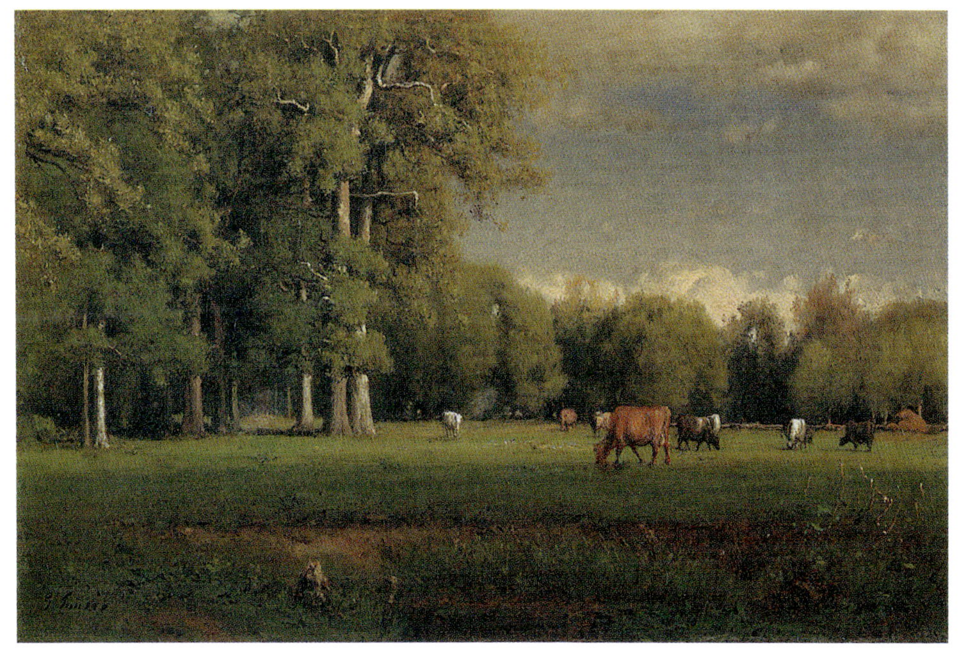

18

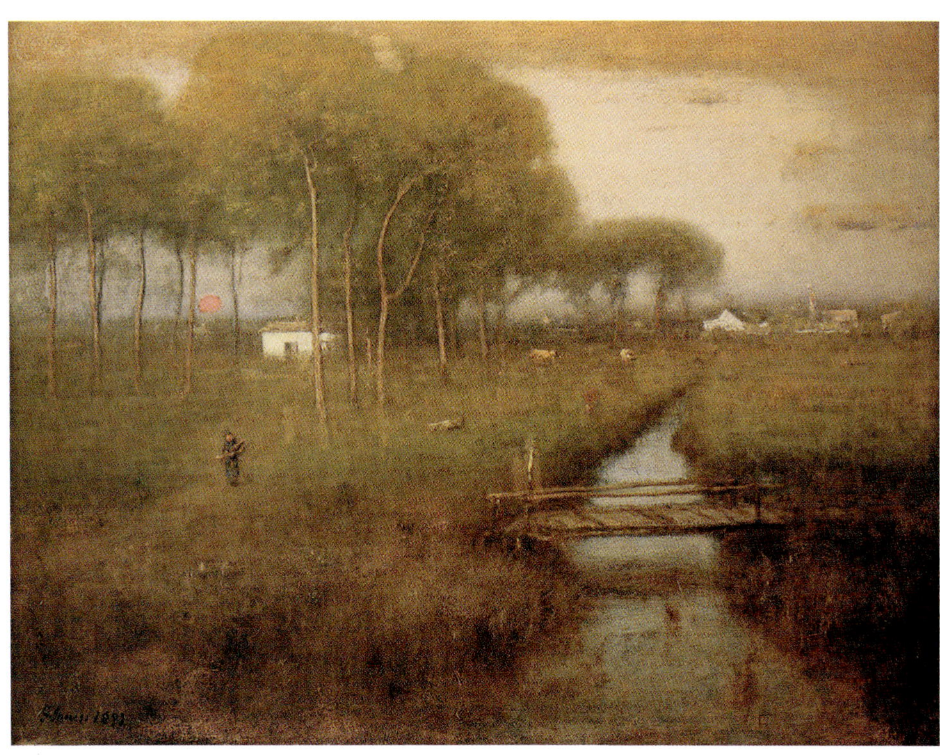

19

20. WINTER EVENING

1887, oil on canvas, 32 x 50"
Private collection

21. HOME AT MONTCLAIR

1892, oil on canvas, 30⅛ x 45"
Sterling and Francine Clark Art Institute,
Williamstown, Massachusetts, 1955.10

> . . . The squirming facts exceed the squamous mind,
> If one may say so. And yet relation appears,
> A small relation expanding like the shade
> Of a cloud on sand, a shape on the side of a hill. . . .
> —Wallace Stevens, "Connoisseur of Chaos"[1]

A "SMALL RELATION" EXPANDS in the mirror-image compositions of *Winter Evening* (Plate 20) and *Home at Montclair* (Plate 21), a covert affinity between visible nature, replete with "squirming facts," and an invisible force of structure and organization. The fiery orange-yellow sky in *Winter Evening,* incarnated with sweeping brushstrokes, offsets the muted gray-blues of the snow-covered terrain, which Inness enlivened with deep brown flecks and scratches that signify dried grasses and trees. Snow nearly buries two houses—one to the right of center and another at the far right—but fails to sublimate three human figures, the largest of whom sports a Corot-inspired red hat. In the exquisitely calibrated *Home at Montclair,* the sky is slightly more muted, the houses more prominent, and the observing figure is secreted to the left-hand edge of the scene.

Another "small relation" appears when the nearly unbroken horizon line counterbalances the sharply sloping hillside (in *Winter Evening*) and the graceful curve of the wood fence (in *Home at Montclair*). Here, Inness alludes to the trigonometric function of the sine curve, used for surveying, navigation, and astronomy. Whether he derived inspiration for his allusion to nature's clandestine structures from art (notably Renaissance art and architecture), from science, or from Swedenborg, remains unknown.[2] It is likely that all three bolstered his ambitious intentions.

Of particular interest is the "small relation" in *Home at Montclair* between nature's ideal forms and the artist's virtuosic brush marks, which spawn tiny black birds that peck for buried seeds, or his scraffito marks in the snow at the far left, which pull contrasting and enlivening whites from under gray shadows. They incise a record of the artist's presence, his free will, into the texture of his canvas. To be sure, order lurks behind nature's façade but order cannot suppress nature's "squirming facts," conveyed through the haptic marks from Inness's dynamic brush.

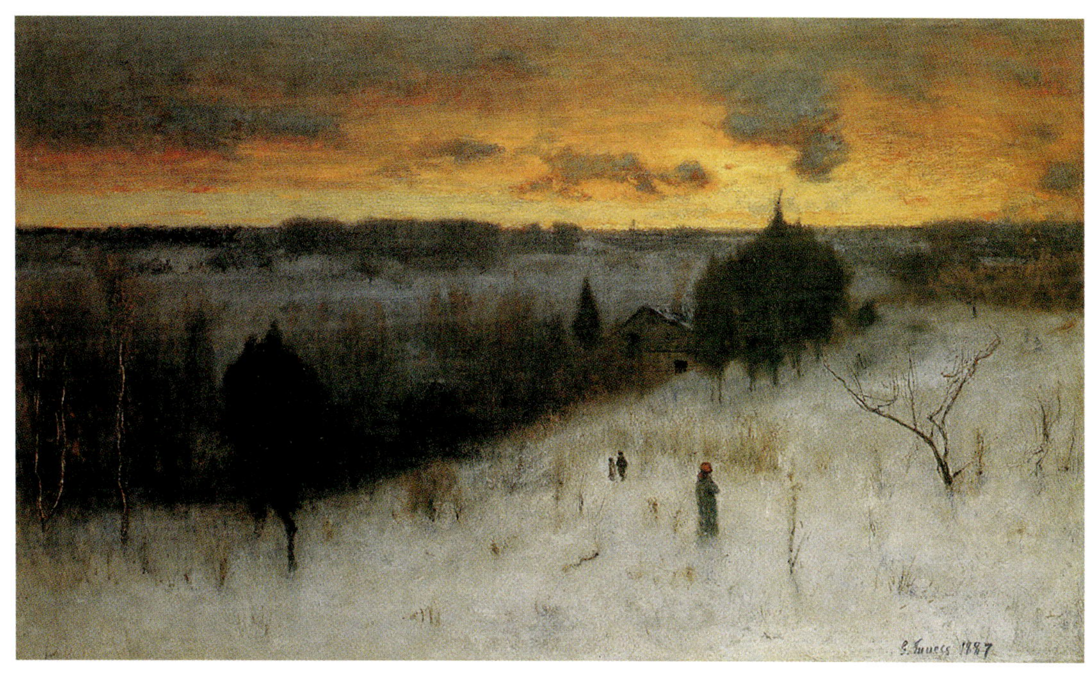

20

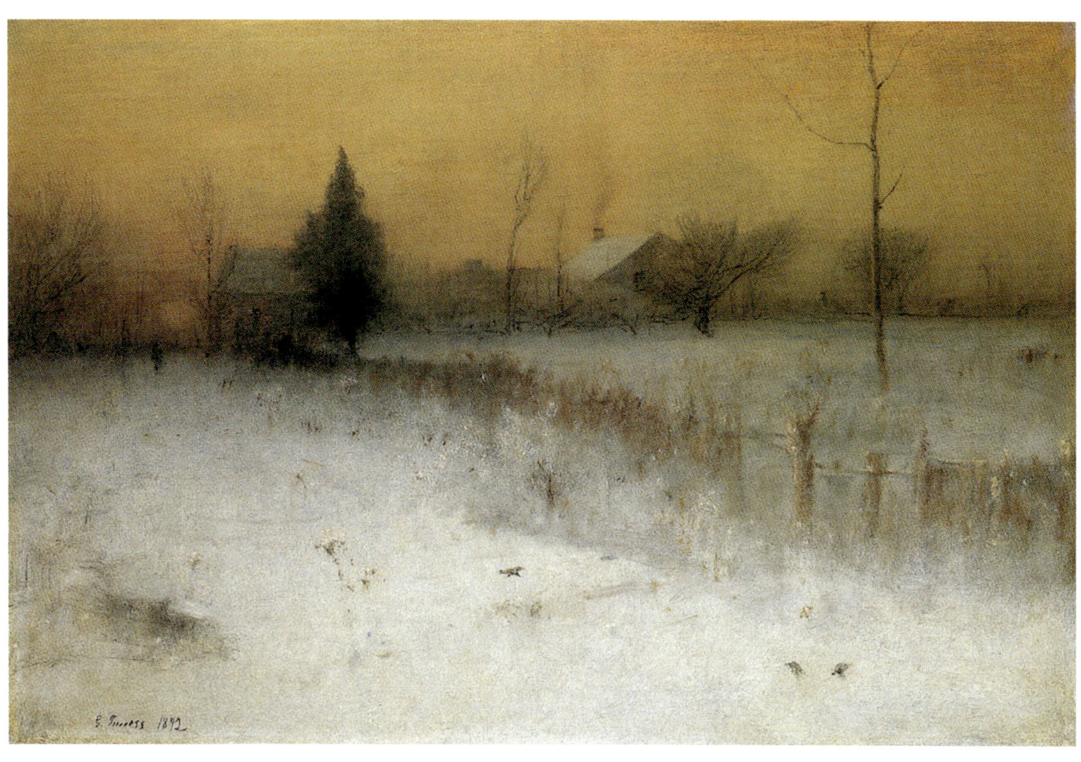

21

22. AUTUMN GOLD

1888, oil on canvas, 29 15/16 x 44 15/16"
Wadsworth Atheneum, Hartford, Connecticut
Purchased through the gift of Henry and Walter Keney

AS IN THE ALIGNMENT OF *Winter Evening* (Plate 20) with *Home at Montclair* (Plate 21), *Autumn Gold* (Plate 22) and *Moonrise* (Plate 23) reveal kindred compositional structures. Here, too, Inness explored the purposiveness of geometric forms: circles (the sun and the moon), verticals (a tree and the mast of a small boat, respectively), rectangles (banks of trees), and irregular shapes (reflections in the water). To reinstate his commitment to the indefinable, Inness bathes *Autumn Gold* in a pale, tenuous light that transforms the uppermost patch of sky into a swatch of shot silk. Falling leaves, incarnated with tiny daubs of orange paint, evolve into fragile specks of gold leaf. A filmic blue sky veils the rising moon. Rather than view this painting, we absorb its atmosphere. As Frank Fowler memorably remarked, Inness "brought us into communion with the splendors of the sky, . . . the mystery of twilight, the witchery of the moon, and the very secrets of the air."[1]

23. MOONRISE

1888, oil on canvas, 29 x 44"
Guild Hall Museum, Easthampton, New York
Gift of Mrs. Victor Harris

ON 11 MARCH 1917, the American Impressionist painter Childe Hassam expressed his admiration for Inness's *Moonrise* to the art dealer Roland Knoedler:

> The Moonrise that I saw for the first time in your gallery the other day is one of the very beautiful pictures of the world. To me George Inness has painted this wonderful effect in nature as no one else in the history of art ever has, and there are only one or two other moonlight pictures that I know of in art that can rank with it, one by Whistler, and the small picture of the waning moon, (called the Sheepfold, I think) by Millet. There may be Moonrises, more modern ones, too, that I have not seen yet, but this canvas will remain one of the great Moonlight pictures of the world.[1]

Elliott Daingerfield, a painter and close friend of Inness's, remarked about this painting, "Mr. Inness, himself, thought it a very high achievement in his art."[2]

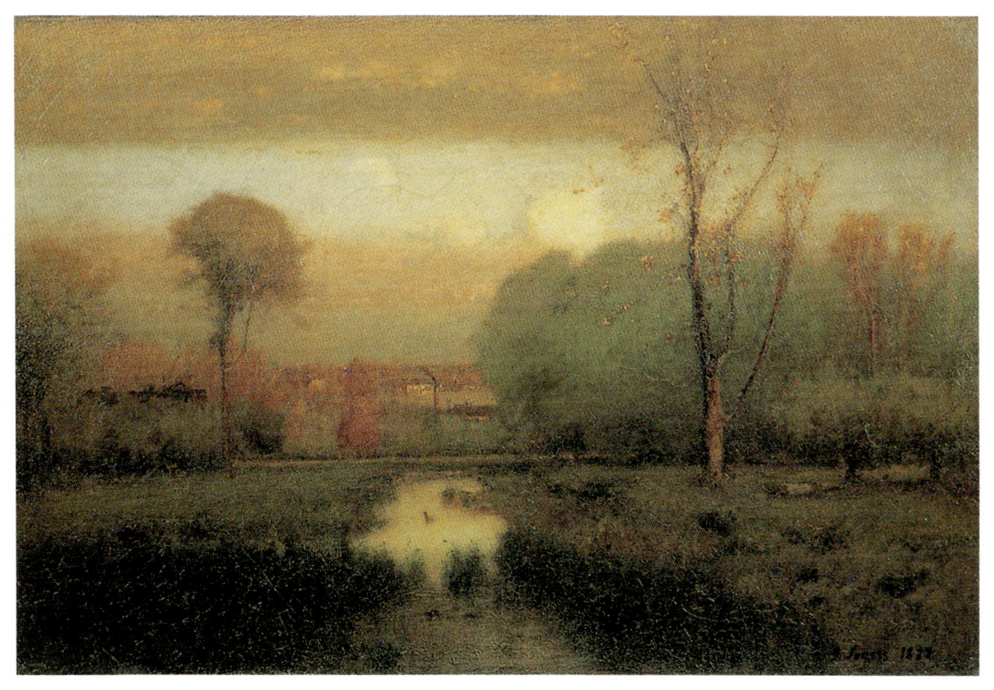

22

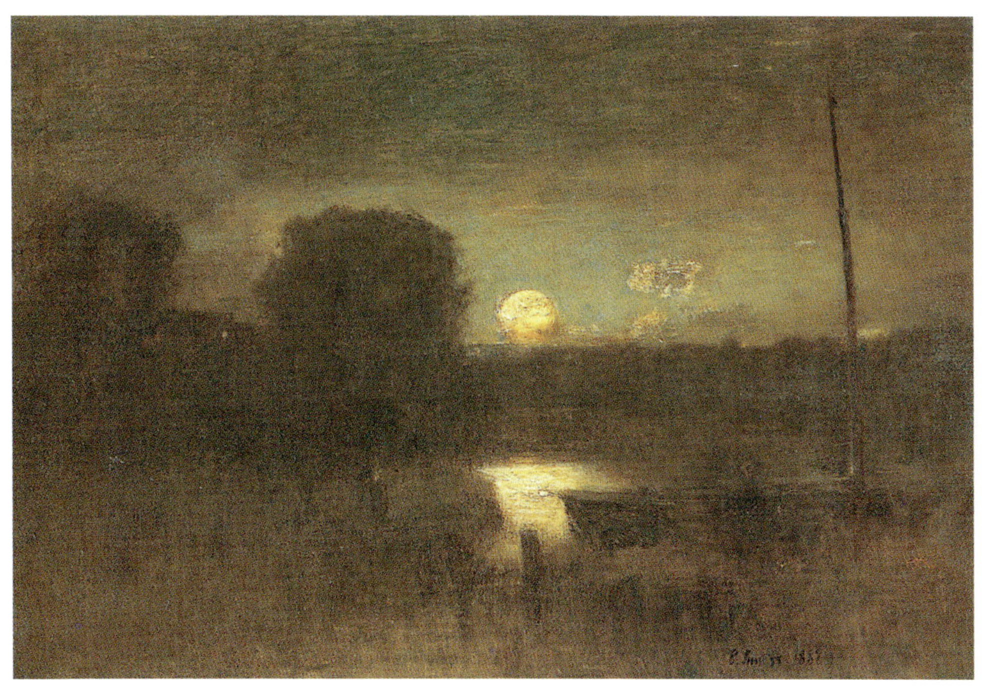

23

24. SUMMER, MONTCLAIR (NEW JERSEY LANDSCAPE)

1891, oil on canvas, 30¼ x 45"
Sterling and Francine Clark Art Institute, Williamstown, Massachusetts
Gift of Frank and Katherine Martucci, 2013.1.17

25. OCTOBER NOON

1891, oil on canvas, 30 x 45"
The Fogg Art Museum, Harvard University, Cambridge, Massachusetts
Bequest of Grenville L. Winthrop

FOR WILLIAM JAMES, the mystical experience possesses two main characteristics: ineffability—the capacity to defy expression—and noesis, or the ability to provide knowledge of "depths of truth unplumbed by the discursive intellect."[1] Mystical insight is distinguished from waking consciousness by only "the filmiest of screens."[2] When this "screen" or margin is breached, mystical experiences "soften nature's outlines and open out the strangest possibilities and perspectives."[3] They lead the believer to feel that his life is "continuous . . . with a wider self from which saving experiences flow in."[4] Questioning the validity of these experiences is futile, for believers have had their "vision and they *know*—that is enough—that we inhabit a spiritual environment from which help comes, our soul being mysteriously one with a larger soul whose instruments we are."[5]

In *Summer, Montclair (New Jersey Landscape)* (Plate 24) and *October Noon* (Plate 25), Inness uses a similar compositional structure to reflect the ineffability and the noesis of the mystical experience. In the former painting, trees and grasses generated by sharp daubs of paint inhabit an ineffable ontological state between clarity—in that we recognize their basic identities—and obscurity—in that details are all but absent. Subtle olive greens, pale blues, and golden ochers colonize a filmy, intermediate range of hues and tones. Scorings with the brush handle in the wet bluish-white of the sky and in its reflection in the water below blend foreground and distance. They reduce the illusion of depth and "open out the strangest possibilities and perspectives." By contrast, the heightened clarity of forms in *October Noon* reverberates with an otherworldly sense of order. Mirror-image L-shaped patches of blue sky and brownish trees interlock above a rectangular swath of grass. The triangle of tiny clouds mirrors the triangle of cleared grasses, which points to a woman in red. (The corresponding figure in *Summer, Montclair* resides near the far left-hand tree.) Inness "softens nature's outlines" in *Summer, Montclair* to embody the ineffability of the mystical experience. He structures forms in *October Noon* to allude to the mystical perfection and legibility of heaven's forms. In so doing, Inness invites his viewers to "submit" their intellect "to the fact that there is such a thing as the undefinable [*sic*],"[6] that is, to experience a form of visionary consciousness.

24

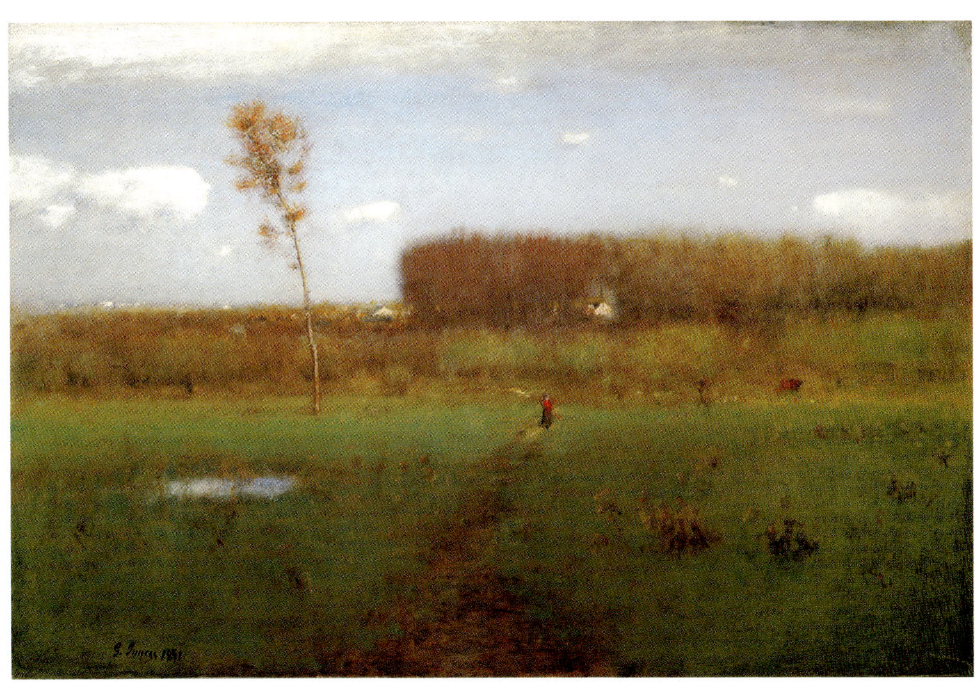

25

26. THE LONE FARM, NANTUCKET

1892, oil on canvas, 30¼ x 45¼"
The Art Institute of Chicago, Edward B. Butler Collection, 1914.189

27. HARVEST MOON

1891, oil on canvas, 30 x 44½"
The Corcoran Gallery of Art, Washington, D.C.
Bequest of Mable Stevens Smithers, the Frances Sydney Smithers Memorial

INNESS EXTENDED HIS USE OF GEOMETRIC FORMS to evoke spiritual spaces into *The Lone Farm, Nantucket* (Plate 26) and *Harvest Moon* (Plate 27) by bifurcating compositional space. In *The Lone Farm,* he divides space into equal parts of thinly applied greenish terrain and bluish sky. A thicker patch of golden yellow at the center signals the rising or setting of the sun. Within this sharp division of space, Inness aligns three, roughly triangular structures in a rhythmic pattern, from left to right, of diminishing sizes. The middle and right-hand structures appear simply as triangles—the former slightly larger than the latter—along an unbroken horizon line.

As in *Summer, Montclair (New Jersey Landscape)* (Plate 24), Inness leaves the lower half of *The Lone Farm, Nantucket* nearly devoid of the familiar, naturalistic details that might establish the illusion of three-dimensional space. Through this deliberate omission, Inness signaled his desire to shun the kinds of pictorial details that would anchor his works to the realm of the quotidian, to the known. "The overlove of knowing," Inness once explained, "is a chronic trouble of artists. . . . This abominable tendency to believe only in what can be defined, this desire to realize all things of life sensuously, is the cause of human misery."[1] (For William James, reality exists not in things made but in "things in the making," in the combination of the known *and* the unknown, the certainties *and* uncertainties of life.) Again, Inness found his greatest source of inspiration in the search for the indefinable, in the reflection of the divine that "hides itself that we may feel after it."

The Lone Farm may be an unfinished work, but Inness almost certainly did not view it in pejorative terms. For Inness, the unfinished state embodied his ongoing relationship to the work and his own status as "dough," as an artist continuously open to the possibility of divine inspiration.[2] A hallmark of modernism, this attitude distinguished Inness from the majority of his American artist-contemporaries. Moreover, the pictorial forms of *The Lone Farm*—its rectangular masses of color, nearly devoid of mediating imagery—and the evocation of the visionary experience through these forms anticipated, in part, the numinosity of Mark Rothko's late, geometric paintings of the 1950s and 1960s.[3]

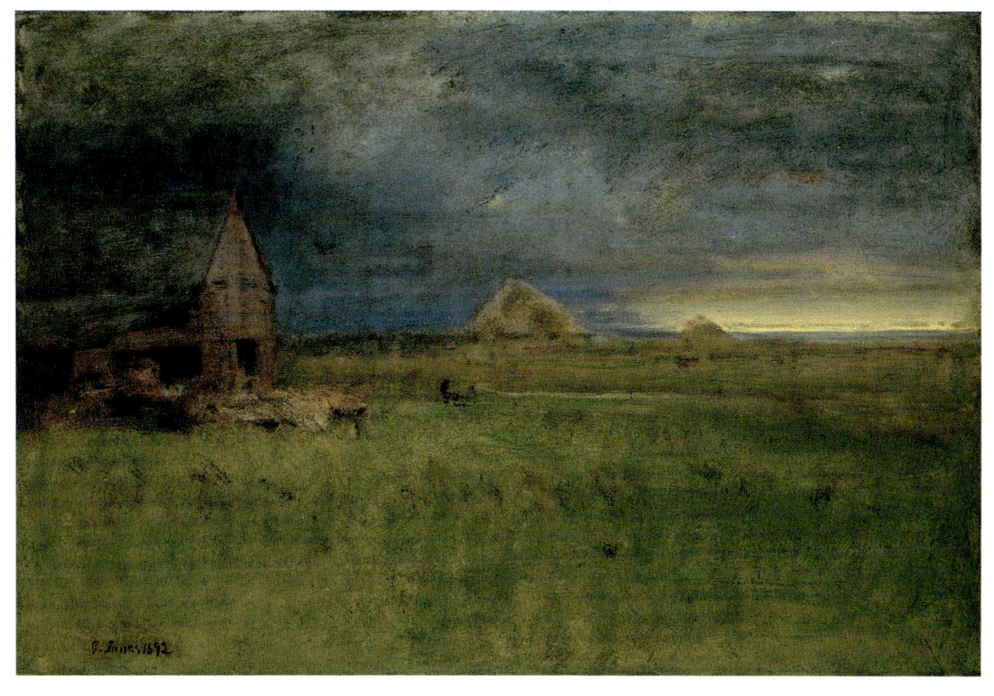

26

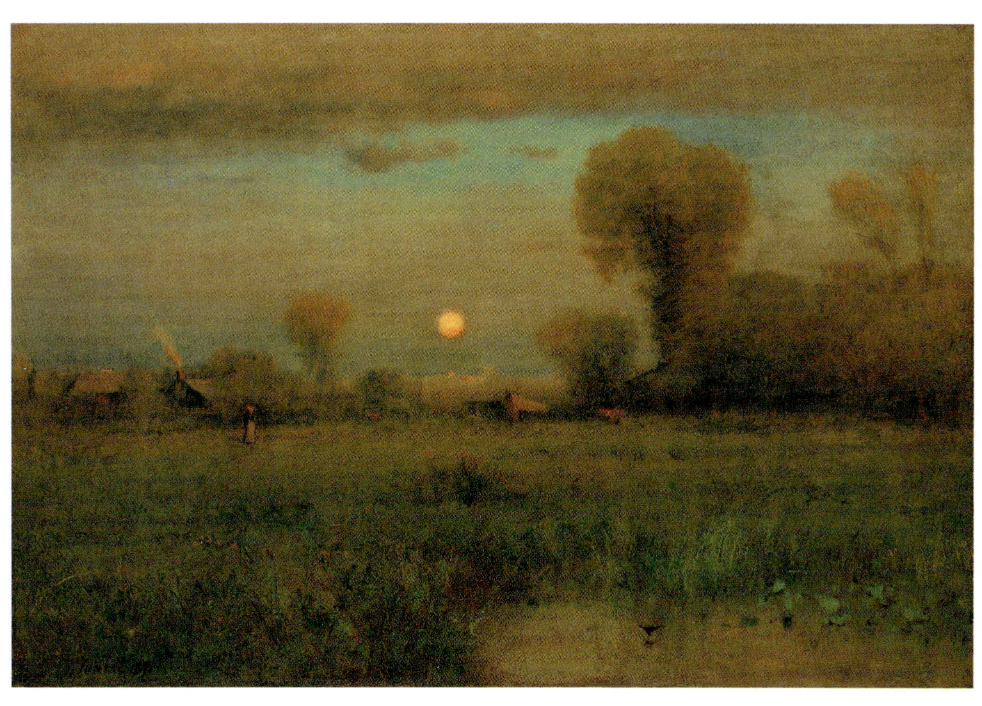

27

The Rhythm of the Working Hand

AS WITH MANY ARTISTS, Inness often spent his summers painting outside of the city. On 1 June 1875, he left Boston for the White Mountains near North Conway, New Hampshire, a region frequented by generations of American artists.[1] He resided first at the Kiarsarge House, but later moved into an "old school house near the Kiarsarge" where he displayed many of his sketches.[2] He returned to Boston on or about 15 September.[3]

The success of Inness's paintings from the summer of 1875 stems not from his ability to represent topographical details or typical events of the setting. Inness left this challenge to artists such as Winslow Homer, who, during his visits to the region in 1868 and 1869, produced drawings and paintings of tourists on their horses and artists sketching at the top of the White Mountains.[4] As always, Inness's interest lay in conveying his sentient responses to his surroundings. As a critic for *Appleton's Journal* observed of these paintings, "the artistic instinct and the human feeling which dominate them [are] so much more impressive than their realistic forms. . . ."[5]

In *Saco Ford: Conway Meadows* (1876; Plate 28), Inness conveys distinctive feelings associated with an oncoming storm: the turbulence of wind through pale gray-and-white storm clouds; the surreptitious rustling of leaves on elm trees; the ambiguity of figures and forms. By focusing on these naturalistic effects, Inness makes nature's process—and, therefore, his own pictorial process—the subject of his painting. Moreover, Inness's process resembles William James's description of consciousness as a process of selection. James explains that the world of sensations and movements that surrounds us is an "indistinguishable, swarming *continuum*, devoid of distinction and emphasis." From this tsunami of sensations, we derive meaning by "attending to this motion and ignoring that"; in so doing, our senses create "a world full of contrasts, of sharp accents, of abrupt changes, of picturesque lights and darks."[6] These contrasts help us define what we see and what we know.

Inness seems to mirror this process of cognitive selection in his construction of *Saco Ford: Conway Meadows*. We identify the two human figures in the foreground not because a plethora of details supplies information on their identities and actions. Rather, they seem human because Inness's judicious daubs of color—his "picturesque lights and darks"—precisely identify their most elemental human characteristics. In this way, Inness activates our threshold of recognition, the psychological capacity that allows us to identity forms by means of the fewest naturalistic details. Likewise, leaves seem to rustle on the trees not because Inness has carefully delineated the characteristics of each naturalistic form but because the sharp flecks of color from his brush, which created these arbors, mimic the physical activity of the leaves in the wind. In these ways, Inness's art of selection resembles the selecting processes of human mind.

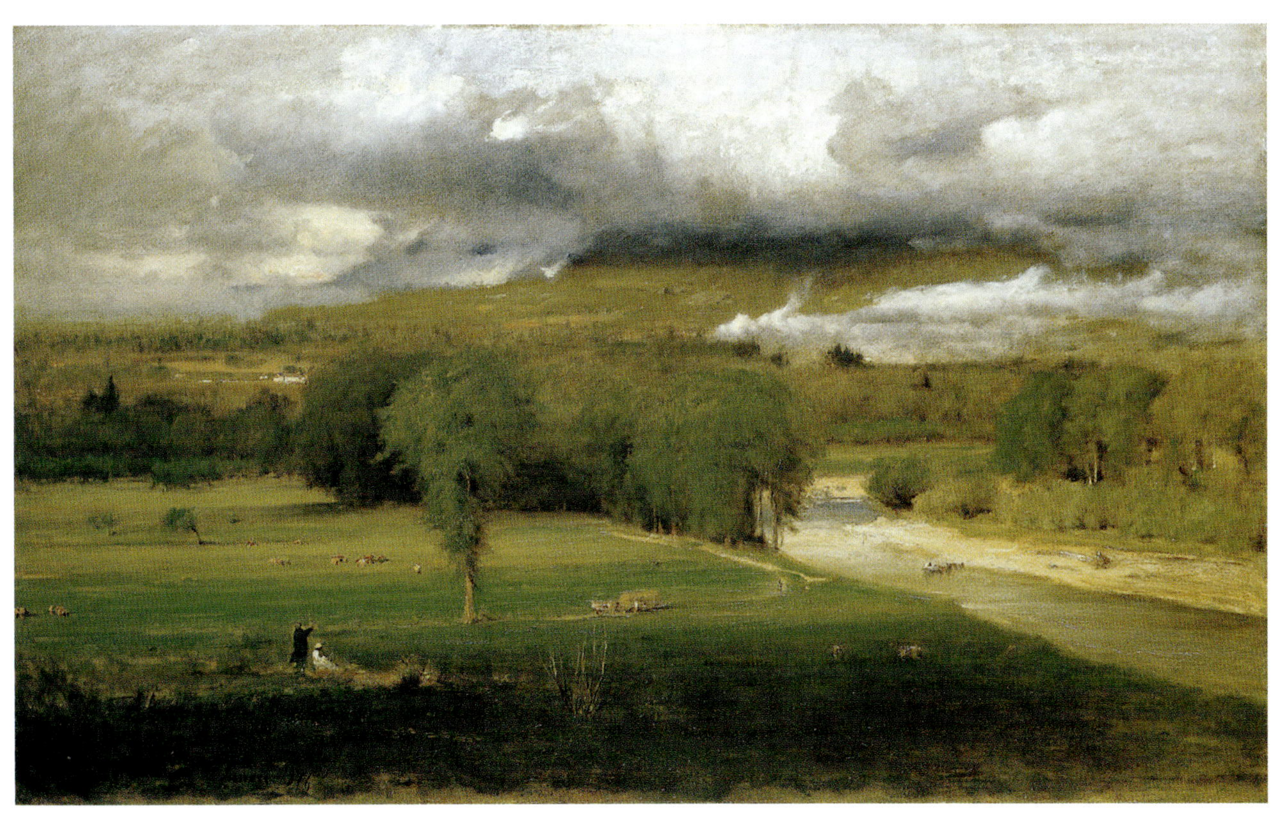

28

28. SACO FORD: CONWAY MEADOWS

1876, oil on canvas, 38 x 63¼"
Mount Holyoke College Art Museum, South Hadley, Massachusetts
Gift of Ellen W. Ayer, 1883

29. THE COMING STORM

1878, oil on canvas, 26 x 39"
Albright-Knox Art Gallery, Buffalo, New York
Albert H. Tracy Fund, 1900

THE YEAR 1878, during which Inness painted *The Coming Storm* (Plate 29), was one of the most important in the artist's career. In February, he gave an extended interview to *Harper's New Monthly Magazine*, entitled "A Painter on Painting," in which he presented his thoughts on a wide array of topics in the history of art, religion, and morality. It marked the first time that readers could gain insight into the complexity of his investment in these subjects. In March, he argued, in a letter to *The [New York] Evening Post*, for the superiority of painting over engraving. Inness asserted several points. First, "the painter does original work. The creative impulse is always urgent in him, leading him to choose the means that will enable him to convey his ideas in the most rapid way." Second, he represents "distances, spaces, etc., directly from nature" while the engraver "produces an imitation, but not a translation" of nature. Third, he is a colorist—"the most difficult thing in the world." "No artist," Inness admitted, "feels that he perfectly succeeds with his color—with that which is the soul of his painting." Finally, for Inness,

> It is evident to everyone that the engraver as an engraver merely does not possess the creative power in the degree that the artist does. And the presence of the creative power is always acknowledged to be the quality essential to great art.[1]

In *The Coming Storm,* we sense all of the qualities for which Inness expressed admiration in his letter: the rapidity of execution, the translation (as opposed to imitation) of nature, the harmonies of nature, and the adroit use of color. Even more clearly than in *Saco Ford: Conway Meadows* (Plate 28), we see in the representation of dark gray clouds how Inness's dexterous use of thinned oil paints conveys the bridled energy of the tempest; how his tempered flecks of golden brown call to mind the swirling of wind through the tress; and how his tiny touches of white and black paint invoke the presence of a trembling birch tree on the foreground coulisse. Nowhere do we witness more clearly Inness's exacting pictorial methods at work; nowhere do we perceive more clearly, in Inness's words, "the presence of the creative power."

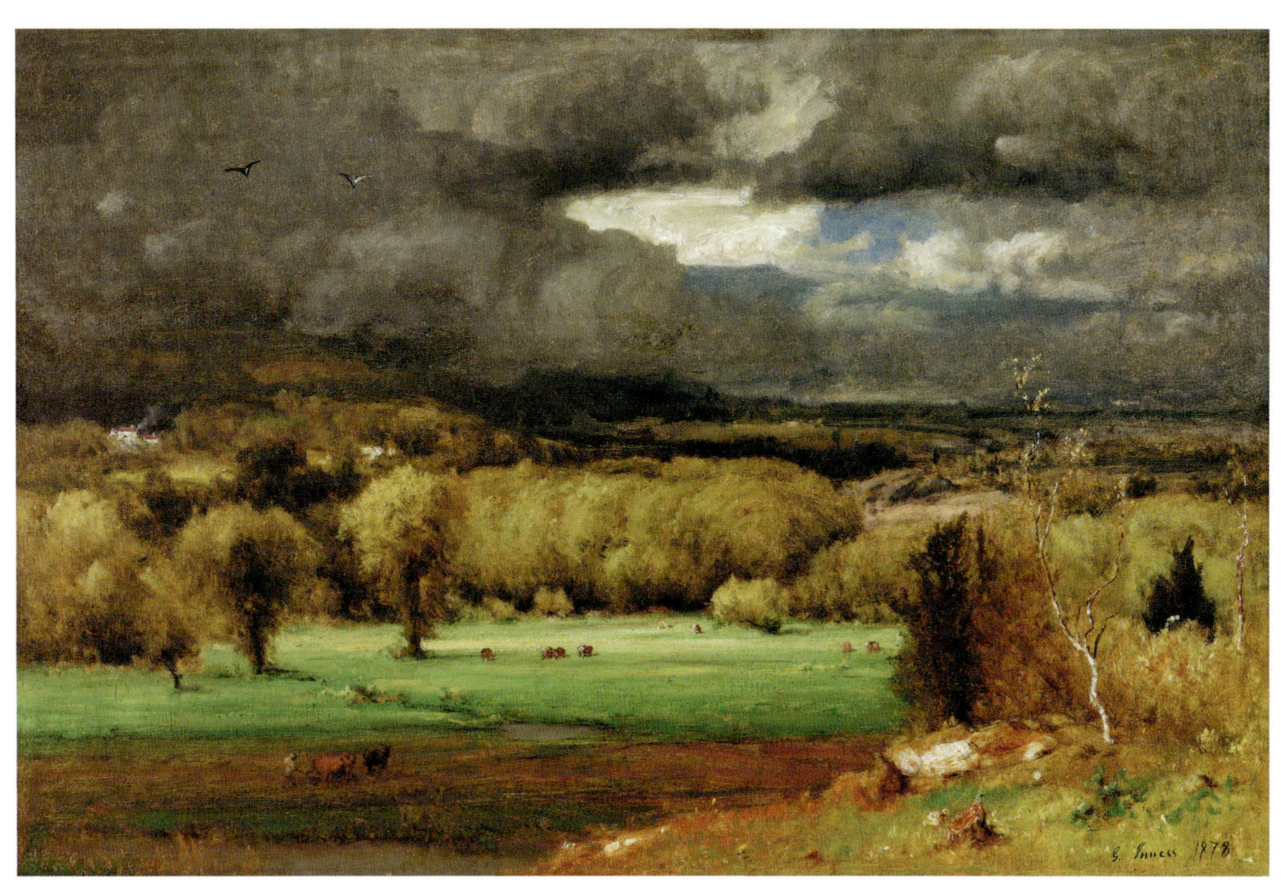
G. Inness 1878

30. THE OLD BARN

c. 1888, oil on canvas, 30 x 45"
Private collection, courtesy of Thomas Colville Fine Art

THE OLD BARN (Plate 30), which likely represents a scene in the backyard of Inness's Montclair, New Jersey, property, embodies one of the artist's highest and most appealing achievements.[1] Here, Inness presents a vignette from a private setting, one warmed by the intimacy of daily chores done in the company of family members. Rachel Hartley, one of Inness's granddaughters, recalled that the Montclair property—known first as "The Dodgery" and later as "The Pines"—"abounded in beautiful trees and rare shrubs." Inness celebrated the fecundity of this terrain in lush greens, golden ochers, and undiluted yellow and white paint.[2]

The most interesting feature of *The Old Barn* is not what we might recognize in the setting but, rather, the way in which Inness activates our imagination as we peruse the represented landscape. His forms inhabit a liminal region of semi-clarity and semi-obscurity. The somewhat more lucid ones function as stabilizing forces. The wheelbarrow pusher, glancing behind him, in the lower left-hand corner; the tree partially struck by sunlight just left of center; and the woman in turquoise next to the barn visually align to stabilize the scene. Regions of greater uncertainty resonate with the dynamic activity of Inness's brushstrokes. Masses of green and ocher strokes form a filmic veil over the right side of the barn and blanket the upper-left quadrant of the composition. In these nebulous passages, we see evidence of Inness's direct encounters with the surface of the canvas—his jabbing, flecking, and swirling of paint. Here, again, Inness weakened the habitual alliance between the medium of paint and the ontological identities of forms it ordinarily conveys.

By opening up new possibilities for pictorial expression, Inness opened new avenues for visual contemplation. *The Old Barn* is, therefore, an immensely inviting work not simply for the opulent beauty of its colors and the charm of its domestic setting. Its success resides in the nature of the thoughtful engagement that it solicits from its viewers and the type of probing examination that it can sustain. The novelist Henry James focused on this rare quality when he described the process of examining a work of art:

> The enjoyment of a work of art, the acceptance of an irresistible illusion, constituting, to my sense, our highest experience of 'luxury,' the luxury is not greatest, by my consequent measure, when the work asks for as little attention as possible. It is greatest, it is delightfully, divinely great, when we feel the surface, like the thick ice of the skater's pond, bear without cracking the strongest pressure we throw on it.[3]

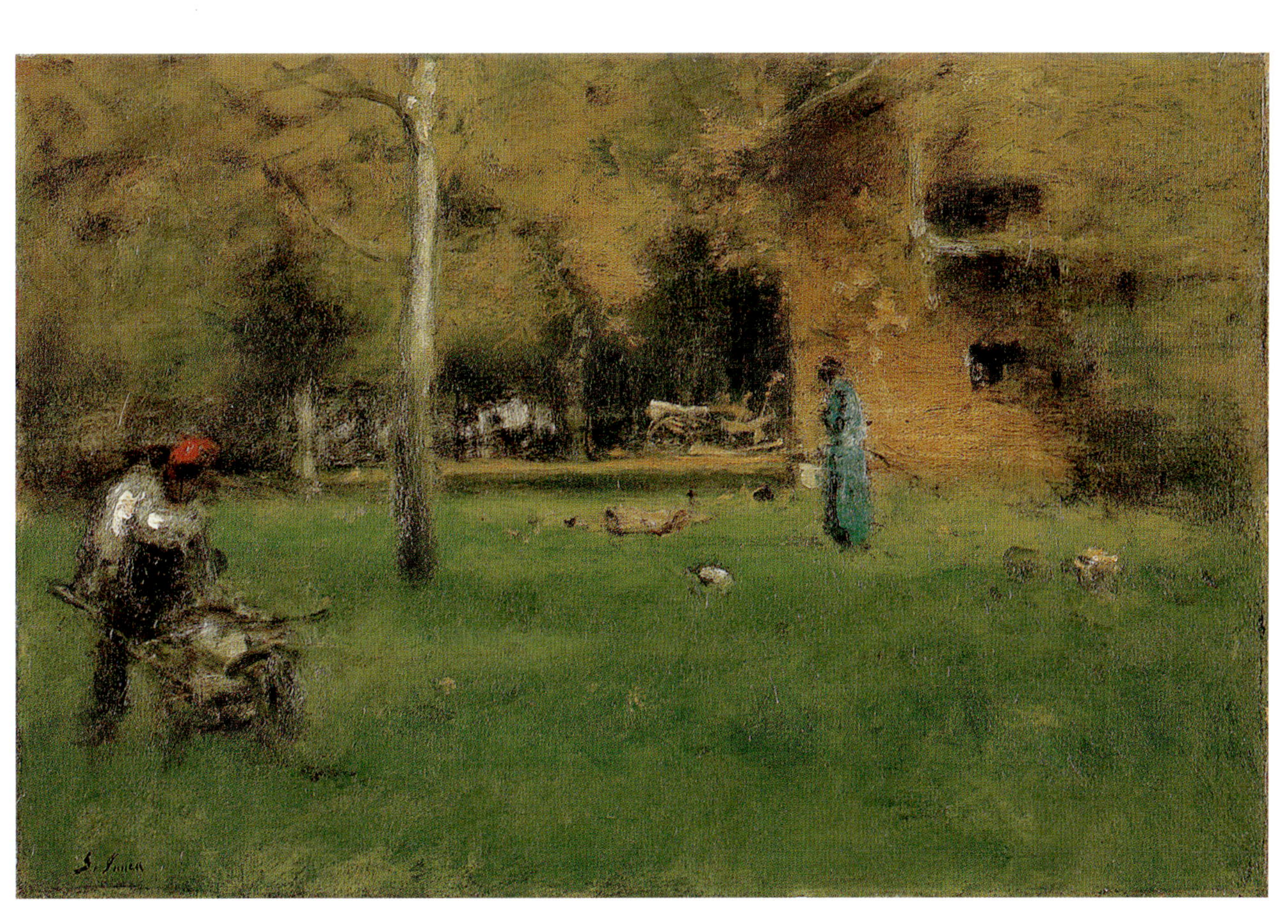

30

31. WOMAN WITH CALF

1886, oil on canvas, 30 x 40"
Sterling and Francine Clark Art Institute, Williamstown, Massachusetts
Gift of Frank and Katherine Martucci, 2013.1.5

IN ONE OF HIS MOST COGENT but understated comments, Inness observed, "I have a method of handling my brush that is all my own."[1] Inness's characteristic "handling" of his brush is nowhere more apparent than in the extraordinary *Woman with Calf* (Plate 31), one of his most vibrant and ambitious pastoral vignettes. Captivated by the liveliness and communicative power of myriad shades of green, Inness's brush nearly runs riot as it dabs, flicks, swirls, and scratches a vast and diverse range of emerald, celadon, and lemony greens throughout the canvas. It possesses a full, dynamic range as it captures and plays with light. So infectious is this spirited activity that the branches of the large, aslant tree bend into similarly irregular, although always graceful, arabesques that slide into and behind billowy clouds of paint. As the French portrait painter Benjamin Constant observed after viewing one of Inness's late landscapes, "The coloring of the green tones is positively delightful, for it may be said that no eye was ever more sensitive than Inness's to the richness of the green tones brought about by the Summer light."[2] In *Woman with Calf*, the rhythms of Inness's working hand have become so activated by a passion for color and the process of painting that, in places, it becomes impossible to distinguish individual forms. Only the judicious allocation of tonal changes—alternating patches of light and dark green behind the woman, highlights on and behind the stone wall—generates distinctions between foreground, middle ground, and distance, the illusion, that is, of naturalistic spaces between individual forms. Absent the few narrative elements of the painting and absent these subtle highlights, Inness's vibrant brushstrokes would merge grass and leaves, land and sky, field and frame into a single wall of paint.

Woman with Calf also resonates with a timeless sense of pleasure in the investigatory process of painting; it possesses the Rococo identity of the work of art as an arena for play. Cognizant of the rules of painting, Inness also challenged those rules by depositing patches of pure color on the canvas, patches that refuse to submit to the rules of foreshortening that guide three-dimensional illusionistic representation. He seems to have engaged, at least in part, in an activity that was limited, until the twentieth century, to drawing, that is, the search for new pictorial ideas within a somewhat chaotic form of artistic production. Just as Leonardo heralded the potential for the discovery of new ideas in random stains on walls, Giovanni Battista Piranesi (1720–1788) used the etching plate, notably in his *Carcieri* series (1749–50), as a field for invention. "Col sporcar si trova," Piranesi inscribed in the corner of one of his prints from another series: "messing about, one finds."[3] In this vascular activity, the action of the hand guided Piranesi's search for new forms and new ideas; for Inness, more than a century later, the expressive vehicle was his characteristic "handling" of the brush. In a modest way, then, Inness extended the productive legacy of pictorial invention into American landscape painting.

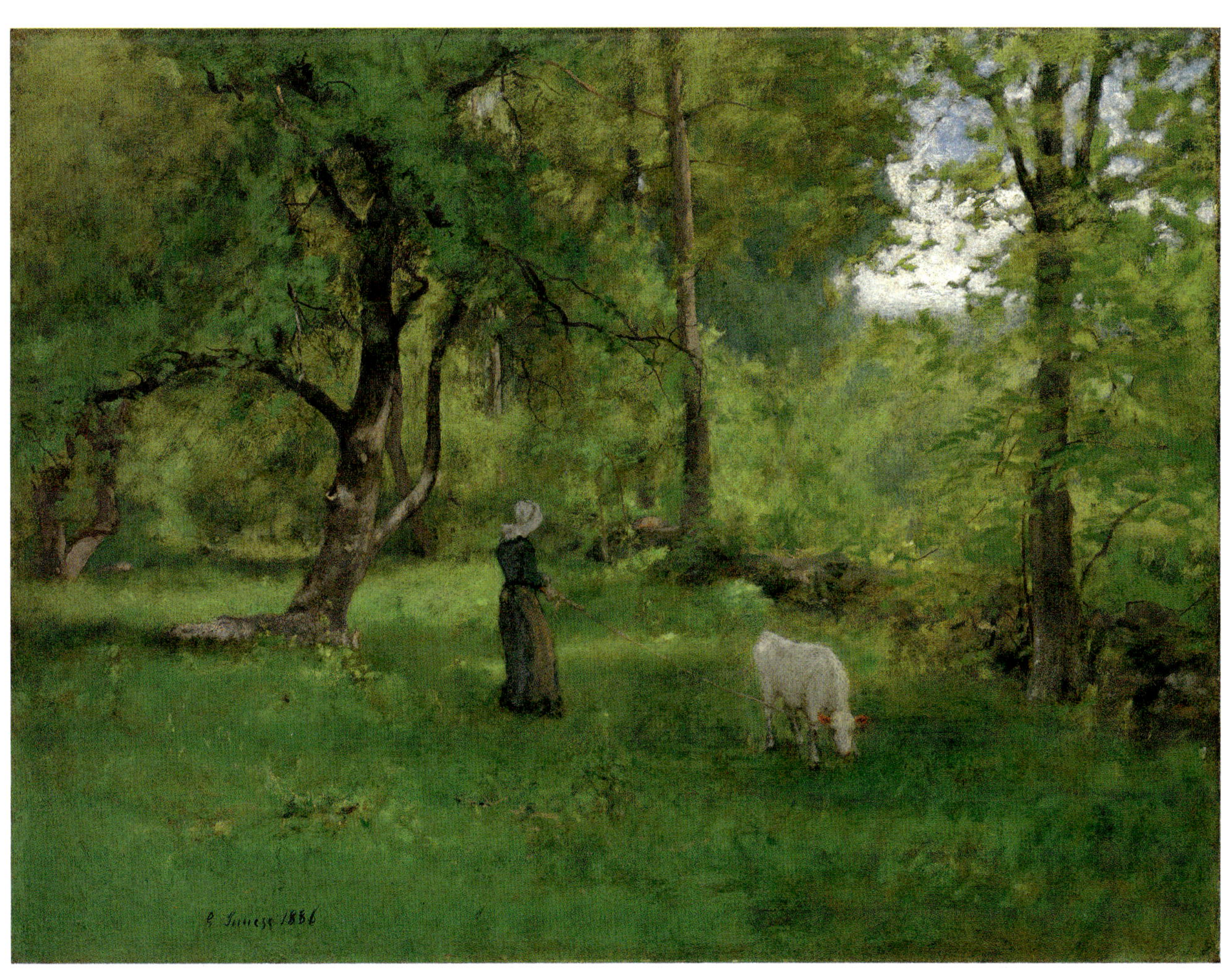
G. Inness 1886

32. HOMEWARD

1881, oil on canvas, 20¼ x 30¼"
Brooklyn Museum of Art, New York
Gift of the Executors of the Estate of Colonel Michael Friedsam, 32.827

> ". . . all at once the glory of God shone upon and round about me, in a manner most marvellous. . . . a light perfectly ineffable shone in my soul, that almost prostrated me to the ground. . . . This light seemed to be like the brightness of the sun in every direction. It was too intense for the eyes. . . . I think I knew something then, by actual experience, of that light that prostrated Paul on his way to Damascus. It was surely a light such as I could not have endured long.
>
> —conversion account in *The Varieties of Religious Experience*

AS DESCRIBED BY WILLIAM JAMES, the "conversion" experience often arrived in the form of "hallucinatory or pseudo-hallucinatory luminous phenomena," or *photisms*—visions of light. In *The Varieties of Religious Experience*, James cites several cases of conversion, such as that of Charles Grandison Finney (cited above), as well as the more familiar examples of Saint Paul on the road to Damascus, and the Roman emperor Constantine, who, having seen a vision of the Holy Cross in a dream, converted himself and his kingdom to Christianity.[1] Each time, the subject of the conversion witnesses an effluence of light, be it "blazing light" or "strange light" or a "flash of light," that wholly transformed his state of mind and spirit. Therefore, the stream or river of light has long symbolized spiritual enlightenment, the process through which conversion takes place.

In *Homeward* (Plate 32), Inness appears to have engaged the symbolic identity of light, specifically of *photisms*, to allude to spiritual enlightenment. Set in a desolate terrain, two farmers return home after a day's labor that has left them hunched in fatigue. Accompanied by his two oxen, the blue-shirted farmer in the foreground is seen stepping into an unnaturally bright patch of yellow light—a light nearly "too intense for the eyes." Inness makes no effort to conform the yellow paint of this light to the illusion of a three-dimensional setting; instead, it rests uncomfortably on the surface of the canvas. It disengages itself from illusionism and, conversely, embraces a somewhat otherworldly identity. At the far left, the phantasmic double of the farmer extends this allusion in that he is surrounded by another form that traditionally symbolizes spirituality: a nimbus, or holy aura.

Well known as one of Inness's finest unfinished works of art, *Homeward* remained in the artist's studio until his death.[2] That Inness kept the painting close suggests that it possessed several especially important qualities. In addition to its evocations of spiritual enlightenment,

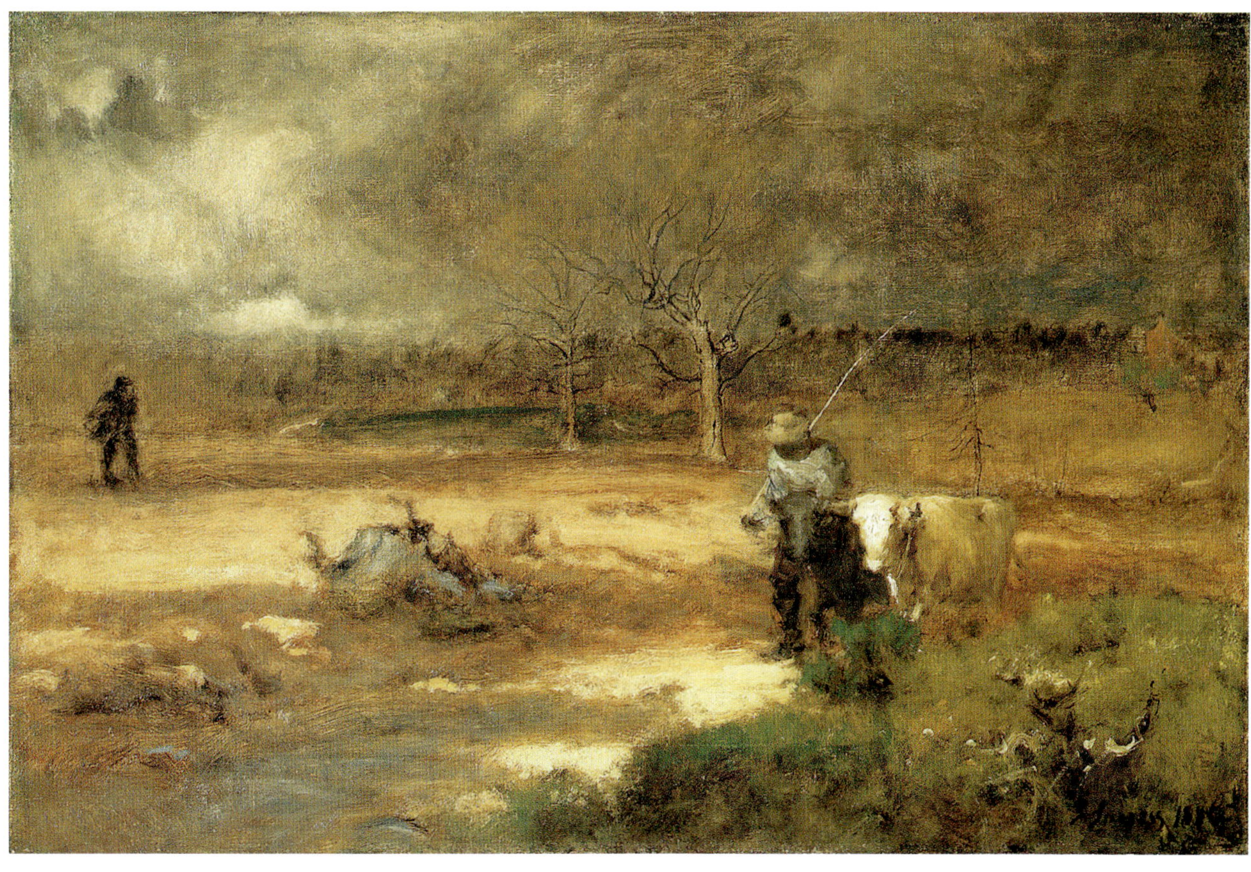

32

Homeward may have aligned with Inness's profound concern for the plight of laborers. During the last fifteen years of his life, Inness engaged deeply with the theories of the political economist Henry George (1839–1897). He became a stalwart follower of George's ideas and even delivered a speech in his honor when George visited New York in 1890.[3] It may have been, therefore, that by using light to allude to spiritual enlightenment, Inness hoped—in the spirit of, for example, Caravaggio's *Calling of St. Matthew* (1599–1600; S. Luigi dei Francesi, Rome) and *Conversion of Paul* (1600–01; S. M. del Popolo, Rome)—to show how enlightenment was available even to the most humble, most unsuspecting of individuals.

33. INDIAN SUMMER

1894, oil on canvas, 30 x 42"
Collection of Fayez Sarofim

PAINTED DURING THE FINAL YEAR OF HIS LIFE, Inness's *Indian Summer* (Plate 33) resonates with the wistful mood of memory, of easy, languid recollection. As in all "Indian summers," occasions in which a fleeting experience from the past (a summer day) unexpectedly appears in the present (the fall), this enchanting painting alters the rhythms and patterns of thought, leaving us expectant with the possibility of new revelations.

Set in an anonymous patch of farmland, the few recognizable objects and forms of *Indian Summer* provide the viewer with little indication of overt meaning. Indeed, it is the paucity of familiar forms that dislocates the viewer from the realm of the quotidian. Reinforcing the sense of distance from the ordinary, the thin applications of pale blue, rust, and muted green paints adhere loosely to the core identities of sky and land; at the same time, they generate a cohesive, abstract, planar unity within the composition. Similarly, staccato flecks of orange, green, and black paint allude, rather tenuously, to branches, rocks, and other bits of nature's detritus. A more convincing reading sees them forming a lively, harmonious counterpoint on the tensile surface of the canvas. Within this fragile alliance of illusionism and abstraction, the most beguiling mark is the daub of white paint near the center foreground. For reasons that defy expression, it possesses a humanistic identity.

During his late landscape painting period (c. 1877–94), Inness maintained a subtle balance between memory and experience in his paintings. His self-possessed disregard for the illusionistic appearance of nature's forms reveals his reliance on memory as a source of inspiration. Indeed, Inness once referred to memory as "the daguerreotype shop of the soul which treasures all that God created to consciousness through eye and touch."[1] On the other hand, Inness acknowledged memory's frailties. He once recalled that, when he relied exclusively on memory to paint, the resulting picture "had no charm—nothing about it that was beautiful."[2] Memory contained a record of our (divinely inspired) sensible experiences. And yet, we must "keep the shop" of memory closed before nature so that we may experience each perception anew, so that, in Inness's words, we may "see, and not think we see."[3] William James described this metaphysical condition as a desire to know "reality's thickness," to experience the passing events of one's life and, also, "to conceive eternities." As he put it more succinctly, "Direct acquaintance and conceptual knowledge are thus complementary to each other; each remedies the other's defects."[4] This seamless blending of immediacy and timelessness, of present and past, of consciousness and memory generates the meditative—even metaphysical—aura that envelops *Indian Summer*.

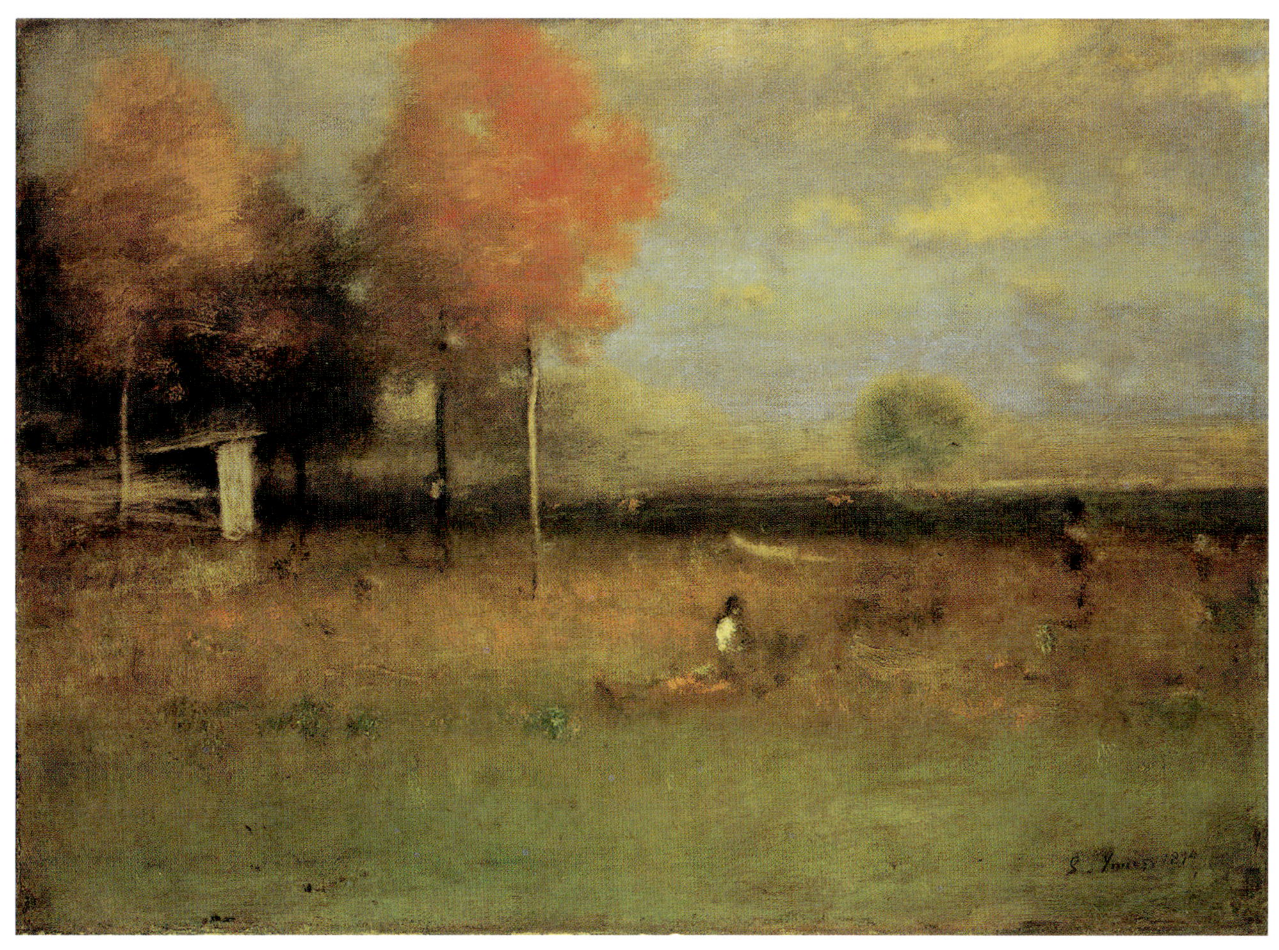

The Anonymous Figure

I SUGGESTED EARLIER that the single figures that we often see in Inness's landscape paintings represent more than traditional staffage, or accessories to the landscape. They are not intended simply to advance a narrative, and they could not be eliminated or altered without destroying the integrity of the scene. They are often our first point of interest in the represented landscape, and in particularly abstracted settings, they tend to anchor our cognitive capacities to the realm of the human, the familiar. We have observed this type of figure in works as early as the late 1850s—for example, in *The Huntsman* (1859; Plate 4). We will observe him repeatedly throughout Inness's body of work, even in paintings from the last year of the artist's life (possibly in *Indian Summer*, Plate 33). This figure, which I have termed the "anonymous figure," therefore represents a critically important facet of Inness's aesthetics and pictorial schema.

To be sure, Inness will still paint figures in markedly narrative settings well into the mid-1880s. With its bold strokes of orange and yellow in the fiery sky, its flecks and jabs of green in the trees at the right, *Shades of Evening* (Plate 34) bears all of the most provocative hallmarks of Inness's brilliant gestural compositions of this period. As its central character, a woman in white with her dog, waves a handkerchief to three figures in a boat, it remains anchored in the realm of narration.

Inness's "anonymous figures" tend to disengage the paintings in which they appear from narrative institutionality. Often represented in silhouette, or with their backs turned to the viewer, or gazing into the landscape (see, for example, Plates 16, 20, 25, 37), these lone, contemplative beings seem to be thinking about something that we cannot see in the landscape, even something beyond the three-dimensional domain in which physical sight functions. Incarnated in two or three summary dashes of paint (see Plates 26, 33, 39), their very beings—as ephemeral as any in art—mirror the transience of the activity in which they appear to be deeply engaged. No longer guided and limited by the "structural imperative" of narration, the "anonymous figure" embodies narrative's emergent operational disintegration.[1]

By using highly discriminating brushstrokes to incarnate these figures, Inness highlights his own role as creator of nature. He suggests that free will—not only the forces of the divine—shapes the character of what we see and what we know. By engaging our own memory in the challenge of identifying the hieroglyphic forms of the "anonymous figures," he makes our own contribution central to that epistemological process.[2]

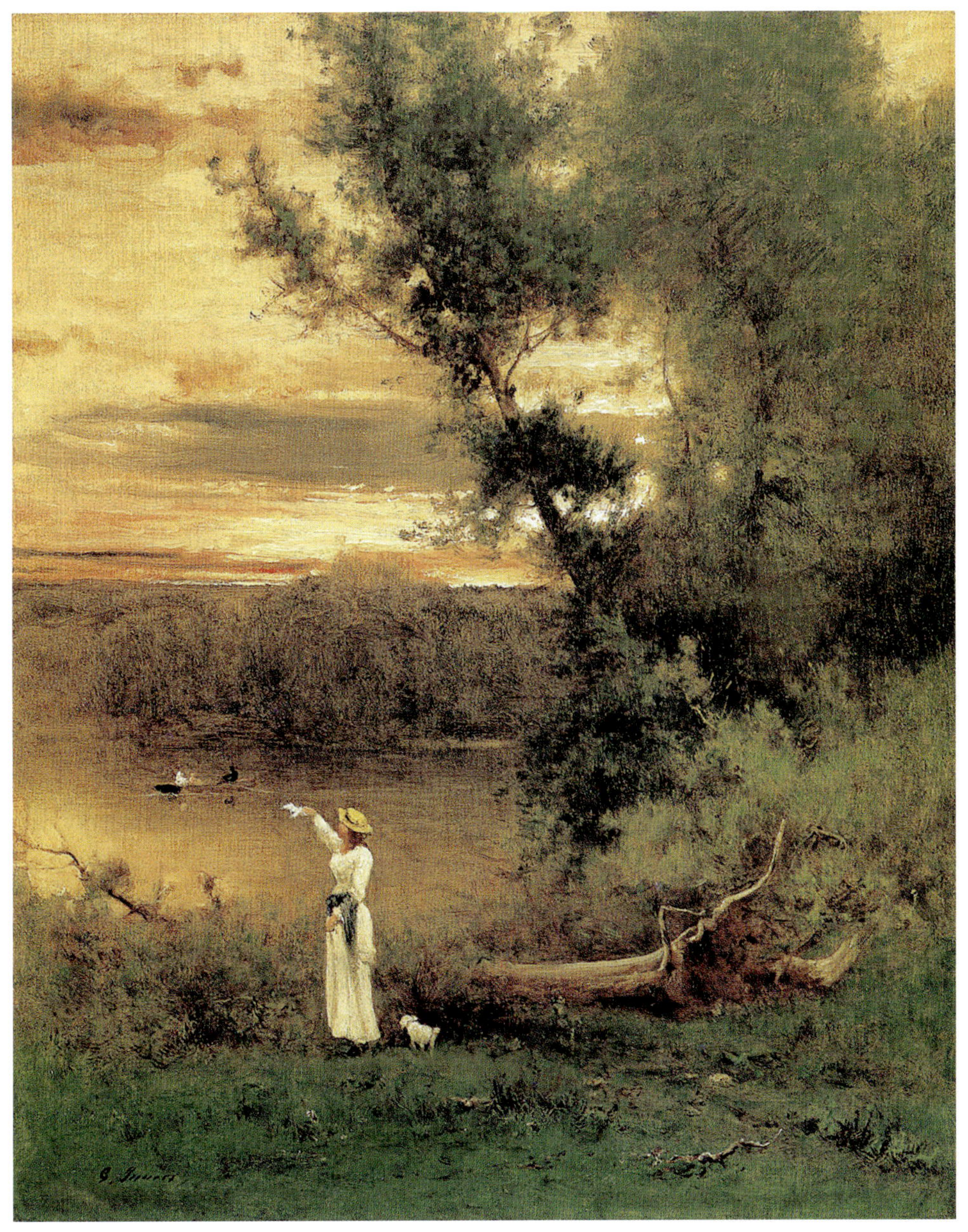

34. SHADES OF EVENING 34

c. 1877, oil on canvas, 27 x 22"
Private collection

35. SUNSET GLOW

1883, oil on panel, 16 x 24⅛"
Montclair Art Museum, Montclair, New Jersey
Gift of Mrs. Francis M. Weld, 1946.1

ACCORDING TO SWEDENBORG, the natural realm, the realm of earthly existence, represents the domain of appearances. Forms exist in this region—they are extended in space and time—and yet, as they are continually imbued with divine spirit through the process of influx, they are, essentially, insubstantial. By contrast, the domain of reality is the domain of truth, of permanence, of eternal spirit. Forms in the natural world may be mirrors of the divine but they are at best imperfect ones.

In a letter of February 13, 1877, to his daughter Helen ("Nellie"), Inness referred to Swedenborg's distinctions between reality and appearance. He wrote that the world we live in

> we eventually find to be a continual changing state, but a state which forms the basis of all our knowledges. . . . Now, what the spirit sees is not the truth, but only an appearance of truth. For instance, we say that the sun rises and the sun sets, but this is not true except as an appearance, and so it is with every fact of the natural world.[1]

When creating *Sunset Glow* (Plate 35), a painting of modest scale that remains one of his most intriguing and inviting, Inness seems to have borne Swedenborg's characterizations of appearance and reality in mind. Filtering these interpretations through his pictorial process, Inness used them to generate a new vision, one that disrupts our mundane assumptions about what we think we see and what we think we know.

Certain features of *Sunset Glow* seem evident enough: set in a forest clearing, the sun blazes an orange radiance at the horizon. And yet, the horizon line, raised from the lower third to the center of the composition, weakens the illusion of three-dimensional depth. In the same vein, Inness challenges the physical integrity of nature's forms. His bristly daubs of brownish-green paint amalgamate the otherwise defining features of trees, bushes, and grasses into tremulous patches of pure color. Disassociated from their corporeal identities, these forms seem to exist in, as Inness described it, a "continual changing state." Epitomizing this sense of dislocation are the phantasmal man and his equally ghostly dog in the central foreground. Tethered loosely to the familiar, *Sunset Glow* seems to peer across an imaginary threshold into a new metaphysical realm, one that reflects Inness's Swedenborgian interpretation of nature as the domain of "appearances."

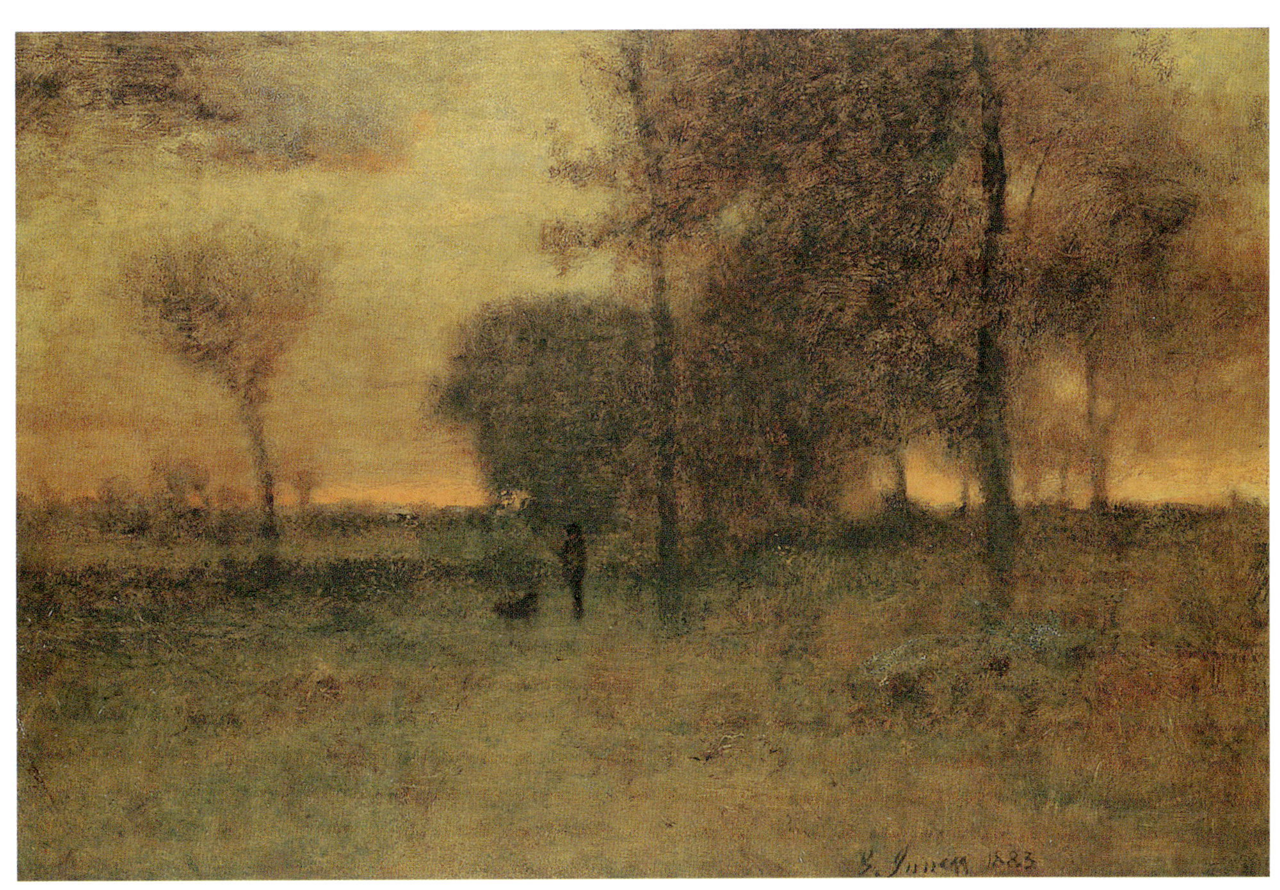

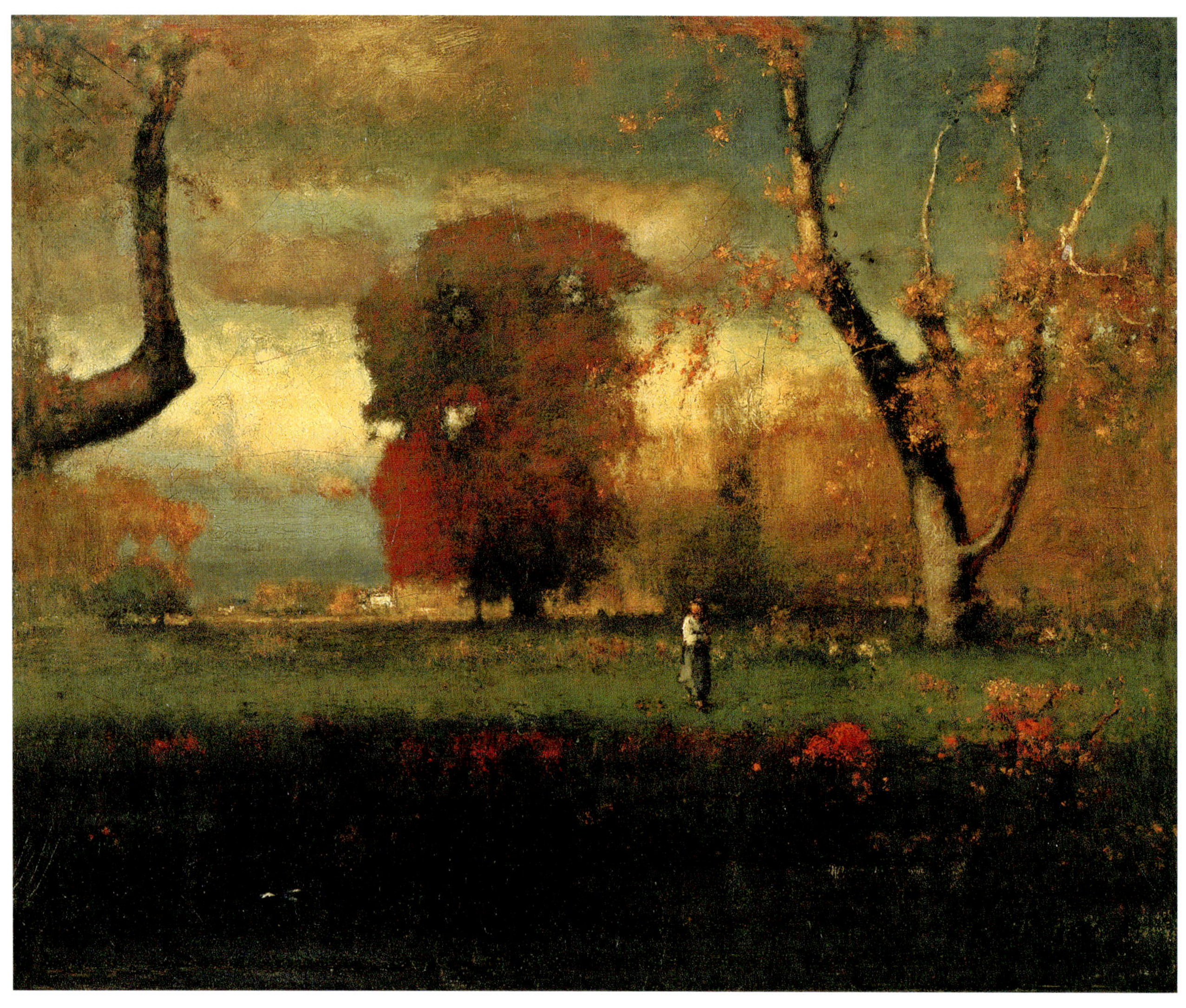

36

36. LANDSCAPE

1888, oil on canvas, 22⅛ x 27½"
The Cleveland Museum of Art
Gift of the Estate of Charles F. Brush, 1929.464

37. SUNRISE

1887, oil on canvas, 30 x 45¼"
The Metropolitan Museum of Art, New York
Anonymous gift in memory of Emile Thiele, 1954 (54.156)

38. NEAR THE VILLAGE, OCTOBER

1892, oil on canvas, 30 x 45"
Cincinnati Art Museum
Gift of Emilie L. Heine in memory of Mr. and Mrs. John Hauck, 1940.943

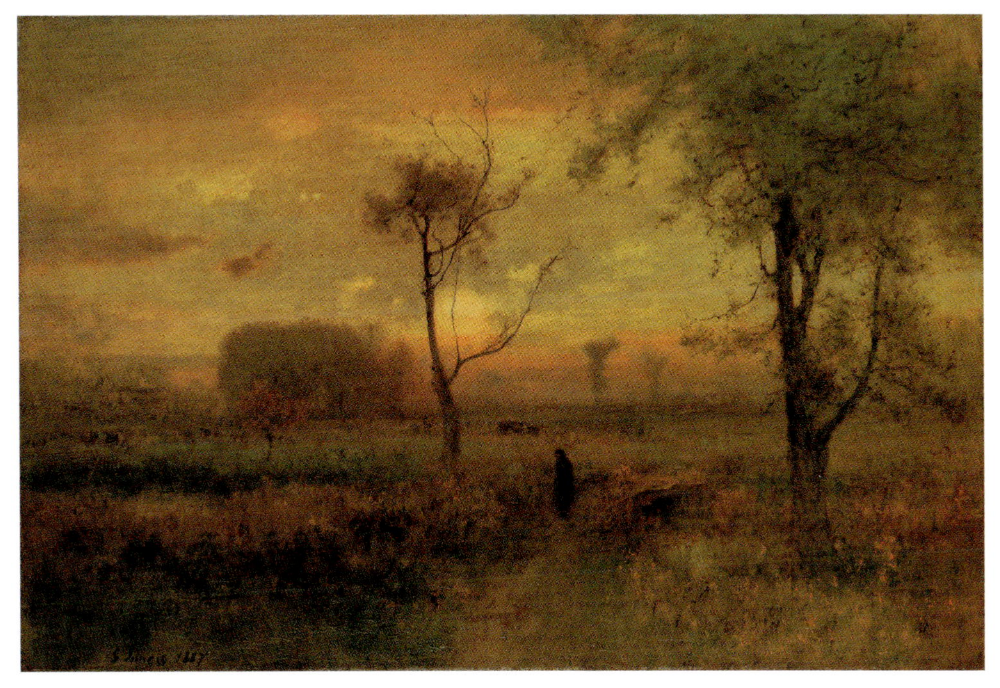

37

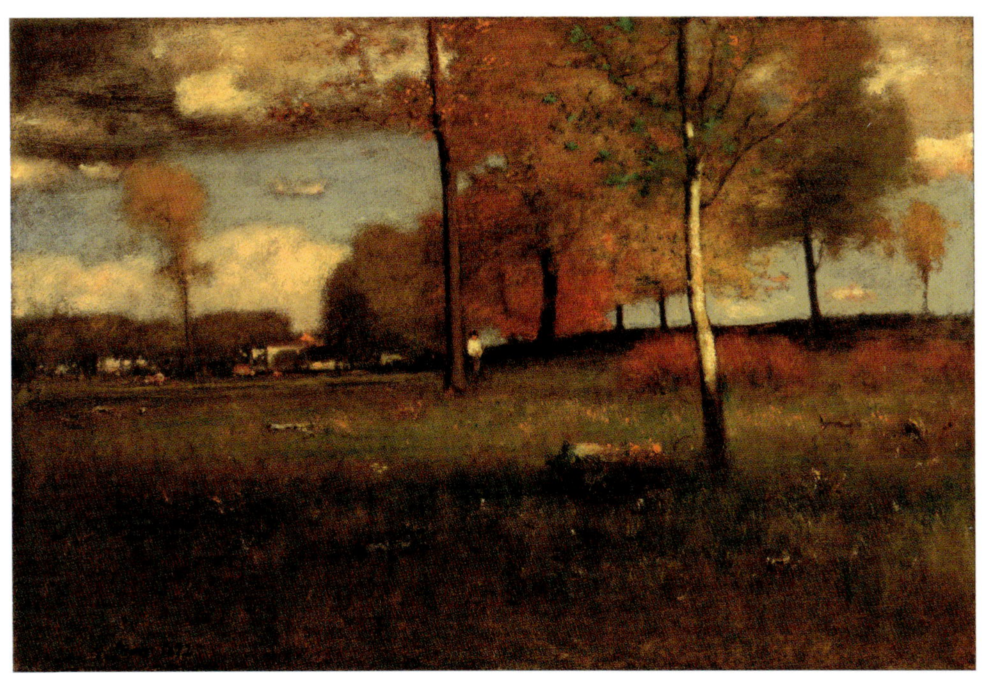

38

39. HAZY MORNING, MONTCLAIR

1893, oil on canvas, 30 x 50"
The Butler Institute of American Art, Youngstown, Ohio

HAZY MORNING, MONTCLAIR (Plate 39) and *The Home of the Heron* (Plate 40) embody the finest achievements of Inness's late landscape painting period. At the same time, they allude to aspects of Inness's biography. The setting of *Hazy Morning, Montclair* may be the grounds of Inness's home on Grove Street in Montclair, New Jersey. The fragment of the obscured structure at the far left probably represents part of the barn featured in *The Old Barn* (Plate 30). The slender, nearly branchless trees in *The Home of the Heron* are characteristic of Tarpon Springs, Florida, where Inness resided during the final winters of his life. They emerged as one of the artist's favorite subjects, as he featured them in such evocative paintings as *Eventide, Tarpon Springs, Florida* (1893; The Art Complex Museum, Duxbury, Massachusetts). In this work and in *The Home of the Heron*, Inness clearly derived great pleasure from conveying the nearly musical rhythms created by the judicious placement of these trees along horizontal axes.

The staccato rhythms of the trees in *The Home of the Heron* reflect a central aspect of Inness's metaphysical investigations: his desire to 'resolve' his theology into a "scientific form." Inness is known to have studied and written about spiritual identities in mathematics ("the science of numbers"); he seems, also, to have investigated Swedenborg's affiliation of spiritual principles with certain geometric forms. Although Inness may have initiated his researches during the early 1850s, perhaps in the company of the Swedenborgian portraitist William Page, indications of his research emerged shortly before his baptism in the Swedenborgian church in 1868, that is, just prior to his four-year stay in Italy (1870–74). The construction of many of the works from this prolific period remains unprecedented in subtlety and refinement. The triangular portions of land and water in *Lake Nemi* (Plate 15), the refined formalism of *The Monk* (Plate 16), and the judicious segmentation of the terrain in *Castel Gandolfo* (Plate 17) all heighten the somewhat otherworldly aura that envelops these settings. Inness would extend the rich legacy of these works into many of his finest late landscapes.

A resolute structure stabilizes the obscured features of *Hazy Morning, Montclair*. Here, again, Inness has bisected his composition into two equal segments of land and sky and re-bisected

(continued on page 126)

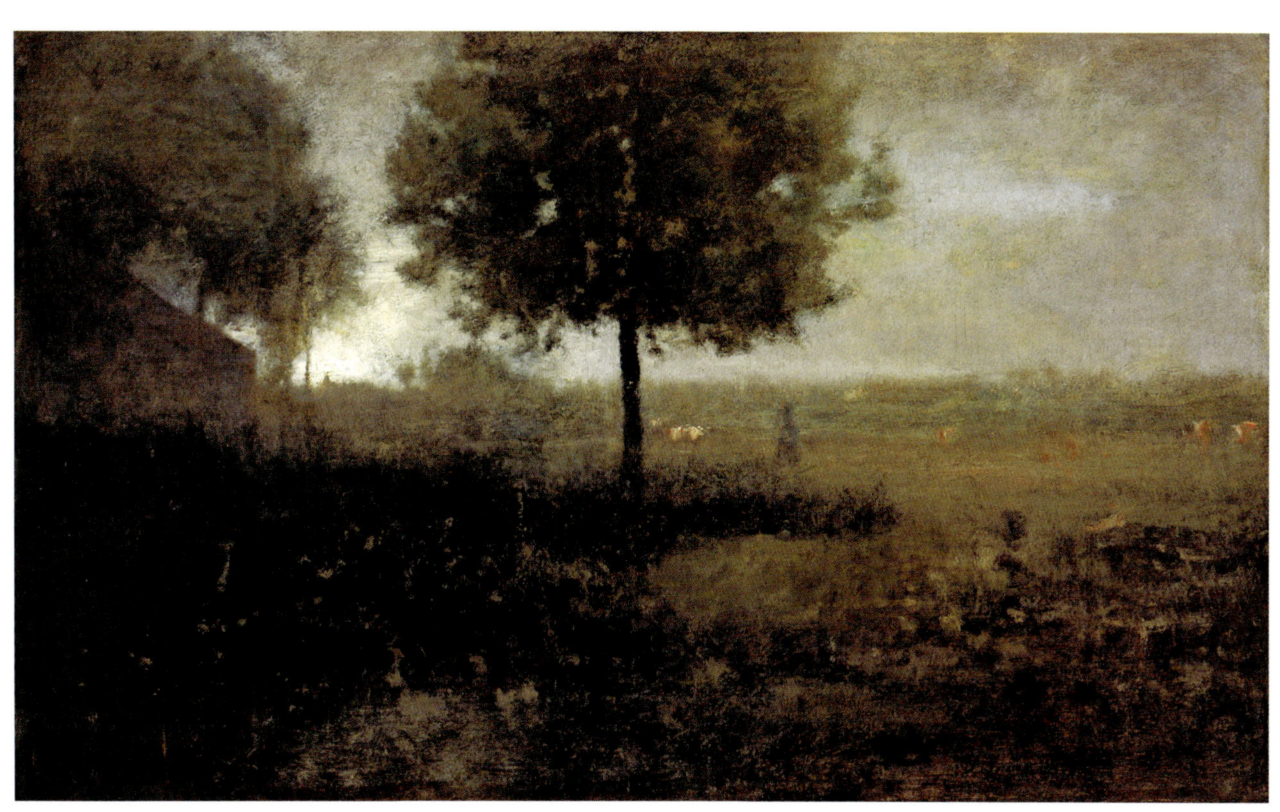

40. THE HOME OF THE HERON

1893, oil on canvas, 30 x 45"
The Art Institute of Chicago
Edward B. Butler Collection, 1911.31

(continued from page 124)
the upper half with a centrally located tree, a formula activated, to great dramatic effect, in *Sunset at Montclair* (Plate 12). Instead of employing overt symbols of divinity, Inness engages these structures to allude to hidden but powerful organizing forces in nature. In the same way, the spaces among the trees in *The Home of the Heron* generate a sequence of mathematically consistent intervals. As we visually link the trees in the foreground to those along the horizon, triangular segments of land—segments that evoke kindred spaces in *Lake Nemi* and *Castel Gandolfo*—seem to emerge.

Although, like the Luminist artists Martin Johnson Heade and Fitz Hugh Lane, Inness pursued his interest in the evocative capacity of geometric and mathematical principles of compositional construction, Inness did not adopt the Luminist's restrained brushstroke techniques. Counterbalancing the refined structure of *The Home of the Heron* are myriad gestures—almost stains—of deep blackish-brown paint, marks generated by the artist's brush, rag, or even fingers. Recalling the enigmatic tissues of brownish green paint that suffuse *Sunset Glow* (Plate 35), these smudges evoke shadows, rocks, and patches of dried grasses. More important, they reassert the artist's determining presence in his pictorial project. As humanistic semaphores, they draw our attention to the heron in flight, which, in turn, leads our gaze to the house with a smoking chimney in the distance. In *Hazy Morning, Montclair,* Inness's facility with the synoptic mark presents the most eidolic of all anonymous figures, an individual seen at the right of the central tree. The anonymous figures of Inness's late work tether the artist's worldview to humanistic concerns. For this reason, they resonate with William James's myriad efforts to validate, for the scientific community, individual spiritual experiences.

Through their geometric schemas and tactile marks, their inclusions (and omissions) of familiar narrative devices, and their efficiently restricted palettes, *Hazy Morning, Montclair* and *The Home of the Heron* embody many of the enigmas of Inness's search for the elusive "moving spirit" that inspired much of his artistic work, indeed, much of his life. Through these details, which invite more analysis than they satisfy, we gladly follow Inness's quest to know, as he put it, "what it is that is in myself, what is this thing we call life, and how does it operate."

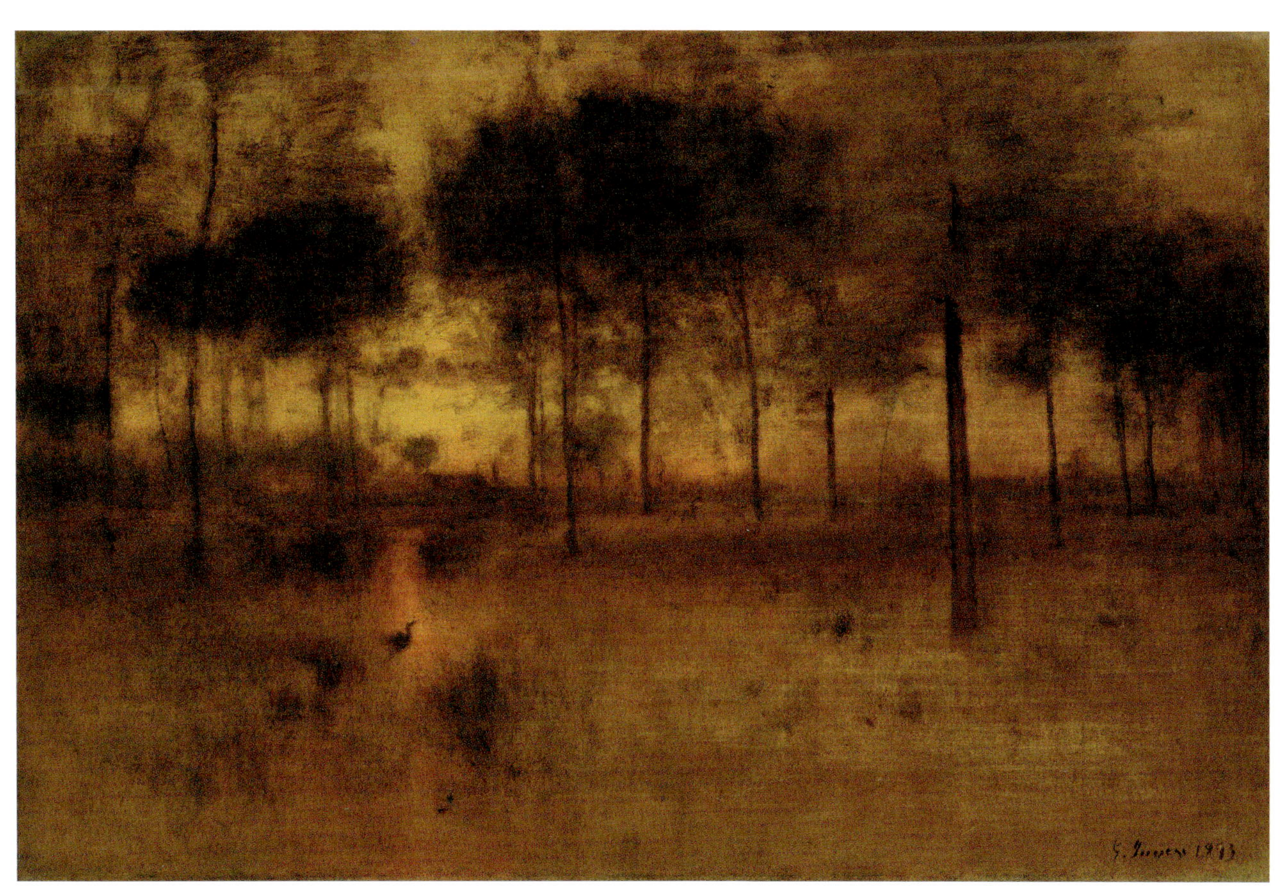

40

ARTISTS AND INNESS'S COLLEAGUES MENTIONED IN THE TEXT

Washington Allston (1779–1843)
Thomas Anshutz (1851–1912)
David Maitland Armstrong (1836–1918)
Albert Bierstadt (1830–1902)
Ralph Albert Blakelock (1847–1919)
Frederic Edwin Church (1826–1900)
Thomas Cole (1801–1848)
Jean-Baptiste-Camille Corot (1796–1875)
Elliott Daingerfield (1859–1932)
Charles-François Daubigny (1817–1878)
Thomas Eakins (1844–1916)
John Flaxman (1755–1826)
Sanford Robertson Gifford (1823–1880)
Régis-François Gignoux (1816–1882)
William Michael Harnett (1848–1892)
Martin Johnson Heade (1819–1904)
Winslow Homer (1836–1913)
Harriet Goodhue Hosmer (1830–1908)
William Keith (1838–1911)
Miner Kellogg (1823–1889)
John Frederick Kensett (1816–1872)
František Kupka (1871–1957)
Fitz Hugh Lane (1804–1865)
Claude Lorrain (1600–1682)
Thomas Moran (1837–1926)
William Sidney Mount (1807–1868)
Edvard Munch (1863–1944)
John Francis Murphy (1853–1921)
George Ward Nichols (1831–1885)
William Page (1811–1885)
John Frederick Peto (1854–1907)
Hiram Powers (1805–1873)
Théodore Rousseau (1812–1867)
John Ruskin (1814–1900)
Albert Pinkham Ryder (1847–1917)
Dwight William Tryon (1849–1925)
Elihu Vedder (1836–1923)
James McNeill Whistler (1834–1903)

Notes to "George Inness and the Visionary Landscape"

1. Inness quoted in E., "Mr. Inness on Art-Matters," *The Art Journal* 5 (1879): 377.
2. Napoleon Sarony (1821–1896) took Inness's portrait. The photograph, recently rediscovered, bears Sarony's signature on the reverse. I thank Harriet Culver for locating it and Leo G. Mazow for originally alerting me to this inscription.

   During the last third of the nineteenth century, Sarony was one of the most sought-after and prolific photographers in the United States. In 1866, he established a studio on Broadway in New York; he later moved it to 37 Union Square. Sarony is best known for his portraits of famous actors and actresses, although he would photograph anyone who wanted to be transformed through dramatic poses, gestures, and expressions. To this end, he became famous for creating theatrical settings for his subjects, replete with fanciful costumes, painted backgrounds, and lavish accessories. According to Ben Bassham, Sarony's real achievement lay in his ability to function as a producer, director, and stage manager of a photography session. See Ben L. Bassham, *The Theatrical Portraits of Napoleon Sarony* (Kent, Ohio: Kent State University Press, 1978). A founding member of the Salmagundi and Tile Clubs, Sarony was also a friend of many late-nineteenth-century American painters, including Robert Swain Gifford, William Merritt Chase, and F. Hopkinson Smith. It is possible that he met Inness at one of these clubs or through a mutual friend. See George Inness, Jr., *Life, Art, and Letters of George Inness* (New York: The Century Co., 1917), p. 119.
3. Booth had represented Hamlet twice in 1870 before the weeklong performance in January 1878. See Thomas Allston Brown, *A History of the New York Stage: From the First Performance in 1732 to 1901*, 3 vols. (New York, 1908; reprint, New York: Benjamin Blom, Inc., 1962), pp. 99, 115. Furthermore, Inness befriended George Waldo Hill, who was an amateur actor and friend of several well-known actors, including Booth and Charlotte Cushman. In May 1875, while both Inness and Hill were sketching in North Conway, New Hampshire, Hill organized a series of theatrical performances, one of which was *Richard the Third*. Arthur Turnbull Hill, "Early Recollections of George Inness and George Waldo Hill," *New Salmagundi Papers, Series of 1922* (New York: The Library of the Salmagundi Club, 1922), p. 112.
4. George Inness quoted in [Anonymous], "His Art His Religion," *New York Herald* (12 August 1894): sect. 4:9: "I have written piles upon piles of manuscripts upon it [the relationship between his art and theology] and my method is to take these piles and re-write them in a very condensed form. Gradually this grows and is 'boiled down,' and all the first essays destroyed."

   Excerpts from the manuscripts were published during Inness's lifetime. Selections from "Suggestions by an Artist" and "The Mathematics of Psychology" were reprinted in G. W. Sheldon, "George Inness," *Harper's Weekly Magazine* 26:1322 (22 April 1882): 244–46 (hereafter: Sheldon 1882).

   In a letter to the Montclair Art Museum (7 May 1956), Rose Inness Hartley, one of Inness's granddaughters, described how all of the artist's personal effects were destroyed in a house fire in 1942 (George Inness files, Le Brun Library, Montclair Art Museum, Montclair, New Jersey). A descendant of Inness's confirmed that the effects were destroyed "in a house fire during the 1940s." (Conversation with the author, 23 February 1998.)
5. John C. Van Dyke, "George Inness," *The Outlook* 73:10 (7 March 1903): 536.
6. In furnishing some details to Alfred Trumble for a biography of Inness that accompanied the catalogue of the executor's sale of the artist's works, James A. Inness remarked, "I have alluded to my brother's

metaphysical labors. These were taken up more as a relaxation after excessive efforts in the field of art, than as a regular pursuit. However, he was at all times fond of discussion on social and theological problems, and at one time told me that in his early days, if his health had permitted, he would have become absorbed in metaphysical studies." Quoted in Alfred Trumble, *George Inness, N.A., A Memorial of The Student, the Artist, and the Man* (New York: "The Collector," 1895), p. 23.

7. George Sheldon observed, "From theology to metaphysics, also, the passage is easy; and Inness is a metaphysician, too." Sheldon 1882, p. 246.
8. Inness quoted in "His Art His Religion," op. cit., p. 9.
9. Barnett B. Newman, "The First Man Was an Artist," *The Tiger's Eye* (New York) 1:1 (October 1947): 59.
10. Vincent van Gogh to Émile Bernard, Arles, end of July 1888, in *The Complete Letters of Vincent van Gogh* (Greenwich, Conn.: New York Graphic Society, 1959), vol. 3, p. 504.
11. Cited in Lloyd Goodrich, *Albert Pinkham Ryder* (New York: George Braziller, Inc., 1960), p. 22.
12. [George Inness], *A Letter from George Inness to Ripley Hitchcock* [23 March 1884] (New York: privately printed, 1928), unpaginated (MS, p. 4). The letter was a reply to a request for information from Ripley Hitchcock, art critic for *The [New York] Daily Tribune*, for his essay "An American Landscape Painter—George Inness," in *Special Exhibition of Oil Paintings, Works of Mr. George Inness* (New York: American Art Gallery, 1884).
13. On this topic see, for example, Perry Miller, *Errand into the Wilderness* (Cambridge, Mass., and London: The Belknap Press of Harvard University Press, 1956) and Sacvan Bercovitch, *The American Jeremiad* (Madison: The University of Wisconsin Press, 1978).
14. Sally M. Promey, "Pictorial Ambivalence and American Protestantism," in *Crossroads: Art and Religion in American Life*, ed. Alberta Arthurs and Glenn Wallach (New York: The New Press, 2001), p. 203.
15. Ibid.
16. Linda C. Hults, "Pilgrim's Progress in the West: *Moran's* The Mountain of the Holy Cross," *American Art* 5:1–2 (winter/spring 1991): 69–85.
17. The leading cultural study on the subject of technology and the American landscape is Leo Marx, *The Machine in the Garden: Technology and the Pastoral Ideal in America* (New York and London: Oxford University Press, 1964). See also Kenneth W. Maddox, *The Railroad in the American Landscape: 1850–1950* (Wellesley, Mass.: Wellesley College Museum, 1981). On *The Lackawanna Valley*, see Nicolai Cikovsky, Jr., "George Inness's *The Lackawanna Valley*: 'Type of the Modern,'" in *The Railroad in American Art: Representations of Technological Change* (Cambridge, Mass., and London: The MIT Press, 1988), pp. 71–91.
18. Inness quoted in [Anonymous], "A Painter on Painting," *Harper's New Monthly Magazine* 56 (February 1878): 458, 459.
19. Nichols was also an art editor for *The [New York] Evening Post* and wrote for the *New York World*. See, for example, "Fine Arts. Return of the Artists," *New York World* (26 September 1860): 5, in which the anonymous writer, probably Nichols, wonders "why [Inness] has not been given his place in the first rank of our landscape painters."
20. Théodore Rousseau quoted in Robert L. Herbert, *Barbizon Revisited* (New York: Clarke & Way, Inc., 1962), p. 66.
21. The finest treatments of this legacy may be found in Barbara Novak, *American Painting of the Nineteenth Century: Realism, Idealism, and the American Experience* (New York: Harper & Row, Publishers, 1969, 2nd ed., 1979) and, by the same author, *Nature and Culture: American Landscape and Painting, 1835–1875* (New York and Toronto: Oxford University Press, 1980).

22. There are exceptions within Inness's corpus of paintings: the *Triumph of the Cross* series, for which Inness derived inspiration from such literary sources as John Bunyan's *Pilgrim's Progress,* the Twenty-third Psalm, and the mystical writings of Swedenborg (see Plate 11), and *The Triumph of the Cross* (also known as *The Triumph of Calvary* and *The Crucifixion*) (c. 1874; oil on canvas, 20 x 30"; Ireland 672). For "Ireland" references, see Selected Bibliography.
23. A rare and useful account is Abraham A. Davidson, *The Eccentrics and Other American Visionary Painters* (New York: E. P. Dutton, 1978). On the visionary tradition in late-nineteenth to twentieth-century European and American art, see Maurice Tuchman et al., *The Spiritual in Art: Abstract Painting 1890–1985* (New York: Abbeville Press, 1986). In the latter, see the excellent essay by Charles C. Eldredge, "Nature Symbolized: American Painting from Ryder to Hartley," pp. 113–29.
24. On Allston's Masonic beliefs, see David Bjelajac, *Millenial Desire and the Apocalyptic Vision of Washington Allston* (Washington, D.C., and London: Smithsonian Institution Press, 1988).
25. On Vedder, see Regina Soria, *Elihu Vedder: American Visionary Artist in Rome (1836–1923)* (Cranbury, N.J.: Associated University Presses, Inc., 1970) and Regina Soria et al., *Perceptions and Evocations: The Art of Elihu Vedder* (Washington, D.C.: Smithsonian Institution Press, 1979); on Blakelock, see, most recently, Glyn Vincent, *The Unknown Night: The Madness and Genius of R. A. Blakelock, an American Painter* (New York: Grove Press, 2003).
26. Among Inness scholars, Nicolai Cikovsky, Jr., was the first to discuss, in detail, the relevance of Swedenborgian doctrine to Inness's life and work. See Cikovsky, "The Life and Work of George Inness" (Ph.D. thesis, Harvard University, 1965); *George Inness* (New York: Praeger, 1971); and *George Inness* (New York: Harry N. Abrams, 1992).

    For a recent and extremely thoughtful analysis of Inness's paintings as products of his investigation into the individual's relationships to the natural and spiritual realms as established through the act of vision, an investigation with roots in seventeenth-century scientific and philosophic theories of perception, see Rachael Ziady DeLue, "George Inness: Landscape, Representation, and the Struggle of Vision" (Ph.D. thesis, The Johns Hopkins University, 2000).

    For additional texts on Inness and Swedenborg, see my Selected Bibliography.
27. "American Artists. George Inness," *Harper's Weekly: A Journal of Civilization* 11:550 (13 July 1867): 433: "In his religious faith he is a disciple of Swedenborg, and believes that all material objects in form and color have a spiritual significance and correspondence."
28. George Inness, "Colors and Their Correspondences," *New Jerusalem Messenger* 13 (13 November 1867): 78–79. Inness authored the article in response to *The Ribband of Blue,* a New Church tract by the British Swedenborgian minister the Reverend Dr. Jonathan Bayley, published first by the Swedenborgian Publishing House in New York in 1866 and reprinted by E. Hazzard Swinney in 1872. It remained unknown in Inness scholarship until Louise Woofenden discovered it in the early 1990s. In 1994, Dr. Sally M. Promey reprinted it in her analysis of the possible influences of Swedenborgian doctrine on Inness's work; see Sally M. Promey, "The Ribband of Faith: George Inness, Color Theory, and the Swedenborgian Church," *The American Art Journal* 26:1 & 2 (1994): 44–65.

    For an intriguing analysis of the historically sacred identity of the color blue, see Roald Hoffman and Shira Leibowitz Schmidt, "The Flag That Came Out of the Blue: A Play in Three Acts and Two Intermezzi," in *Old Wine, New Flasks: Reflections on Science and Jewish Tradition* (New York: W. H. Freeman and Company, 1997), pp. 159–211, esp. pp. 159–60, 165–74.

29. Dr. Sally M. Promey discovered the membership/baptismal records of the Innesses and published them in Promey, "The Ribband of Faith," op. cit., p. 57. A reference in the *New Jerusalem Messenger*, which published excerpts from Inness's writings ("criticisms") in one of its issues, underscored Inness's engagement with Swedenborgian doctrine during the late 1860s. Prefacing the excerpts were the following comments: "Mr. Inness is a New Churchman, and was a member of the Brooklyn society prior to his removal to Europe some three years since [1870]. To those in the Church who have not known this before, the present criticism will possess a double interest. We have the authority of a personal friend of the artist for saying that Mr. Inness acknowledges his indebtedness to the heavenly doctrines not only for benefits of a more interior kind, but for enlarged perceptions of the beauties and requirements of art." [Untitled Notice], *New Jerusalem Messenger* 24:15 (9 April 1873): 175.

    Inness appears not to have regularly attended church services, although Swedenborgian churches were accessible to him near his homes in New York and Montclair, New Jersey. In Brooklyn, he might have attended the church where he was baptized; originally Universalist, it was purchased by Swedenborgians in 1868. See "News and Correspondence," *New Jerusalem Messenger* (21 October 1868): 265. After settling permanently in Montclair in February 1885, Inness might have attended The Orange Society of the New Jerusalem, which served the Oranges, Bloomfield, Montclair, and other neighboring towns in New Jersey. There are no records that he attended services there, although his daughter Helen Hart Inness Hartley (1861–1931), her daughter Helen R. Hartley, and Rose Inness Hartley (the daughter of Helen Hart Inness Hartley's sister Rose Bonheur Inness and stepsister to Helen R. Hartley), were members of the New Church Society of Orange in 1899. See "Members of Orange New Church Society, 1899," manuscript, Church Archives, The New Church (Swedenborgian), New York. We may surmise that Inness studied Swedenborgian doctrine on his own or under the direction of Ager or William Page.
30. Quoted in Reginald Coxe, "Homage to George Inness. Memorial Services in the National Academy of Design," *The New-York Times* (24 August 1894): 8.
31. In his foreword to LeRoy Ireland's catalogue raisonné, Robert McIntyre states that William Page introduced Inness to the writings of Swedenborg while Inness was in his "early thirties," which would have been in the mid- to late 1850s. See LeRoy Ireland, *The Works of George Inness: An Illustrated Catalogue Raisonné* (Austin: University of Texas Press, 1965), p. xi. Following George Inness, Jr. (see Inness, Jr., op. cit., p. 61), several scholars have adhered to the idea that Inness became involved with Swedenborgian doctrine only during the 1860s. See, for example, Mary Phillips, "The Effect of Swedenborgianism on the Later Paintings of George Inness," in Erland J. Brock, gen. ed., *Swedenborg and his Influence* (Bryn Athyn, Pa.: The Academy of the New Church, 1988), p. 427.
32. Page had arrived in Florence in the summer of 1850. On 10 July 1850, he and his friend Abel Nichols leased a suite of rooms from a Signora Eufemia Cabbani on the Via Sant'Apollonia. For a citation of the location of the studios of Page and Inness, see "American Artists Abroad," *Bulletin of the American Art-Union* (August 1851): 80. See also Joshua C. Taylor, *William Page: The American Titian* (Chicago: University of Chicago Press, 1957), p. 106, n. 20. It is unclear why Taylor held that "the two men [Page and Inness] evidently did not become friends until Page's return to the United States." Inness may have learned of the vacancy of the studio in Florence through the New York auctioneer Ogden Haggerty, who financed Inness's trip and who was also a patron of Page's.
33. Early in 1850, Powers, a native of the Swedenborgian stronghold of Cincinnati, had been baptized in the Swedenborgian Church by the Rev. Thomas Worcester, who subsequently sat for a bust portrait

by Powers while in Florence on his honeymoon. See "Notes from Abroad," *New Jerusalem Messenger* 25 (August 1850): 438. See also Ednah C. Silver, *Sketches of the New Church in America on a Background of Civic and Social Life* (Boston: The Massachusetts New Church Union, 1910), pp. 22, 110. Although he had little to say on why he took up the doctrine or what it had to do with his ideas on art, Powers remained a faithful follower of the New Church. Joshua C. Taylor believed that Powers "must have imparted his interest [in Swedenborg] to Page with some enthusiasm." See Joshua C. Taylor, ibid., p. 111. Worcester subsequently left Florence to set up a Swedenborgian congregation in Rome. In April 1851, Powers wrote to Worcester in Rome to say that Page had embraced Swedenborgian doctrine "with great earnestness and pleasure." Quoted in Richard P. Wunder, *Hiram Powers: Vermont Sculptor, 1805–1873* (Newark, Delaware: University of Delaware Press, 1991), vol. 1, p. 168.

34. Journal of James Russell Lowell, 28 September 1851, Lowell Papers, Houghton Library, Harvard University, Cambridge, Mass. At the time, Lowell was staying at Casa Guidi with Robert Browning and Elizabeth Barrett Browning. Page would later develop a close friendship with Mrs. Browning, a fellow admirer of Swedenborg's ideas. See Robert W. Gladish, "Tre Amici Artistici: E. B. Browning, Hiram Powers, and William Page in Florence and Rome," *Covenant: A Journal Devoted to the Study of the Five Churches* 1:4 (spring 1998): 273–91.
35. Joshua C. Taylor, op. cit., p. 29.
36. The basic studies of Swedenborg's life and work include Signe Toksvig, *Emanuel Swedenborg: Scientist and Mystic* (New Haven: Yale University Press, 1948), Inge Jonsson, *Emanuel Swedenborg* (New York: The Swedenborg Society, 1971), and Cyriel Sigstedt, *The Swedenborg Epic: The Life and Works of Emanuel Swedenborg* (London: The Swedenborg Society, 1981). The most comprehensive examination of Swedenborg's influence in America remains Marguerite Beck Block, *The New Church in the New World* (New York: Swedenborg Publishing Association, 1964). A useful collection of essays on Swedenborg—his life, his ideas, and his widespread cultural influence—is Robin Larsen, ed., *Emanuel Swedenborg: A Continuing Vision* (New York: Swedenborg Foundation, Inc., 1988).
37. Ralph Waldo Emerson, "Swedenborg; or, the Mystic," in *Representative Men: Seven Lectures* (Boston: Phillips, Sampson, and Company, 1849), p. 100.
38. See Emanuel Swedenborg, *On the Height of Waters and Strong Tides in the Primeval World* (1718), in A. Stroh, ed., *Opera Quaedam aut Inedita aut Obsoleta de Rebus Naturalibus, nunc edita sub auspiciis Regiae Academiae Scientarum Suecicae*, 3 vols.: vol. 1, *Geologica et Epistolae*, preface by G. Retzius, introduction by A. Nathorst; vol. 2, *Cosmologica*, introduction by S. Arrhenius; vol. 3, *Miscellanea*, preface, introduction, and notes by A. Stroh (Stockholm: Ex Officina Aftonbladet, 1907, 1908, 1911); Emanuel Swedenborg, *Prodromus Principiorum Rerum Naturalium* (*Principles of Chemistry*), trans. by C. E. Strutt (1721; London: William Newbery, 1847; Bryn Athyn, Pa.: Swedenborg Scientific Association, 1976); Emanuel Swedenborg, *Opera Philosophica et Mineralia* (*Philosophical and Mineralogical Works*), 3 vols. (Dresden and Leipzig: Friedrich Hekel, 1734); Emanuel Swedenborg, *Oeconomia Regni Animalis in transactions divisa, quarum haec tertia de Fibra, de Tunica Arachnoidea, et de Morbis Fibrarum agit, anatomice, physice, et philosophice perlustrata* (*Economy of the Animal Kingdom*), trans. A. Clissold, 2 vols. (Amsterdam, 1740; London: W. Newbery, 1845; New York: New Church Press, 1903; Philadelphia: Swedenborg Scientific Association, 1955); Emanuel Swedenborg, *Regnum Animale, Anatomice, Physice, et Philophice Perlustratum* (The Hague, 1744); trans. J. J. G. Wilkinson as *Animal Kingdom* (the widely preferred translation of the title is *Soul's Domain*), 2 vols. (London: William Newbery, 1843; reprint, Bryn Athyn, Pa.: Swedenborg Scientific Association, 1960).

39. Block (op. cit., p. 11) describes Swedenborg's experiences as "strange dreams and phantasies, tremors, prostrations, trances, sweatings, and swoonings." She believed that Swedenborg "alternated between moods of deepest gloom and states of ecstatic joy." Elsewhere, she identified Swedenborg as "an extreme type of 'visualizer' who actually *saw* his ideas in symbolic pictures." Quoted in Frederic Harold Young, *The Philosophy of Henry James, Sr.* (New York: Bookman Associates, 1951), pp. 65–66, n. 11.

    The use of the term "vastation" to describe a "crisis of selfhood" is particularly important because of its reappearance in the literature on both Henry James, Sr., and his son William James. The elder James is said to have experienced a "vastation" while living with his family near Windsor, England, toward the end of May 1844 (almost exactly one hundred years after Swedenborg's "vastation"). For his account of this experience, see Henry James, Sr., *Society the Redeemed Form of Man, and the Earnest of God's Omnipotence in Human Nature: Affirmed in Letters to a Friend* (Boston, Mass.: Houghton, Osgood, 1879), pp. 44–45. The central role that this experience played in shaping Henry James, Sr.'s philosophy is discussed in Raymond H. Deck, Jr., "The 'Vastation' of Henry James, Sr.: New Light on James's Theological Career," *Bulletin of Research in the Humanities* 83:2 (summer 1980): 216–47, and in Alfred Habegger, *The Father: A Life of Henry James, Sr.* (New York: Farrar, Straus and Giroux, 1994). It is widely believed that William James provided a veiled account of his own vastation in his description of a nervous breakdown suffered by an unidentified "Frenchman" in "The Sick Soul," in *The Varieties of Religious Experience* (Boston: Longmans, Green, and Co., 1902; reprint, New York: Viking Penguin, 1982), p. 160. According to Ralph Barton Perry, the vastation "might have occurred any time between [James's] return from Europe [in January 1870] and the definitive improvement of his health in 1872." See Ralph Barton Perry, *The Thought and Character of William James*, 2 vols. (Boston: Little, Brown, 1935), vol. 1, p. 322.

40. Emanuel Swedenborg, *Swedenborg's Journal of Dreams*, commentary by W. Van Dusen, edited from the original Swedish by G. E. Klemming, translated into English in 1860 by J. J. G. Wilkinson, edited by W. R. Woofenden (New York: Swedenborg Foundation, 1986).

    Contrary to Emerson, I prefer the description of Swedenborg as a "visionary" rather than a "mystic" because he appears to have been aware of his own identity during his interactions with inhabitants of the spiritual world, whereas the mystical experience is traditionally identified when the self is *subsumed* into the divine. See Emerson, op. cit., pp. 95–145.

41. Swedenborg, *Swedenborg's Journal of Dreams*, op. cit., nos. 58–59. This particular aspect of his experiences produced Swedenborg's *Arcana Coelestia, the Heavenly Arcana Contained in the Holy Scripture or Word of the Lord Unfolded, Beginning with the Book of Genesis: together with wonderful things seen in the world of spirits and in the heaven of angels*, trans. revised and edited by J. F. Potts, 12 vols. (New York: American Swedenborg Printing and Publishing Society, 1905–10); originally published as *Arcana Coelestia, quae in Scriptura Sacra, seu Verbo Domini sunt, detecta: Hic Primum quae in Genesi. Una cum Mirabilibus Quae visa sunt In Mundo Spirituum, & Coelo Angelorum*, 8 vols. (London: John Lewis, 1749–56).

42. See also Eugene Taylor, "The Interior Landscape: George Inness and William James on Art from a Swedenborgian Point of View," *Archives of American Art Journal* 37:1–2 (1997): 2–10. Affinities between James's ideas and the works of John La Farge have been explored in Henry Adams, "Henry James, William James, John La Farge, and the Foundations of Radical Empiricism," *The American Art Journal* 17:1 (winter 1985): 60–67.

43. Several of James's biographers have posited theories on the degree to which Henry James, Sr.'s Swedenborgian ideas helped, both positively and negatively, to shape William James's ideas. Only a

decade after James's death, Woodbridge Riley made the case for a clear connection between the two. See Woodbridge Riley, *American Thought: From Puritanism to Pragmatism and Beyond* (New York: Henry Holt and Company, 1923). Riley saw the influence of Swedenborg in nearly all of James's later philosophical studies on mysticism. Riley observed, ". . . in the case of [William] James an American might prefer to trace the latter's mystic leanings to a directly inherited interest in Swedenborg." (p. 336) Riley targeted the father's influence to *The Varieties of Religious Experience*, *The Will to Believe,* and *A Pluralistic Universe*: "Among the *Varieties of Religious Experience,"* Riley observed, "we find many cases like those of the seer of Stockholm. In the *Will to Believe* there is also advocated the 'right to believe' in the celestial world. Finally in the *Pluralistic Universe* there is presented that hierarchy of superhuman beings, which have a family likeness to the Swedenborgian conception of the world as a progressive spiral of perfectibility. To read the chapter 'Concerning Fechner,' with its earth-soul and its multi-verses, is like reading [Swedenborg's] *Earths in the Universe* and the *Heavenly Arcana*" (ibid., p. 329).

For a penetrating examination of the topic, see Armi Värilä, *The Swedenborgian Background of William James' Philosophy* (Helsinki: Suomalainen Tiedeakatemia, 1977).

The Swedenborgian community clearly envisioned William James as a kindred spirit. In an obituary for the philosopher, it praised James for his "open mind toward mysticism" and for refusing to be "drawn by the materialistic aspects of physiological psychology away from the contemplation of that world which lies around us beyond the reach of our physical senses." It especially appreciated James as a "conspicuous, distinguished, and influential advocate and illustration of the open mind." See "William James," *New-Church Messenger* 94:11 (14 September 1910): 162.

44. "Lessons in the Science of Correspondence. 1. What is Correspondence?" *New Jerusalem Messenger* 12:37 (27 March 1867): 154.
45. A correspondence is deeper kind of relationship than a figure of speech, such as a metaphor, in which a term is transferred from the object it ordinary designates by implicit comparison or analogy, or a simile, in which two ostensibly different things are compared. It is more powerful and more stable than a symbol, a material object used to represent an operation, element, quantity, or relation. The use of the crown to symbolize authority, for example, is a fundamentally arbitrary representation, just as words are arbitrary symbols for ideas (they change in every language). When Swedenborgians say that light corresponds to truth, it means that light in the natural world *derives its existence* from truth in the spiritual world, the material realm being the realm of effects and the spiritual realm being the realm of causes. These designations are permanent, hence the "scientific" nature of the Swedenborgian doctrine of correspondence.
46. George Sheldon, "Characteristics of George Inness," *The Century Illustrated Monthly Magazine* 49 (February 1895): 530.
47. Emanuel Swedenborg, *Heaven and Hell*, rev. trans. George F. Dole (West Chester, Pa.: Swedenborg Foundation, 1979), Part 5 ("There are Three Heavens") and Part 15 ("Light and Warmth in Heaven"); originally published as *De Coelo et ejus mirabilibus, et de Inferno, ex auditis et visis* (London, 1758).
48. Emanuel Swedenborg, *On the Intercourse Between the Soul and The Body, Which is Supposed to Take Place Either by Physical Influx, or by Spiritual Influx, or by Pre-Established Harmony* (New York: The General Convention of the New Jerusalem in the United States of America, 1865), see esp. nos. II, IV–VIII. See also Emanuel Swedenborg, *Divine Love and Wisdom*, trans. George Dole (New York: Swedenborg Foundation, Inc., 1986), no. 340: "There is a continual influx from the spiritual world into the natural. He who does not know that there is a spiritual world and that it is distinct from the natural world . . . can know nothing of this influx." Originally published as *Sapientia Angelica de Divino Amore et Divina Sapientia* (Amsterdam, 1764).

49. Walt Whitman, "Song of Myself" (1855; rev. ed. 1891–92), in *Leaves of Grass and Selected Prose*, edited with an introduction by Sculley Bradley (New York and Toronto: Rinehart & Co, 1949), verse 22.
50. [Walt Whitman], "Who Was Swedenborg?" *Brooklyn Daily Times* (15 May 1858): [2]; excerpt reprinted in *The Uncollected Poetry and Prose of Walt Whitman*. Collected and edited by Emory Holloway, 2 vols. (Gloucester, Mass.: Peter Smith, 1972), vol. 2, pp. 16–18.
51. Inness quoted in E., "Mr. Inness on Art-Matters," op. cit., p. 377.
52. Ibid.
53. [George Inness], *A Letter from George Inness to Ripley Hitchcock*, op. cit., MS, p. 5.
54. Inness quoted in "His Art His Religion," op. cit., p. 9.
55. In his Doctrine of Forms (also known as his Doctrine of Series and Degrees), Swedenborg affiliated spiritual and psychological properties with the most complex of nature's forms. He ranked them from the least to the most complex. The lowest form is the angle, as it most accurately represents the planar nature of earthly substances, while the highest and most complex is the perpetually rotating vortex, a form, according to the early-twentieth-century Swedenborgian scientist Frank Very, "in which almost all boundaries are, as it were, erased. . . ." This most complex of forms lies in a realm beyond sight, although it is accessible through consciousness in that we may conceive of it without being able to see it. For this reason, Very describes it as "the psychical, or superspatial form." See Frank Very, "Swedenborg's Doctrine of Forms," *An Epitome of Swedenborg's Science* (Boston: The Four Seasons Company, 1927), vol. 1, pp. 612–13.

    There is evidence that Inness ruminated on aspects of Swedenborg's Doctrine of Forms, specifically on the psychospiritual identity of the vortical form. In a 1917 essay on Inness, Elliott Daingerfield recalled that Inness "once expounded to me what he called the ascent of a fleck of soot to the pure diamond by the vortexical progress, and he proved, to himself at least, divinity." Daingerfield, who was not a Swedenborgian, added that he found himself baffled by the remark. "Frankly I could not follow either the thought or the reasoning," he confessed, although, he added, "it seemed eminently interesting." "I begged him to write it down," Daingerfield declared. "He said that he had spent the night doing so, but I have never heard of the writing and inquiry did not reveal it." (See Elliott Daingerfield, "Introduction," in Inness, Jr., op. cit., p. xiii.) Daingerfield later visited Inness in Montclair and recorded one of Inness's final remarks: "I am trying to adjust the principle of construction in my work so that the nearest spiral of the vortex shall strike at my feet—so that I shall be able to paint all that is within the scene, including the objects which are at my very feet." (Quoted in Elliott Daingerfield, "Inness, Genius of American Art," *Cosmopolitan* 55:4 [September 1913]: 524.)

    Although this topic requires more space than I can devote to it here, I will simply mention that the peculiar—and distinctly Swedenborgian—identity of the vortical form engaged Inness's friend William Page, who, I have argued, introduced Inness to the writings of Swedenborg in Florence about 1851–52. Page and Inness continued to discuss Swedenborg during their stay at Eagleswood in the mid-1860s. I would like to suggest that they probably discussed Swedenborg's Doctrine of Forms. During the following decade, while Inness and his family were in Italy, Page and his wife, Sophie, engaged in extended discussions on Swedenborgian topics, notably the Doctrine of Forms. They did so in a diary that Sophie Page maintained. Sophie would pose questions and thoughts to her husband on one page, and on subsequent pages, he would record his replies. (Diary of Sophie C. Page, William Page Papers, Archives of American Art, Smithsonian Institution, Washington, D.C.) In one entry, Sophie, who was an amateur student of astronomy and physics, cited Swedenborg's theory that "the whole sidereal Heaven is in the form of a magnetic sphere," a concept he explicated in *The Principia; or, The First Principles of Natural Things, Being New Attempts Toward a Philosophical Explanation of the Elementary World*, trans. from the Latin by the Rev. Augustus Clissold, M.A., 2 vols. (London: W. Newbery, 1846); originally published as *Principia rerum naturalium sive novorum tentaminum phaenomena mundi elementaris philosophice explicandi* (London, 1734). Sophie mentions that, in *The Principia*, Swedenborg explicates his "Theory of Vortical motion" and "accounts for variable stars—for new & lost stars—& indeed all the phenomena which had been observed to his time." (*Principia*, Part III, Ch. I: "Comparison of the Sidereal Heaven with the Magnetic Sphere," op. cit., vol. 2, pp. 229–50.) She refers on several additional occasions to Swedenborg's exploration of the psychospiritual identity of vortexical forms. In other words, given that William and Sophie Page habitually analyzed Swedenborgian metaphysics, specifically Swedenborg's psychospiritual theory of vortices, it is likely that such theories found their place in Inness's own metaphysical studies, in the "piles upon piles" of manuscripts that he wrote on the relationships between his art and theology (see above, n. 4). Furthermore, it is likely that they played a role in the formation of Inness's middle (Italian) and late (and, possibly, his early) landscape paintings as well.

56. Letter from George Inness to Mrs. A. D. Williams, Albano, 13 August 1872, Object file for *Lake Nemi*, Department of The Art of the Americas, Museum of Fine Arts, Boston.
57. The Palazzo Cesarini, built in 1621 for Prince Giuliano Cesarini, is visible in the distance. See Janet L. Comey, "George Inness: *Lake Nemi*," in Theodore E. Stebbins, Jr., et al., *The Lure of Italy: American Artists and The Italian Experience, 1760–1914* (Museum of Fine Arts, Boston, in association with Harry N. Abrams, Inc., Publishers, 1992), p. 310.
58. Nicolai Cikovsky, Jr., "Inness and Italy," in Irma Jaffe, ed., *The Italian Presence in American Art, 1860–1920* (New York: Fordham University Press, 1992), p. 55; see also Janet L. Comey, "George Inness: *The Monk*," in Stebbins, Jr., et al., op. cit., p. 312.
59. Paintings by Inness and Sanford Gifford, among other artists, were sold at the Crosby Opera House in Philadelphia in August 1866. See "Crosby Opera House, Grand Art Association," *The Philadelphia Inquirer* (1 August 1866): 8. Inness's *Sunset in America (American Sunset)* and *Landscape with Animals* were included, along with two paintings by Gifford and four paintings by Kensett (and works by many other artists), at the Exposition Universelle of 1867 in Paris. See the catalogue for the exhibition, pp. 202–03, and "The Paris Universal Exposition," *The [Philadelphia] Daily Evening Bulletin* (5 April 1867): 1. Kensett and Inness were both represented at the Derby Gallery in New York in an early 1867 exhibition. See "The Derby Gallery," *The [New York] Evening Post* (21 January 1867): 2. The artist and poet (and Swedenborgian) Christopher Pearce Cranch wrote about an Inness painting and a Kensett painting that were exhibited side by side at the National Academy of Design in 1873. See C. P. C. [Christopher Pearce Cranch], "Art. The Kensett Gallery," *The Independent* 25:1269 (27 March 1873): 390. An auction at Clinton Hall on 27 December 1867 included Inness's *Sleepy Hollow* (1849) and Heade's *Sunset*. See "Auction Sale of Paintings," *The [New York] Evening Post* (28 December 1867): 4. Indeed, throughout the 1860s, Williams & Everett, Inness's Boston dealers, handled both Inness's work and the works of Gifford and Heade. See "A Free Gallery Re-Opened," *Boston Daily Evening Traveler* (13 September 1861): 2.
60. Ralph Waldo Emerson, "Nature" (1836), in *The Portable Emerson*, edited by Carl Bode, in collaboration with Malcolm Cowley (New York: Penguin Books, 1981), p. 11. On Luminism and the self, see Barbara Novak, "Man's Traces: Axe, Train, Figure," in *Nature and Culture,* op. cit., pp. 157–200, esp. pp. 184–200.
61. My position differs from that of Gene Veith, who has identified Inness, on two occasions, as a "Luminist." (Gene Edward Veith, *Painters of Faith: The Spiritual Landscape in Nineteenth-Century America*

[Washington, D.C.: Regnery Publishing, Inc., 2001], pp. 14, 126). Veith affiliated Inness with the Swedenborgian belief in the immanence of God in nature. He sees this idea expressed in Luminist painting, in landscapes where "individual details are often effaced and everything blends into a harmonious unity" (p. 126). My reading of Inness's paintings sees "unity" also but not at the expense or effacement of detail. Instead, I suggest that Inness reinvents detail as the gestural mark, leaving permanent reminders of his presence in the engagement of the divine and nature.

62. George Chambers Calvert, "George Inness: Painter and Personality," in *The Bulletin of the Art Association of Indianapolis, Indiana, The John Herron Art Institute* 13:5–8 (November 1926): 45. Calvert is almost certainly referring to the still-life painter Lars Gustav Sellstedt (1819–1911), who lived in Buffalo, New York.
63. Vincent van Gogh to Émile Bernard, end of June 1888, Arles, reprinted in *The Complete Letters of Vincent Van Gogh*, op. cit., vol. 3, p. 499.
64. Pictorial evidence suggests that Inness initiated this kind of brushstroke even earlier, during his Italian trip of 1870–74. In the process of constructing *Old Aqueduct, Campagna, Rome* (1871, oil on canvas, 8 ¾ x 13", Montclair Art Museum, New Jersey), an otherwise modest, intimate pastoral landscape, Inness formulated a shorthand brushstroke technique to represent a herd of grazing sheep. As the sun sets and bathes the landscape in an ocher glow, two Italian herdsmen pause to rest on a small hillside. A fairly large herd of sheep fills the foreground, although the absence of grass begs the question of their source of nourishment. No matter, for the intriguing aspect of the painting is not narration but execution. With flicks of his wrist, and avoiding the temptation to represent detailed ruminant characteristics, Inness daubed paint—white with touches of lemon chrome and black—along the foreground pasture. Each creature in the foreground materialized in no more than five daubs; sheep in the distance required one supremely confident stroke apiece. *Old Aqueduct* is decidedly not an oil sketch; it is a finished composition in which Inness demonstrated a masterful ability to register in the mind, somewhat paradoxically, the identity of tangible, recognizable forms through the most summary, the most conceptual, of means. In this landscape painting, he used the virtuosic brushstroke not so much to represent sheep as to present to his viewers the ontological *essence* of sheep.
65. Works such as *Approaching Storm* (1869, oil on canvas, 30 ¼ x 45 ¼", Collection of Mr. and Mrs. Frederick R. Mayer) confirm that Inness had started to paint storm scenes during the late 1860s. However, he did not fully explore the artistic character of his subject until after his return from Europe in 1875.
66. To support my interpretation of Inness's choice of colors and pictorial techniques, I have also referred to descriptions of colors and techniques characteristic of nineteenth-century landscape painting in Jonathan Stephenson, *The Materials and Techniques of Painting* (London: Thames and Hudson, Ltd., 1989), esp. pp. 99 and 104–5.
67. Inness quoted in "A Painter on Painting," op. cit., p. 458.
68. See Michael Quick's entry for this painting in Nicolai Cikovsky, Jr., and Michael Quick, eds., *George Inness* (New York: Harper & Row, 1985), p. 174. Inness's property, located at 151 Grove Street in the heart of Montclair, New Jersey, consisted of two large houses connected by a covered bridge, a barn, and a painting studio. Making the personal affiliation of the painting even stronger is the fact that Inness gave *The Old Barn* to his daughter Helen Hart Inness Hartley, wife of the sculptor Jonathan Scott Hartley.
69. Quotations from Reginald Cleveland Coxe, "The Field of Art. George Inness," *Scribner's Magazine* 44:4 (October 1908): 511.
70. According to research conducted by Diane Pietrucha Fischer, Inness rented the old Dodge estate ("The Dodgery") in Montclair from 1878 but did not purchase the property until December 1884. In February

1885, Inness and his wife moved into the gate house on the property while their daughter Helen lived in the main house with her husband, Jonathan Scott Hartley. After moving in, the Innesses rechristened the property "The Pines." See Fischer, "The 'Inness' Colony of Montclair," *The Montclair Art Colony: Past and Present* (Montclair, N.J.: Montclair Art Museum, 1997), p. 9. The Innesses constructed a covered bridge between the two houses so that the elderly Mrs. Inness could visit her daughter without having to go outside.

71. S. C. G. Watkins, "Reminiscences of George Inness, the great painter, as I knew him," in *Reminiscences of Montclair* (New York: A. S. Barnes and Company, 1929), p. 109.
72. Elliott Daingerfield, "A Reminiscence of George Inness," *The Monthly Illustrator* 3:2 (March 1895): 262–64.
73. Frederick Stymetz Lamb, "Reminiscences of George Inness," *The Art World* 1:4 (January 1917): 252.
74. Arthur Turnbull Hill, "Early Recollections of George Inness and George Waldo Hill," *New Salmagundi Papers. Series of 1922* (New York: The Library of the Salmagundi Club, 1922), pp. 110–11.
75. By painting with his fingers, Inness joined a legacy of European artists who employed this same technique. The underpainting of Leonardo's *The Virgin of the Rocks* (1491/94–1508, oil on panel, 73⅞ x 46¾", National Gallery, London) reveals traces of the artist's finger- and palm prints. Titian's *The Flaying of Marsyas* (1570–76, oil on canvas, 83½ x 81½", State Museum, Kroměříž, Czech Republic) offers a prime example of how, using both fingers and brush, the elderly Titian constructed a subtle combination of sinuous and bristly marks to create passages of obscurity and clarity, thereby enhancing the oneiric aura of his mythological scene. For Titian's use of his fingers to paint, see David Rosand, "Titian and Pictorial Space," in *Titian: Prince of Painters* (Venice: Marsilio Editori, S.p.A., 1990), p. 100: "The touch of the brush and, indeed, of the artist's own fingers presents us with a new reality that we readily accept and engage." *Thames River Scene* (c. 1805, watercolor on paper, 10¼ x 14⅜", Tate Gallery, London, Turner Bequest XCV47) represents one of many occasions in which Turner used his fingernails to scratch marks into his pictorial surface. For Turner's use of his fingers, see Joyce Townsend, *Turner's Painting Techniques* (London: Tate Gallery, 1993), pp. 52–53: "There is evidence that Turner worked in paint with his fingers, in both water and oil media. In the case of watercolour medium he used the technique less after the 1820s. More late oil paintings show evidence of finger working than earlier ones, probably since Turner applied fewer glazes which conceal the application techniques in the later works. In paintings from the 1820s curved scratch marks are visible, apparently made by Turner's thumbnail. More than one contemporary of Turner's noted that he kept his thumbnail long for the purpose. He used the handles of brushes too, to make straighter, deeper, scratches. Works on paper were scratched with sharp points (pins?) as well as with brush handles and finger nails."
76. See, for example, the lower and right center of *Etretat, Normandy, France* (1892, oil on canvas, 30 x 45", offered for sale at Christie's, New York, 29 November 2000, lot 61), the lower left foreground of *The Lone Farm, Nantucket* (1892; Plate 26), and the trunk of the large tree in *Early Autumn, Montclair* (1891, oil on canvas, 30 x 45", Delaware Art Museum, Wilmington, Delaware. Special Purchase Fund and the Friends of Art).
77. Watkins, op. cit., pp. 110–11.
78. Useful studies on the communicative power of touch include J. J. Gibson, "Observation on active touch," *Psychology Review* 69 (1962): 471–90; J. J. Gibson, *The Senses Considered as Perceptual Systems* (Boston: Houghton Mifflin, 1966); Bruno Bettelheim, "Where Self Begins," *Child and Family* 7 (1967): 5–9; Ashley Montagu, *Touching: The Human Significance of the Skin* (New York: Harper & Row, Publishers, 1971); and Emily W. Bushnell and J. Paul Boudreau, "The Development of Haptic Perception During

Infancy," in Morton A. Heller and William Schiff, eds., *The Psychology of Touch* (Hillsdale, N.J.: Lawrence Erlbaum Associates, Publishers, 1991), pp. 139–61.

79. Inness quoted in "A Painter on Painting," op. cit., p. 461.
80. Quoted in Alexander Lieberman, *The Artist in His Studio* (rev. ed., New York: Random House, 1988), p. 108.
81. Inness, Jr., op. cit., p. 117. See also the comments of William Morris Hunt: "If a bit of canvas uncovered has a better effect than it would have if paint were on it; if something half done looks better than anything finished; in a word, if the Lord helps us in that way, let us say, 'Much obliged!' and take the help; and not, because *we* did not do it, think that we must work over that spot and so spoil it." Quoted in William Morris Hunt, *Talks on Art* (First and Second Series) (Boston: Houghton, Mifflin, and Company, 1883), First Series, p. 9. And later (and more boldly): "To *finish*, stop *fooling* over your work! Don't blister it all over with *facts! Facts are not poetry!* And stop this eternal going back to correct! . . . Avoid certain petty, trivial details which people call 'finish.' They are the nature of things with which one would confuse a child, deceive a fly, or amuse an idiot!" Ibid., p. 20. It is possible that William James, who (with his brother Henry) studied painting with Hunt in Newport in the fall of 1860, later sensed resonances between Hunt's celebration of the unfinished and his own theories of consciousness as an ongoing "stream."
82. George W. Sheldon, "Characteristics of George Inness," *The Century Illustrated Monthly Magazine* 49 (February 1895): 533.
83. A. T. Van Laer, "George Inness," *Arts for America* 5 (February 1896): 19–20.
84. Trumble, op. cit., p. 14.
85. Calvert, op. cit., p. 46.
86. Arthur Hoeber, "A Remarkable Collection of Landscapes by the late George Inness, N.A.," *International Studio* 43 (April 1911): 37.
87. The question as to which of Inness's late paintings are unfinished remains the subject of debate. Regarding *Homeward* (1881; Plate 32), Nicolai Cikovsky, Jr., proposed, "Inness would not have considered this to be a finished painting." Michael Quick has identified *The Lone Farm, Nantucket* (1892; Plate 26) as unfinished though "essentially complete and perhaps even more moving" than a finished work. See the entries for these works in Cikovsky, Jr., and Quick, op. cit., pp. 152 and 188, respectively.
88. Inness quoted in "A Painter on Painting," op. cit., p. 461.
89. Matisse quoted in Maria Luz, "Témoignages: Henri Matisse," *Xxe Siècle* (Paris), n.s. 2 (January 1952): 57; English trans. in Jack D. Flam, ed., *Matisse on Art* (New York: Phaidon Press, Ltd., 1973), p. 137.
90. Inness quoted in Elliott Daingerfield, "Introduction," *Fifty Paintings by George Inness* (New York: privately printed by Frederick Fairchild Sherman, 1913), p. 6.
91. Whistler's engagements with the problem of "finish" were legendary. The best known was played out in the case of *Whistler v. Ruskin*. Upon viewing Whistler's paintings at the Grosvenor Gallery in London during the summer of 1877, notably *Nocturne in Black and Gold: The Falling Rocket* (1875, oil on panel, 23¾ x 18⅜", Detroit Institute of Arts, Gift of Dexter M. Ferry, Jr.), the British art critic John Ruskin famously branded the artist a "coxcomb" who asked "two hundred guineas for flinging a pot of paint in the public's face." Whistler sued for liable and won, although he was awarded a paltry sum. For Ruskin's review, see John Ruskin, *Fors Clavigera* 79 (18 June 1877) in *The Complete Works of John Ruskin*, ed. E. T. Cook and Alexander Wedderburn, Library Edition (London: George Allen, 1903–12), 29:160. Ruskin provided his summary of the trial in "Whistler v. Ruskin," ibid., 29: 580–87. The story and implications of the trial are examined in detail in Linda Merrill, *A Pot of Paint: Aesthetics on Trial in*

Whistler v. Ruskin (Washington, D.C., and London: Smithsonian Institution Press, 1992). Less familiar, but equally important for an understanding of Whistler's—and Inness's—interpretation of the commercial implications of "finish," is the case of *Eden c. Whistler*, which ultimately set an historical precedent, still in place, that legally codified the artist's "moral right" (*droit moral*) to determine when to disclose his or her work. See [James McNeill Whistler], *Eden Versus Whistler: The Baronet & The Butterfly* (Paris: Louis-Henry May, 1899). The story and implications of this trial are described in Albert Elsen, "The Artist's Oldest Right?" *Art History* 2:2 (June 1988): 217–30. For subsequent cases based on *Eden c. Whistler*, see Ralph E. Lerner and Judith Bresler, *Art Law: The Guide for Collectors, Investors, Dealers, and Artists* (New York: Practising Law Institute, rev. ed., 1998), pp. 943–99, esp. p. 945.

92. Inness, Jr., op. cit., p. 140.
93. Ibid., pp. 140–41.
94. Montgomery Schuyler, "George Inness: The Man and His Work," *Forum* 18 (November 1894): 309.
95. According to Arthur Hoeber, Clarke carried away the still-wet paintings "that there might be no mistake and that Inness might have no further chance to experiment." Hoeber, op. cit., p. 37.
96. Schuyler, op. cit.
97. Inness quoted in *A Letter from George Inness to Ripley Hitchcock*, op. cit., MS, pp. 9–10.
98. Gaston Bachelard, *The Poetics of Space*, trans. Maria Jolas (Boston: Beacon Press, 1969), p. 61.
99. Inness quoted in Sheldon 1882, p. 244; reprinted, with slight variations, in E., "Mr. Inness on Art-Matters," op. cit., p. 377.
100. Inness quoted in Sheldon, ibid.
101. James, "Remarks on Spencer's Definition of Mind as Correspondence," *Journal of Speculative Philosophy* 12 (January 1878): 2; reprinted in *Essays in Philosophy (The Works of William James)* (Cambridge, Mass., and London: Harvard University Press, 1978), p. 8.
102. William James, "The Stream of Thought," in *The Principles of Psychology* (New York: Henry Holt and Company, 1890; reprint, Cambridge, Mass.: Harvard University Press, 1950), vol. 1, p. 239.
103. Ibid.
104. In an undated poem, said to be his first and entitled "The Leaves and The Brook," Inness likened the flow of life to the "stream" of thought: "Through that great power which pulsates // Nature into life (truth to its substance // Joined) we form an ever-flowing stream, // Which pours along that conscious shore // Where memory stands, the image of // The past—a present good." Typescript, LeRoy Ireland Papers, Archives of American Art, Smithsonian Institution, Washington, D.C., reel 995, no. 1029. Reprinted in "Poems by the Late George Inness. The American Corot," *The Illustrated American* 17:3, whole no. 257 (for the week ending 19 January 1895): 2.
105. James, *A Pluralistic Universe* (New York: Longmans, Green, and Co., 1909; reprint, Lincoln and London: University of Nebraska Press, 1996), p. 309.
106. See Eugene Taylor, *William James on Exceptional Mental States: The 1896 Lowell Lectures* (New York: Charles Scribner's Sons, 1982).
107. James, *A Pluralistic Universe*, op. cit., p. 307.
108. Ibid., p. 305
109. Ibid., p. 306. Given his experiences as an artist, it is not surprising that James often used the language of art to describe psychological activities. He likened his text on "The Stream of Thought" to "a painter's first charcoal sketch upon his canvas, in which no niceties appear." See James, "The Stream of Thought," op. cit., vol. 1, p. 225.

110. Margaret R. Miles, *Image as Insight: Visual Understanding in Western Christianity and Secular Culture* (Boston: Beacon Press, 1985), p. 32.
111. James, *The Varieties of Religious Experience*, op. cit., pp. 69, 72.
112. Roland Barthes, *Camera Lucida: Reflections on Photography*, trans. Richard Howard (New York: Hill and Wang, 1981), p. 27; originally published as *La Chambre Claire* (Paris: Editions du Seuil, 1980).
113. Elliott Daingerfield, *George Inness: The Man and His Art* (New York: private printing, 1911), p. 26.
114. See Novak, "Man's Traces: Axe, Train, Figure," op. cit.
115. Brian O'Doherty, *American Masters: The Voice and the Myth* (New York: Random House, 1973), p. 159.
116. James joined the American Society for Psychical Research at its founding in 1884 and served as vice president for eighteen years. He served as president from 1894–96. (See Perry, op. cit., vol. 2, p. 160.) Among the many studies on this topic, see *William James on Psychical Research*, comp. and ed. by Gardner Murphy, M.D., and Robert O. Ballou (New York: The Viking Press, 1960). The excellent cultural biography of James by Paul Jerome Croce, *Science and Religion in the Era of William James*, vol. 1, *Eclipse of Certainty, 1820–1880* (Chapel Hill and London: The University of North Carolina Press, 1995), situates James's later work in psychical research and metaphysics at the center of an expanding rift between science and religion in mid- to late-nineteenth-century American culture.
117. His studies of Mrs. Piper's abilities include "Notes on Echolalia in Mrs. Piper" (1886), "A Record of Observations of Certain Phenomena of Trance" (1890), "Letter on Mrs. Piper the Medium" (1898), and "Report on Mrs. Piper's Hodgson-Control" (1909), reprinted in James, *Essays in Psychical Research*, op. cit., pp. 19, 79–88, 184–86, and 253–360, respectively.
118. James, *The Varieties of Religious Experience*, op. cit., p. 428.
119. Ibid., p. 53.
120. William Joseph Gavin, *William James and the Reinstatement of the Vague* (Philadelphia: Temple University Press, 1992), p. 2.
121. Eugene Fontinell, *Self, God, and Immortality: A Jamesian Investigation* (Philadelphia: Temple University Press, 1986), p. 64.
122. James, *A Pluralistic Universe*, op. cit., p. 264.
123. Ibid., p. 315.
124. William James, *Human Immortality: two supposed objections to the doctrine* (New York: Houghton Mifflin & Company, 1898; reprint, New York: Dover Publications, Inc., 1956), p. 27.
125. On the relationship between William and Henry James, Sr., see Daniel Bjork, *The Compromised Scientist: William James and the Development of American Psychology* (New York: Columbia University Press, 1983); Howard M. Feinstein, *Becoming William James* (Ithaca and London: Cornell University Press, 1984); Paul Jerome Croce, "A Scientific Spiritualism: The Elder Henry James's Adaptation of Emanuel Swedenborg," *Swedenborg and his Influence*, op. cit., pp. 251–62; and Perry, op. cit.

    Late in 1882, William wrote a heartfelt letter to his dying father. It read, in part, as follows: "In that mysterious gulf of the past into which the present soon will fall and go back and back, yours is still for me the central figure. All my intellectual life I derive from you; and though we have often seemed at odds in the expression thereof, I'm sure there's a harmony somewhere, and that our strivings will combine. What my debt to you is goes beyond all my power of estimating,—so early, so penetrating and so constant has been the influence." Letter from William James to Henry James, Sr., 14 December 1882; reprinted in *The Letters of William James*, edited by his son Henry James, 2 vols. (Boston: The Atlantic Monthly Press, 1920), vol. 1, p. 219.

126. Henry James, Sr.'s chief text on Swedenborg is *The Secret of Swedenborg: Being an Elucidation of his Doctrine of the Divine Natural Humanity* (Boston: Fields, Osgood, & Co., 1869). See also Frederic Harold Young, *The Philosophy of Henry James, Sr.* (New York: Bookman Associates, 1951).

127. Henry James, Sr., rebelled against the idea and practice of organized religion. Like John Calvin (and unlike Swedenborg), he believed in the inherent sinfulness of mankind. He envisioned the possibility of redemption from original sin through the establishment of new forms of society. In this belief, he followed the principles of the utopian socialist François-Marie-Charles Fourier (1772–1837). For James's views on this subject, see Henry James, Sr., *Society the Redeemed Form of Man, and the Earnest of God's Omnipotence in Human Nature: Affirmed in Letters to a Friend* (Boston, Mass.: Houghton, Osgood, 1879).

Swedenborg did not believe that sin came into the world through a single act of disobedience, or that it could be removed by a single act of conversion. He held, instead, that man was followed by evil spirits and that he was in a continual process of regeneration and deterioration. For this reason, his fate would be decided, in the intermediate state after his death, not by God or by a jury but by himself. His inner self, or *anima,* would choose the society of spirits with which he felt most in harmony. See Inge Jonsson, "Swedenborg and his Influence," in Erland J. Brock, gen. ed., *Swedenborg and his Influence*, op. cit., pp. 29–43.

128. James, *A Pluralistic Universe*, op. cit., p. 299.

129. Ibid., p. 314.

130. See above, note 4.

131. Percy MacKaye, *Epoch: The Life of Steele MacKaye, Genius of the Theatre in Relation to His Times & Contemporaries* (New York: Boni & Liveright, 1927), p. 96. The meeting of Inness and James was first brought to my attention by Taylor in "The Interior Landscape . . . ," op. cit., p. 4.

Steele MacKaye's father, Col. James McKaye (he later changed the spelling to MacKaye) (1805–1888), was, according to Alfred Habegger (op. cit., p. 375), "an early and avid Transcendentalist" who had visited Thomas Carlyle in Chelsea with Henry James, Sr. See also Henry James, Sr.'s recollections in William James, ed., *The Literary Remains of the Late Henry James* (Boston: James R. Osgood Company, 1885), p. 446: "I went to see Carlyle last night to get permission to bring a friend—J. McK.—to see him the next day, who had it much at heart to thank him for the aid and comfort his books had given him, years ago, away out on the shores of Lake Erie." See also pp. 447–48.

Ralph Barton Perry has identified James McKaye as an "artist, abolitionist, [and] man of affairs" (op. cit., vol. 1, p. 84). The McKaye family spent summers in Newport, where they came to know the James family; for two summers (1860 and 1861), the Jameses rented the McKayes' Newport house. When James McKaye allowed Steele to study art with Thomas Couture in Paris, Henry James, Sr., had a more difficult time refusing the opportunity to William. Steele MacKaye became a famous dramatist, actor, and theater manager, the father of the poet Percy MacKaye and the economist James MacKaye.

Louis Comfort Tiffany, who was a student of Inness's during part of his stay at Eagleswood, is said to have overheard "heated exchanges between Inness and fellow painters William Page and James Steele Mackaye." See Michael John Burlingham, *The Last Tiffany: A Biography of Dorothy Tiffany Burlingham* (New York: Atheneum, 1989), p. 43. See also Doreen Bolger Burke, "Louis Comfort Tiffany and his Early Training at Eagleswood, 1862–1865," *The American Art Journal* 19:3 (1987): 29–30.

132. On 21 November 1852, Inness wrote, "I take the liberty of asking you for money[.] I should not do so but that three shillings is all I possess in the world and I know not where to get more[.] I dread asking Mr. Haggert [*sic;* Ogden Haggerty, an early patron of Inness's] as I [have] been almost entire[ly] supported by

him since I have been back from Europe." Letter from George Inness to Samuel Gray Ward, 21 November 1852, Samuel Gray Ward Papers, bMS Am 1465, no. 708, Houghton Library, Harvard University, Cambridge, Mass. See also letters from Inness to Ward dated 7 January 1852 and 30 November 1852, bMS Am 1465, nos. 707, 709, Houghton Library, Harvard University, Cambridge, Mass.

133. See, for example, the letter from Henry James, Sr., to Samuel Gray Ward, 9 March 1854, bMS Am 1093.1, Houghton Library, Harvard University, Cambridge, Mass.

Ward, the American agent for London's Baring Brothers, was Henry James, Sr.'s friend and banker. See Habegger, op. cit., p. 401. Ward's son, Thomas W. (Tom) Ward, was one of William James's best friends; the two young men were companions on the Thayer Expedition of 1865–66. Ultimately, the James and Ward families would be united through marriage. See Perry, op. cit., p. 39, note 1; Louis Menand, *The Metaphysical Club* (New York: Farrar, Straus, and Giroux, 2001), p. 119. Henry James, Sr.'s sister, Jeanette, married William H. Barker, the brother of Anna Hazard Barker Ward (Mrs. Samuel Gray Ward).

134. Ward may also have served as a liaison for the James family to William Morris Hunt. Hunt and Ward were members of the Saturday Club, a dining and literary club that began regular meetings in the winter of 1855–56. Among the founding members were Emerson (who, during the 1850s, was corresponding regularly with Henry James, Sr.), Hawthorne, Longfellow, Richard Henry Dana, Jr., James Russell Lowell, Charles Eliot Norton, Louis Agassiz, and Benjamin Peirce (the father of the philosopher and mathematician Charles Sanders Peirce). Henry James, Sr., would join the Club in 1862. See Menand, op. cit., p. 204.

135. The Inness and James families frequently resided in the same or neighboring cities. In 1854, Inness and his family returned from a yearlong trip to France to reside in Brooklyn, New York. In between their own lengthy visits to Europe, the James family resided in Manhattan. In 1859, Inness moved to Medfield, Massachusetts, a suburb of Boston. In late September 1860, the James family relocated to Newport, Rhode Island, where Henry and William studied painting under Hunt's direction. In the spring of 1864, after William had enrolled in Harvard Medical School, the Jameses settled in a house at 13 Ashburton Place in Boston. In the autumn of 1866, the family moved again, this time to 20 Quincy Street in Cambridge, where they resided for fifteen years. The synchronic physical proximity of the Inness and James families makes the possibility of one or more early meetings all the more likely.

136. Inness quoted in "His Art His Religion," op. cit., p. 9.

137. As described in Inness, Jr., op. cit., pp. 209–10.

138. Meyer Schapiro, "Eugène Fromentin as Critic," in *Theory and Philosophy of Art: Style, Artist, and Society (Selected Papers, Vol. IV)* (New York: George Braziller, 1994), p. 106.

139. James, *A Pluralistic Universe,* op. cit., p. 309.

Notes to the Commentaries

Page 67: Elliott Daingerfield, "George Inness," *The Century* 95:1 (November 1917): 76.

INNESS'S ARTISTIC SELF-EDUCATION

1. Quoted in George Chambers Calvert, "George Inness: Painter and Personality," *The Bulletin of the Art Association of Indianapolis Indiana. The John Herron Art Institute* 13:5–8 (November 1926): 37.
2. Robert L. Herbert, *Barbizon Revisited* (New York: Clarke & Way, Inc., 1962), p. 24.

ART AND POETRY: INNESS AND SWEDENBORG ON SPIRITUAL SPACE

1. Emanuel Swedenborg, *Heaven and Hell*, trans. George F. Dole, introduction by Colin Wilson (West Chester, Pa.: Swedenborg Foundation, 1994), nos. 192, 195 (pp. 145, 146).
2. Elizabeth Barrett Browning, *Letters to Her Sister: 1846–1859*, ed. Leonard Huxley (New York: E. P. Dutton, 1930), p. 283.
3. Robert W. Gladish, "Tre Amici Artistici: E. B. Browning, Hiram Powers, and William Page in Florence and Rome," *Covenant: A Journal Devoted to the Study of the Five Churches* 1:4 (spring 1998): 285–89.
4. *The Poetical Works of Elizabeth Barrett Browning* (New York: James Miller, Publisher, 1875), p. 399.
5. Walt Whitman, *Leaves of Grass* (1885; reprint, New York: Random House, Inc., 1992), [verse 6], p. 32.
6. [Walt Whitman], "Who Was Swedenborg?" *[Brooklyn] Daily Times* (15 May 1858): [2].
7. Whitman, *Leaves of Grass* (1891–92 edition), op. cit., verse 20, p. 206.
8. Reprinted in George Inness, Jr., *Life, Art, and Letters of George Inness* (New York: The Century Co., 1917), pp. 97–98.

PLATE 10. WINTER, CLOSE OF DAY (A WINTER SKY)

1. Essential biographies of Henry Ward Beecher include Paxton Hibben, *Henry Ward Beecher: An American Portrait* (New York: George H. Doran Company, 1927); William McLoughlin, *The Meaning of Henry Ward Beecher* (New York: Alfred A. Knopf, 1970); and Clifford E. Clark, Jr., *Henry Ward Beecher: Spokesman for a Middle-Class America* (Chicago: University of Chicago Press, 1978). On the Beecher family within the context of nineteenth-century evangelical reform movements, see Marie Caskey, *Chariot of Fire: Religion and the Beecher Family* (New Haven: Yale University Press, 1978) and Milton Rugoff, *The Beechers: An American Family in the 19th-Century* (New York: Harper & Row, 1981). See also Lyman Beecher's auto-biography and the many essays and sermons of Henry Ward Beecher.
2. Seven of Inness's paintings were included in Beecher's estate sale of 8–10 November 1887; see *Catalogue of the Bric-a-Brac, Rare Oriental Rugs[,] Oil Paintings, Furniture[,] Fine Curtains[;] Large Collection of Fine Old Engravings and Etchings and the Valuable Library Belonging to the Estate of the Late Rev. Henry Ward Beecher* (New York: American Art Association, Managers, 1887). An eighth painting was exhibited in 1860 (see below, "i"). The works were as follows:
   a. no. 421: *Light Triumphant,* or *Landscape,* signed and dated lower right: G. Inness 1862, 12 x 18", exhibited at the National Academy of Design in 1862 (cat. no. 19); see "The Academy of Design, Second Notice, The Large Room," *The [New York] Evening Post* (17 April 1862): [1]; Ireland no. 240.
   b. no. 422: *Pool in the Woods,* 7 x 9"; no work matches this description in Ireland's catalogue raisonné.

c. no. 427: *Landscape,* or *Summer Landscape,* c. 1861, 12 x 18", Ireland no. 233.
d. no. 428: *Landscape,* 1876, 18 x 12", possibly *Summer Sunshine and Shadow* (12 x 18", Ireland no. 312).
e. no. 439: *English Oaks,* or *Landscape with Sheep,* 15 x 26", Ireland, p. 414.
f. no. 445: *The Old Mill,* 14 x 10"; possibly Ireland no. 448 (although Ireland does not list Beecher as an owner).
g. no. 446: *Landscape,* 12 x 16".
h. no. 440: *Still Life,* 1884, 30 x 47": almost certainly not by Inness.
i. [*View on the Hudson River*]: exhibited at Dodworth's Hall in Brooklyn, New York, in March 1860. See "Art Items," *The [New York] Evening Post* (23 March 1860): [2].

3. All quotations from this lecture are from Henry Ward Beecher, "Landscape Picture," 7 March 1865, inscribed "Before Horticulture Department," in "Sermons, 1860–1865," Henry Ward Beecher Papers, Library of Congress, Box 13, unpaginated. In this transcription, I have retained Beecher's original punctuation.

PLATE 11. THE VALLEY OF THE SHADOW OF DEATH

1. See, for example, "Art Gossip," *Frank Leslie's Illustrated Newspaper* 24:609 (1 June 1867): 163.
2. *The Valley of the Shadow of Death* was owned by Fletcher Harper and then by Charles M. Pratt, who gave it to The Frances Lehman Loeb Art Center, Vassar College, in 1917. According to Inness's son, *The New Jerusalem,* which he calls "The Delectable City," was destroyed or damaged "in an accident at the Madison Square Garden." See Inness, Jr., op. cit., p. 69. It is possible that sections of this painting survived and were reworked by Inness in 1880, after the fire. The location of the third painting, *The Vision of Faith,* is unknown.
3. George F. Dole and Robert H. Kirven, *A Scientist Explores Spirit* (West Chester, Pa.: Swedenborg Foundation, 1992), p. 74.
4. "Inness's Allegorical Pictures," *The [New York] Evening Post* (11 May 1867): [4].
5. Ibid.
6. The body of the pilgrim represents the single exception to Inness's otherwise restrained brushwork in that it is as loosely painted as any of Inness's later "anonymous figures." In other words, Inness maintains the paradoxical nature of his theme by making the subject of primary interest the most ephemeral form in the painting.
7. "Death's Valley," in Walt Whitman, *Leaves of Grass, Including The Annexes, The Prefaces,* A Backward Glance O'er Travel'd Roads, Old Age Echoes, *The Excluded Poems and Fragments, The Uncollected Poems and Fragments* (Comprehensive Reader's Edition), ed. Harold W. Blodgett and Sculley Bradley (New York: New York University Press, 1965), pp. 580–81. The version of the poem published in the Comprehensive Reader's Edition differs somewhat from Horace Traubel's reproduction of Whitman's manuscript of the poem. For Traubel's facsimile, see Horace Traubel, *With Walt Whitman in Camden: April 8 to September 14, 1889,* ed. Gertrude Traubel (Carbondale, Ill.: Southern Illinois University Press, 1964), after p. 242.

   Whitman made note of the poem in his Daybook with the following entry: "Harpers' Monthly has a poemet illustrating 'the Valley of the Shadow of Death' picture by Innes [*sic*] –paid $25 // pub'd. . . . " See William White, ed., *Walt Whitman: Daybooks and Notebooks, Vol. II: Daybooks, December 1881–1891* (New York: New York University Press, 1978), p. 540 (entry for December 9, 1889). See also related entries on p. 525, n. 2869; p. 530, n. 2897, p. 532. Whitman wrote a first stanza for the poem, which he subsequently deleted: "Aye, well I know tis ghastly to descend in that valley // Preachers, musicians, poets, painters always render'd it // Philosophs exploit—the battle-field, the ship at sea, the myriad beds of death. // All, all the past have entered—the ancientest humanity we know. // Syria's, India's,

Egypt's, Greece's, Rome's, // Till now, for us, under our very eyes, spreading the same to-day, // Grim, ready for entrance yours and mine, // Here, here 'tis limned."

PLATE 14. THE TROUT BROOK

1. Marcel Proust, *Remembrance of Things Past* (New York: Random House, 1927), vol. 2, pp. 1122–23.
2. Swedenborg, *Heaven and Hell*, op. cit., no. 191 ("Space in Heaven").

SCIENCE, ART, AND THE VISIONARY IN ITALY

1. Inness, Jr., op. cit., p. 284.
2. William James, *The Varieties of Religious Experience* (Boston: Longmans, Green, and Co., 1902; reprint New York: Viking Penguin, 1982), p. 515.

PLATE 16. THE MONK

1. For the identification of the setting of *The Monk*, see Nicolai Cikovsky, Jr., "Inness and Italy," in Irma Jaffe, ed., *The Italian Presence in American Art, 1860–1920* (New York: Fordham University Press, 1992), p. 55; see also Janet L. Comey, "George Inness: *The Monk*," in Theodore E. Stebbins, Jr., et al., *The Lure of Italy: American Artists and The Italian Experience, 1760–1914* (Museum of Fine Arts, Boston, in association with Harry N. Abrams, Inc., Publishers, New York, 1992), p. 312.
2. Regina Soria, *Elihu Vedder: American Visionary Artist in Rome (1836-1923)* (Cranbury, N.J.: Associated University Presses, 1970), p. 94.

PLATE 17. CASTEL GANDOLFO

1. Built from the designs by Carlo Maderno (1556–1629), Castel Gandolfo was enlarged by Alexander VII in 1660 and altered in the eighteenth century by Clement XII. Around 1870, nuns, established in the area by Pius IX, came to occupy the residence. See Norwood Young, ed., *Handbook for Rome and the Campagna* (London: Edward Stanford, 1908), p. 499. According to Young, Castel Gandolfo became famous for its extremely picturesque eminence above the north-west margin of Lake Albano.
2. "The Fine Arts," *The Boston Daily Globe* (19 June 1875): 2.
3. Jorge Luis Borges, *Seven Nights*, trans. Eliot Weinberger (New York: New Directions, 1984), p. 80.

PLATES 18. LANDSCAPE WITH CATTLE AND 19. EARLY MOONRISE, TARPON SPRINGS

1. [Anonymous], "A Painter on Painting," *Harper's New Monthly Magazine* 56 (February 1878): 458–61; E., "Mr. Inness on Art-Matters," *The Art Journal* 5 (December 1879): 374–77; [Anonymous],"Strong Talk on Art," *The [New York] Evening Post* (3 June 1879): [3].
2. Since the 1880s, the Inness family made its winter home in Tarpon Springs in a large frame house located about two blocks from the Church of the Good Shepherd (Universalist). When a storm blew out several of the windows of the church in September 1918, George Inness, Jr., a painter in his own right, created canvases to cover the unsightly holes inside the church. See Richard Wagner, "Church Has Rare View of Easter," *The [Cleveland] Plain Dealer* (26 March 1967): 8–F.

PLATES 20. WINTER EVENING AND 21. HOME AT MONTCLAIR

1. Reprinted in *The Collected Poems of Wallace Stevens* (New York: Vintage Books, 1990), p. 215.
2. On hidden structures in science, see, for example, Ilya Prigogine and Isabelle Stengers, *Order Out of*

Chaos (New York: Bantam Books, 1984); Roald Hoffmann, "Molecular Beauty," *The Journal of Aesthetics and Art Criticism* 48:3 (Summer 1990): 191–204; and Frank Close, *Lucifer's Legacy: The Meaning of Asymmetry* (New York: Oxford University Press, 2000).

On the earliest affiliations between geometric forms and spiritual identities, see Henry Schaefer-Simmern, "Basic Structures in the Earliest Beginnings of Artistic Activity," in Mary Henle, ed., *Vision and Artifact* (New York: Springer Publishing Company, 1976), pp. 87–90. On hidden structures in Renaissance art, see, for example, Michael Baxandall, "Truth and Other Cultures: Piero della Francesca's *Baptism of Christ*," in *Patterns of Intention* (New Haven and London: Yale University Press, 1985); and James Elkins, "The Case Against Surface Geometry," *Art History* 14:2 (June 1991): 143–74.

On Swedenborg's Doctrine of Forms, see Inge Jonsson, *Visionary Scientist: The Effects of Science and Philosophy on Swedenborg's Cosmology* (West Chester, Pa.: Swedenborg Foundation Publishers, 1971, reprint 1999), esp. pp. 69–91; and E. R. Edson, *Swedenborg's Vortex-rings and Some of their Applications in the Realm of Natural Science, with Especial Reference to the Subject of Thought* (Seattle: Washington Medical Library Association, 1904). See also pp. 136–37, n. 55, above.

PLATE 22. AUTUMN GOLD

1. Frank Fowler, "A Master Landscape Painter: The Late George Inness," *Harper's Weekly: A Journal of Civilization* 38:1984 (29 December 1894): 1240.

PLATE 23. MOONRISE

1. Childe Hassam to Roland Knoedler, Esq., New York, 11 March 1917, Archives, Guild Hall, Easthampton, New York. I thank Frank Martucci for bringing this letter to my attention.
2. Elliott Daingerfield to Messrs. M. Knoedler & Co., 5 November 1914, Archives, Guild Hall, Easthampton, New York. George Inness, Jr., added, "This canvas, 'Moonrise,' is one of the most beautiful things my father ever did. In subtlety of tone and richness of quality it is surpassed by none." Inness, Jr., op. cit., p. 276.

PLATES 24. SUMMER, MONTCLAIR (NEW JERSEY LANDSCAPE) AND 25. OCTOBER NOON

1. William James, *The Varieties of Religious Experience*, op. cit., p. 380.
2. Ibid., p. 388.
3. William James, *A Pluralistic Universe* (New York: Longmans, Green, 1909; reprint, Lincoln and London: The University of Nebraska Press, 1996), p. 306
4. Ibid., p. 307.
5. Ibid., p. 308.
6. Inness quoted in G. W. Sheldon, "George Inness," *Harper's Weekly Magazine* 26:1322 (22 April 1882): 244 (hereafter: Sheldon 1882); reprinted, with slight variations, in E., "Mr. Inness on Art-Matters," op. cit., p. 377.

PLATES 26. THE LONE FARM, NANTUCKET AND 27. HARVEST MOON

1. Quoted in Sheldon 1882, p. 244.
2. Quoted in George Inness, *A Letter from George Inness to Ripley Hitchcock* [23 March 1884] (New York: privately printed, 1928), unpaginated (MS, p. 9).
3. For a sensitive examination of the concepts of image-making and abstraction, of humanism and religion in Rothko's paintings, see Anna C. Chave, *Mark Rothko: Subjects in Abstraction* (New Haven and London: Yale University Press, 1989).

THE RHYTHM OF THE WORKING HAND

1. See "Art and Artists," *Boston Evening Transcript* (1 June 1875): 6. Joining Inness were his son, George Inness, Jr., and John A. (Jack) Monks In 1875, the two Innesses and Monks collaborated to create *Barberini Pines* (The Metropolitan Museum of Art, New York). Monks was later identified as a "pupil" of Inness (see "The Collection at Williams & Everett," *Boston Daily Evening Transcript* [23 May 1876]: 8), although, when asked later, Inness never admitted having any students. See J. Walker McSpadden, *Famous Painters of America* (New York: Thomas Y. Crowell & Co., 1907), p. 137.
2. Kiarsarge House (alternatively spelled Kiarsage and Kearsarge) was "a large and commodious first-class hotel accommodating 300 guests." See "The Summer Exodus. No. V," *Boston Evening Transcript* (28 June 1875): 6. For a description of the schoolhouse, see B., "White Mountain Travel," *Boston Evening Transcript* (13 August 1875): 4. The close proximity of the famous residence to the railroad station made it extremely popular and convenient for businessmen commuting from the city on the weekends. See "The Arts," *Appleton's Journal* 14:339 (18 September 1875): 375–76.
3. See "Art and Artists," *Boston Daily Traveller* (16 September 1875): 6.
4. For example: *Bridle Path, Mount Washington* (1868; oil on canvas, 24⅛ x 38", Sterling and Francine Clark Art Institute, Williamstown, Massachusetts), *Mount Washington* (1869; oil on canvas, 16¼ x 24$\frac{5}{16}$", The Art Institute of Chicago), and *Mountain Climber Resting* (1869; oil on canvas, 10¾ x 14¾", Private collection, Washington, D.C.). See the entries for these paintings and other related works in Nicolai Cikovsky, Jr., and Franklin Kelly, *Winslow Homer* (New Haven and London: Yale University Press, in association with the National Gallery of Art, Washington, D.C., 1995), pp. 72–78.
5. "The Arts," *Appleton's Journal* 14:339 (18 September 1875): 376.
6. William James, "The Stream of Thought," in *The Principles of Psychology* (New York: Henry Holt, 1890; reprint, New York: Dover Publications, Inc., 1950), vol. 1, pp. 284–85.

PLATE 29. THE COMING STORM

1. George Inness, "A Plea for the Painters. Letter from the Artist Inness," *The [New York] Evening Post* (21 March 1878): 2.

PLATE 30. THE OLD BARN

1. Inness purchased the property in December 1884 and moved in permanently the following February. For a note on Inness's initial move to Montclair, see "Personal," *The [New York] Evening Post* (4 June 1878): [2]. For the date of his final move, see above, pp. 138–39, n. 70. The buildings on Inness's property were razed shortly after 1911. See "Innes [*sic*] Studio to be Razed," *The Montclair Times* (11 July 1911): 5.
2. Notes made by Rachel Hartley at the request of Miss Gladys Segar, Reference Librarian, Montclair Library, early 1940s, typescript copy, Heritage File, Montclair Public Library, Montclair, New Jersey. Rachel, who died in 1963, was the daughter of Helen, Inness's daughter (1861–1931), and the sculptor Jonathan Scott Hartley (1845–1912). The barn is visible in an undated survey of the Inness property. See copy in the Montclair Historical Society, Montclair, New Jersey.

   The Old Barn remained in Inness's family until Louise Hartley Norton, one of Rachel's sisters, sold it in 1975. See letter from Mrs. Norton to the Montclair Art Museum, undated but about 21 February 1975, copy in George Inness file, Le Brun Library, Montclair Art Museum, Montclair, New Jersey.
3. Henry James, "Preface," *The Wings of the Dove* (1902; reprint, New York, Random House, 1946), p. xxvii–xxviii.

PLATE 31. WOMAN WITH CALF

1. Quoted in Elliott Daingerfield, "George Inness, N.A., An Appreciation," in *Catalogue of the Loan Exhibition of Important Works by George Inness, Alexander Wyant, Ralph Blakelock* (Chicago: Moulton & Ricketts, 1913), n.p. [p. 7].
2. Benjamin Constant, "Inness's Work Judged by an Artist [Letter to the Editor]," *The New-York Times* (6 January 1895): 4.
3. Quoted and described in David Rosand, *Drawing Acts: Studies in Graphic Expression and Representation* (Cambridge: Cambridge University Press, 2002), pp. 278–98, esp. p. 294.

PLATE 32. HOMEWARD

1. James, *The Varieties of Religious Experience*, op. cit., pp. 251–52. Transcription from *Memoirs of Rev. Charles G. Finney. Written by Himself* (New York: A. S. Barnes & Company, 1876), p. 34.
2. We will never know if the artist found himself unable to complete the painting or if he preferred the painting in its unfinished state and kept it for his own purposes; in either case, he refused to destroy it or repaint it, and he refused to sell it or give it away, all of which suggests that Inness regarded *Homeward* as an especially meaningful painting. Nicolai Cikovsky, Jr., proposed that Inness "clearly liked" this painting, "or it would not have survived." He asserted that, owing to the unfinished condition of the painting, Inness "would never have exhibited it in its present state." See Cikovsky and Quick 1985, op. cit., p. 152.
3. See "The George Dinner. The Great Banquet at the Metropolitan Hotel. . . . George Inness," *The Standard* 7:4 (22 January 1890): 10. Discovered and first discussed by Mazow in "George Inness: Problems in Antimodernism" (see below). Furthermore, Inness authored a short article on the importance of the eight-hour day. See "Unite and Succeed," *The American Federationist* 1 (1894): 119. For assessments of Inness's identity as an advocate for social reform, see Jane Morley, "George Inness—Friend of Labor," *Labor History* 25:2 (Spring 1984): 252–57, and Leo G. Mazow, "George Inness: Problems in Antimodernism" (Ph.D. dissertation, University of North Carolina, Chapel Hill, 1996).

PLATE 33. INDIAN SUMMER

1. Inness quoted in Sheldon 1882, p. 244.
2. Inness quoted in [Anonymous], "His Art His Religion," *New York Herald* (12 August 1894): sect. 4:9.
3. Inness quoted in Sheldon 1882, op. cit.
4. James, *A Pluralistic Universe*, op. cit., p. 250–51.

THE ANONYMOUS FIGURE

1. Roland Barthes, *The Rustle of Language*, trans. Richard Howard (New York: Hill and Wang, 1986), p. 145.
2. For a theoretical analysis, nearly concurrent with Inness's late landscape painting period, of the role of memory in identifying the hieroglyphic form—specifically, the scratches that call to mind "some vast horizon of open plain, masses of trees" in Rembrandt's etched landscapes—see John La Farge, *Considerations on Painting* (New York: Macmillan and Co., 1895), p. 101.

PLATE 35. SUNSET GLOW

1. George Inness quoted in Inness, Jr., op. cit., p. 200.

Chronology

1825 1 May: Born on a farm near Newburgh, New York, to Clarissa Baldwin (1795–1841) and John Williams Inness (1793–1873), whom George Inness later described as "a well to do farmer."[1] George Inness is the fifth of thirteen children. Family soon moves to home on Green and Centre Streets in New York City.[2]

1830–31[3] Family moves to Newark, New Jersey, where Inness receives some schooling; returns to New York City. May have suffered from epilepsy.[4]

1839 Takes drawing lessons "for a few months" from John Jesse Barker (active 1815–56), an itinerant painter living in Newark.[5] Inness later remarked of Barker, "I used to wonder if I should ever be able to do what he did."[6]

1841 Works at the map engravers Sherman & Smith, New York City, "on and off for two years."[7]

1843 Summer: Studies with the French itinerant landscape painter Régis-François Gignoux (1816–1882), a student of Paul Delaroche (1797–1856).[8]

1843–44 Registers for antique class at the National Academy of Design; registers again for the same class in 1845–46 and 1846–47.[9]

mid-1840s Gains first exposure, through prints, to works of the old masters. Also studies works by Thomas Cole (1801–1848) and Asher B. Durand (1789–1886). "There was a lofty striving in Cole," Inness later recalled, "although he did not technically realize that for which he reached. There was in Durand a more intimate feeling of nature. 'If,' thought I, 'these two can be combined. I will try.'"[10]

1844 Spring: First exhibition at the National Academy of Design, New York; shows *Evening, a Composition* (Ireland 2) and *Sunset* (Ireland 3).[11] Begins lifelong affiliation with the Academy.

after 1844 Opens first studio in New York; Ogden Haggerty, a New York auctioneer, becomes first patron.[12]

1847 First review in *Literary World* for *View on the Passaic*.[13] Sells paintings to the American Art-Union.[14]

1848 October: Seen sketching in the neighborhood of Peekskill, New York.[15]

1849 Joins Baptist Church and is baptized in the North River (part of the Hudson River estuary separating New Jersey and New York City);[16] marries Delia Francis Miller, of Newark, who dies a few months later.[17]

1850 Marries Elizabeth Abigail Hart (1833–1903); together they will have six children.[18] On his father's relationship to his mother, George Inness, Jr., recalled, "He depended on her for everything, from the arranging of his necktie to the solving of his deep metaphysical problems."[19]

1851 Shortly after 27 February: Departs for first trip to Europe; resides mainly in Florence.[20] Ogden Haggerty defrays costs.[21]

August: Rents studio space on the Via Sant'Apollonia directly above the portraitist William Page (1811–1885).[22] Page probably introduced Inness to Swedenborgian doctrine at this time.[23] Known for his copies of paintings by Titian, Page probably examined and discussed Titian's work with Inness.

1852 January: Corresponds with patron Samuel Gray Ward (1817–1907).[24] Ward, the American agent for London's Baring Brothers, is also Henry James, Sr.'s banker.[25]

Before 25 April: In Rome; refuses to remove his hat in the presence of the pope; engages in altercation with French policeman; is arrested and briefly jailed.[26]

May: Returns to New York via Paris, where he sees paintings by Théodore Rousseau at the Salon.[27]

1853 Elected Associate Member at the National Academy of Design.[28]

Second trip to Europe, mainly Paris. Stays in the Latin Quarter. Gains greater exposure to works of the Barbizon School.[29]

1854 24 June: Applies for passport at the U.S. Embassy in Paris to visit England.[30]

19 July: Visits Rijksmuseum in Amsterdam.[31]

Resides in Brooklyn, New York. Probably converses with Protestant theologian Henry Ward Beecher (1813–1887), renowned pastor of Plymouth Church in Brooklyn

(1847–87). Beecher is an active collector of artworks, including Inness's paintings; later delivers a lecture entitled "Landscape Picture" in which he identifies Inness as "the first of American landscape painters."[32]

1860 March: Takes over studio formerly occupied by "Coleman," probably the decorative and landscape painter Charles Caryl Coleman (1840–1928), in Montague Place, Brooklyn.[33]

June: Settles in Medfield, Massachusetts.[34] Encouraged by Ogden Haggerty, Williams & Everett become Inness's dealers.[35]

Spring to Fall: Continues to exhibit in New York at the Crayon Art Gallery[36] and the Athenaeum Club.[37]

1861 April: Unable to enlist in the army because of his fragile health, Inness, an ardent abolitionist, offers the proceeds from one of his paintings, *The Mill Stream*, for the benefit of the volunteers of Norfolk County, near Boston.[38]

1862 August: Organizes rally to collect funds that will offset the quota of ten soldiers from Medfield ($100 per soldier) for the Civil War.[39] Inness, Jr., adds that during the war his father "made speeches in front of the meeting-house nearly every night."[40]

1863 June: Accompanied by their mutual friend James (Steele) MacKaye, Inness and William James (1842–1910) embark on a sketching trip to Mount Desert, Maine.[41]

Publishes text to accompany the exhibition of *The Sign of Promise*, which he will repaint in 1865 and retitle *Peace and Plenty* (The Metropolitan Museum of Art, New York).[42]

1864 Accepts teaching post (painting instructor) at Eagleswood, a social reform community led by Marcus Spring (1810–1874) and Rebecca Buffum Spring (1811–1911) in Perth Amboy, New Jersey.[43] The Springs have a house—"Eagleswood Eyry"—constructed for Inness and his family on what is now the west side of Route 35 in Perth Amboy, a few hundred feet to the north of the entrance to the Victory Bridge (fig. 15, p. 156). (Despite protection by the National Registry of Historic Sites, the house was demolished shortly after 1991.)[44] Inness's students include Louis Comfort Tiffany (1848–1933) and Carleton Wiggins (1848–1932).[45] William Page is also in residence. According to George Sheldon, at Eagleswood Inness "fell into the study of theology, which for seven years was almost his only reading."[46]

1866 Summer: In the Catskills.[47]

December: Studio at 927 Broadway, New York.[48] Begins Triumph of the Cross series.[49] Works in the series will include *The Valley of the Shadow of Death* (1867; The Frances Lehman Loeb Art Center, Vassar College, Poughkeepsie, New York; Plate

11); *The Vision of Faith—View from the Delectable Mountains* (later known as *The Vision of Faith*; unlocated); and *The New Jerusalem* (said to have been destroyed in the collapse of the Art Gallery at Madison Square Garden in April 1880).[50]

1867 Exhibits *Golden American Sunset, Catskill Mountains* (Ireland 383: *American Sunset)* at the Universal Exposition, Paris.[51]

July 13: First public citation of Inness's devotion to Swedenborgian theology.[52]

September: Takes John Frederick Kensett's studio in the Waverly Building, New York.[53]

November: Publishes "Colors and Their Correspondences" in the Swedenborgian newspaper *New Jerusalem Messenger*.[54]

1868 Elected Member of the National Academy of Design.

May: Moves studio to Dodworth's Studio Building, at 212 Fifth Avenue, in New York;[55] remains there at least through December 1869 and probably until he leaves for Europe in April 1870.[56]

October 4: The Swedenborgian minister the Rev. John Curtis Ager[57] baptizes Inness and his wife in the New Church (Swedenborgian) in Brooklyn.[58]

1870 6 April: The art critic Earl Marble offers a rare tribute to the "impetuosity" of Inness's painting technique.[59]

19 April: Issued passport for European visit.[60]

Shortly before 29 April: Third trip to Europe.[61] Travel from Liverpool to London, Paris (by the end of May 1870),[62] and to Rome, where he rents the studio on the Via Sistina said to have been occupied by Claude Lorrain.[63]

Summer: Outside of Rome.[64]

1871 January: Exhibits works at Williams & Everett's gallery[65] and the Leeds Art Gallery, in New York.[66]

Summer: Perugia; in the company of Elihu Vedder (1836–1923).[67]

December: Exhibits at the Boston Art Club.[68]

1872 Summer: In Albano, with Charley Griswold (among others).[69]

1873 Paints landscape near Perugia.[70]

Summer: Visits Venice and Pieve di Cadore, the birthplace of Titian;[71] George Inness, Jr., and W. L. Bicknell, of Boston, are identified as artists "under his instruction."[72]

1874 June: To Paris, "chiefly for the education of his son."[73]

Summer: In Brittany.[74]

October: Awarded Gold medal for *View in Medfield* at The Mechanics' Exhibition in Boston.[75]

November: In Paris, at 28 Rue Pauquet.[76]

1875 26 February: Returns to New York on the *Algeria*.[77] Takes studio in the Boylston Bank on Washington Street, Boston.[78]

10 April: Delivers "a paper" at the Boston Art Club entitled, "The Logic of the Real, Aesthetically Considered."[79]

May: Trip to the White Mountains, North Conway; stays at Kearsarge (also known as Kiarsage and Kiarsarge) House; accompanied by George Waldo Hill and his son, Arthur Turnbull Hill;[80] joined by George Inness, Jr., and John A. S. Monks.[81]

Early September: In North Conway; said to be "engaged in writing a work of some kind upon art."[82] Returns to Boston by 17 September.[83]

1876 February: Said to be considering a trip to California.[84]

1877 By January: Studio in Booth Building, at Twenty-third Street and Sixth Avenue, in New York. May have had himself photographed as Hamlet around this time (see fig. 1).[85]

1878 Develops friendship with Thomas B. Clarke (1848–1931) who forms one of the largest collections of his paintings and serves as his manager; Inness is afforded a degree of financial freedom for the first time in his life.[86]

Interview, entitled "A Painter on Painting," is published in *Harper's New Monthly Magazine*.[87]

Becomes founding member of the Society of American Artists (formerly American Art Association), a group of artists—including John La Farge, William Morris Hunt, Homer Martin, G. Alden Weir, and Helena De Kay—that sought freedom from the conservatism of the National Academy and that would later be identified as precursors to the Tonalist movement.[88] Despite his philosophical affinity with the Society, Inness continues to exhibit at the Academy.

February: Exhibits *View Near Medfield, Massachusetts* (Ireland 740) at the Universal Exposition, Paris.[89]

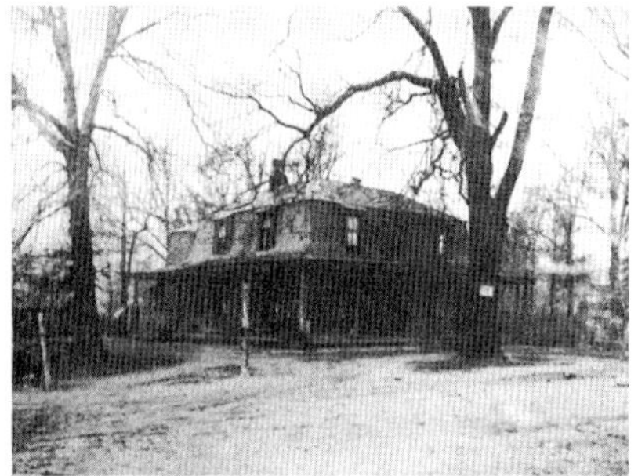

FIG. 15

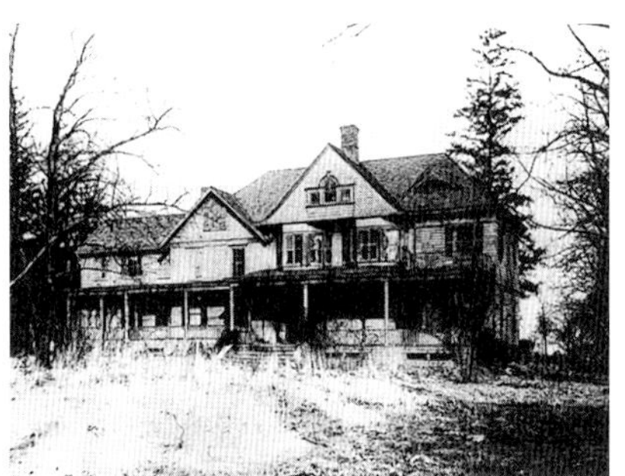

FIG. 16

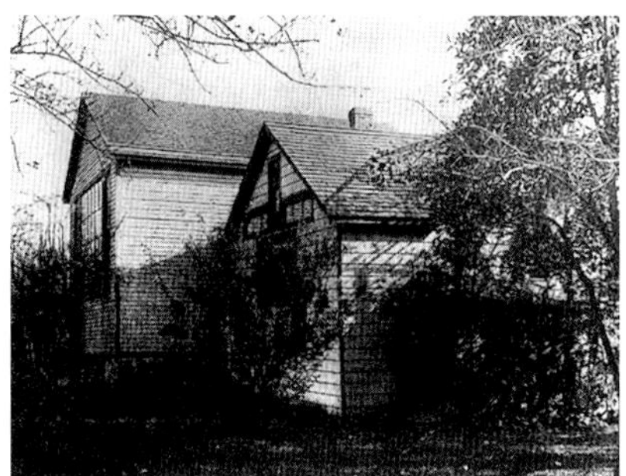

FIG. 17

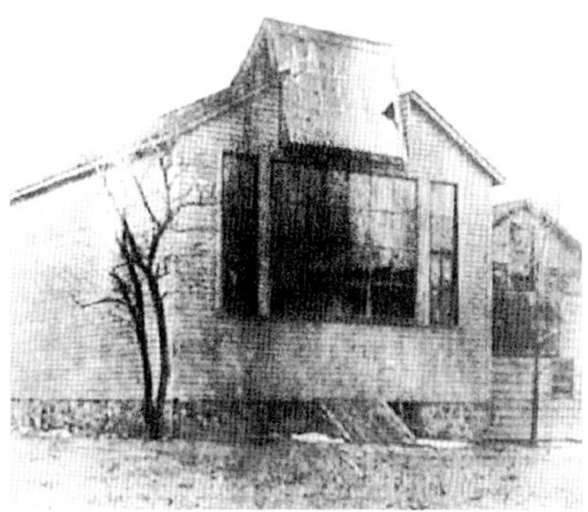

FIG. 18

FIG. 15.
George Inness's home and studio at Eagleswood, Perth Amboy, New Jersey (from 1864–67), 1899, photograph, George Inness file, Le Brun Library, Montclair Art Museum, Montclair, New Jersey.

FIG. 16.
George Inness's home, 151 Grove Street, Montclair, New Jersey (from 1885–94), photograph, n.d. (before 1912), Local History Collection, Montclair Public Library, Montclair, New Jersey.

FIG. 17.
George Inness's studio (north–west side), 151 Grove Street, Montclair, New Jersey (from 1885–94), photograph by W. H. Crocker, c. 1890, Local History Collection, Montclair Public Library, Montclair, New Jersey.

FIG. 18.
George Inness's studio (north side), 151 Grove Street, Montclair, New Jersey (from 1885–94), photograph, n.d. (before 1912), Local History Collection, Montclair Public Library, Montclair, New Jersey.

FIG. 19.
George Inness, Jr. (1854–1926), *George Inness Sketching Outside His Montclair Studio,* c. 1889, oil on canvas board, 14½ x 15¼", Montclair Art Museum, Montclair, New Jersey. Museum Purchase 1945.10.

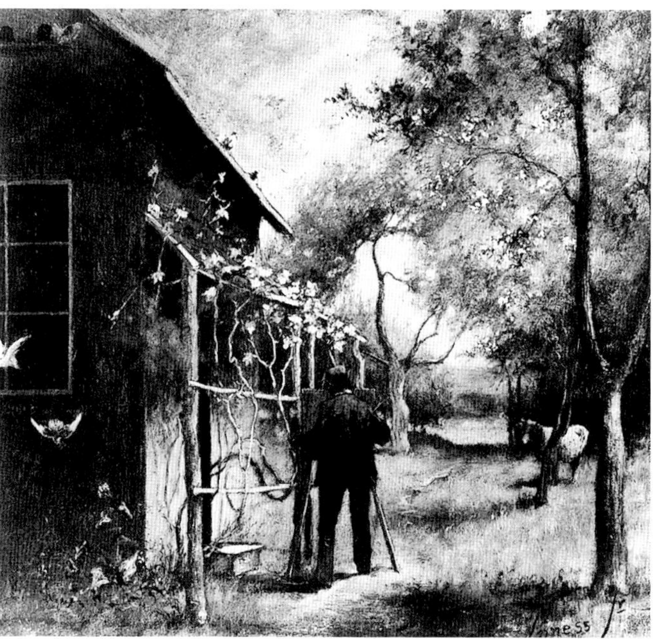

FIG. 19

April: Composes poem, "Whirlwind," that accompanies a sculpture of the same name by Jonathan Scott Hartley, his son-in-law. Also inscribes his own poems on the frames of his paintings included in the 53rd Annual exhibition of the National Academy of Design, New York.[90]

June: Rents gatehouse on an estate at 151 Grove Street in Montclair, New Jersey (see figs. 16–19).[91]

October: Rents studio in the University Building (of New York University) on Washington Square, New York; intends "to give lessons to pupils in the technics [*sic*] of the profession of which he is a master."[92]

November: Awarded Gold Medal ("for excellence in landscape, especially for truthful effect of light and atmosphere") at the Massachusetts Charitable Mechanic Association.[93]

1879 Interview, entitled "Mr. Inness on Art-Matters," is published in *The Art Journal*.[94]

June: Interview, entitled "Strong Talk on Art," is published in *The [New York] Evening Post*.[95]

July: In Connecticut.[96]

August: In Nantucket.[97]

October: Inness's landscapes prominently feature the human figure.[98]

1880 March: Writes poetry.[99]

Summer: Living in Milton, New York.[100]

1882 Moves his studio to the Holbein Building at 141 West 55th Street, New York.[101]

April: Said to have authored manuscripts entitled "Suggestions by an Artist" and "Mathematics of Psychology."[102]

Summer: At home in Milton-on-the-Hudson, near Poughkeepsie, New York.[103]

1883 Summer: Visits Nantucket Island.[104]

1884 April–May: Visits Goochland, Virginia.[105]

January: Roswell Smith, the founder of *The Century Magazine* and the father-in-law of George Inness, Jr., purchases Inness's *Niagara Falls* (Museum of Fine Arts, Boston) for $5,000.[106]

23 March: Responds to request for biographical information from Ripley Hitchcock, art critic for *The New York Daily Tribune*, for his essay "An American Landscape

Painter—George Inness," in *Special Exhibition of Oil Paintings, Works of Mr. George Inness* (New York: American Art Gallery, 1884). Reply published as *A Letter from George Inness to Ripley Hitchcock*.[107]

April: Major retrospective of fifty-eight canvases is held at the American Art Galleries, New York.[108]

December: Purchases the Dodge estate in Montclair; moves permanently to Montclair in February 1885.[109]

1887 To England; paints at Cornwall and Lyndhurst Forest.[110]

10 November: Large sale of the paintings of Henry Ward Beecher, including Inness's *Landscape and Sheep*.[111]

1888 12 August: Staying at Atlantic House, Ocean Beach, New York. Suffers from "neuralgia of the spleen."[112]

1889 January: Eugene W. Glaenzer, the American representative of the house of Boussod, Valadon & Co., purchases seven paintings by Inness, which are sent to Paris for exhibition.[113] The company enters into a contract with Inness for "control of all his work for a term of ten years" and for a "special exhibition" of his work in Paris during the summer.[114]

March: Objects vehemently when *Short Cut, Watchung Station, New Jersey* (Philadelphia Museum of Art; formerly American Art Association) is sent, without his approval, to the American section of the International Exposition in Paris. Identifies the painting as "not fairly representative of my present work."[115] It subsequently wins a bronze medal.[116]

1890s Spends winters in Tarpon Springs, Florida.

1890 20 January: Delivers speech at a banquet at the Metropolitan Hotel in New York in honor of Henry George.[117]

Breaks his right arm while alighting from a railroad car. Intending to fulfill a $12,000 commission from the Chicago millionaire Potter Palmer, Inness learns to paint with his left hand.[118]

18 March, in Thomasville, Georgia: Frederic E. Church writes, "Geo. Inness is here and thinks it very attractive for the artist."[119]

1891 February: Stops off in New Orleans on his way to California.[120] Visits Mexico City; finds *The Lackawanna Valley* (National Gallery of Art, Washington, D.C.; fig. 3) in a "curiosity shop";[121] travels to San Diego, stays at the Hotel Del Coronado in San Diego.[122] Visits Los Angeles and Yosemite.[123] May have visited Pasadena on the way to San Francisco. Shares studio of the painter and fellow Swedenborgian William Keith (1838–1911).[124] Visits Monterey with Keith.[125] Later writes a letter of introduction for Keith to friend and patron Thomas B. Clarke.[126]

Spring: Exhibited *Near Monterey* at the San Francisco Art Association exhibition (painting now lost or overpainted).[127]

August: In ill health; says at Ocean View House in Siasconset, Mass.[128]

1893 Spring: Thomas B. Clarke loans fourteen paintings by Inness to the World's Columbian Exposition in Chicago.[129]

1894 Final trip to Europe; visits Paris, Munich, Baden-Baden, and Scotland.[130]

August: "Unite and Succeed" is published in *The American Federationist.* Praises the newly established journal, advocates an eight-hour workday, and admonishes workers to unite as a means of escaping the "tyranny of combining capitalists and corporations."[131]

3 August: Dies at the Royal Hotel in Bridge-of-Allen, Scotland.[132]

Interview, entitled "His Art His Religion," is published in the *New York Herald* (12 August 1894): 4.

23 August: Funeral, led by the Swedenborgian minister the Rev. John Curtis Ager, at the National Academy of Design; interred at Rosedale Cemetery, West Orange, New Jersey.[133]

1895 February: Executor's Sale; 240 paintings by Inness are offered for sale.[134]

1899 Inness's family members continue to attend services in the New Church Society (Swedenborgian) of Orange, New Jersey.[135]

1903 April 6: Inness's widow, Elizabeth Hart Inness, dies. Services are conducted by the Rev. A. Roeder, pastor of the Swedenborgian Church in Orange, New Jersey, an organization with which she was "prominently identified."[136]

Notes to the Chronology

1. [George Inness], *A Letter from George Inness to Ripley Hitchcock* [23 March 1884]. (New York: privately printed, 1928), MS, p. 2 (hereafter: "Inness 1884").
2. George Inness, Jr., *Life, Art, and Letters of George Inness* (New York: The Century Co., 1917), p. 7; George Sheldon, "George Inness," *Harper's Weekly Magazine* 26:1322 (22 April 1882): 246 (hereafter: "Sheldon 1882") for location of home.
3. Sheldon 1882, p. 246: Inness "lived in Greene Street and Centre Street [in New York] till six or seven years old; went to Newark and staid [*sic*] there till fifteenth year."
4. George Chambers Calvert, "George Inness: Painter and Personality," *The Bulletin of the Art Association of Indianapolis, Indiana, The John Herron Art Institute* 13: 5–8 (November 1926): 36.
5. Inness, Jr., op. cit., p. 13.
6. Quoted in George W. Sheldon, *American Painters, with one hundred and four examples of their work engraved on wood* (New York: D. Appleton, & Co., 1881; reprint, New York: B. Blom, 1972), p. 29 (hereafter: "Sheldon 1881").
7. Sheldon 1882, p. 246.
8. Calvert, op. cit., p. 36.
9. School register, Archives, National Academy of Design, New York.
10. Calvert, op. cit., p. 37.
11. *National Academy of Design Exhibition Record, 1826–1860* (New York: Printed for The New-York Historical Society, 1943), vol. 1, p. 260.
12. Inness, Jr., op. cit., p. 19. According to Ireland, Haggerty purchases his first paintings by Inness in 1848 (Ireland 44, Ireland 46).
13. "The Fine Arts. Exhibition at the National Academy," *The Literary World* 13 (1 May 1847): 304.
14. Letter from George Inness to The Committee of the American Art-Union, 4 October 1867, BV American Art-Union, Manuscript Division, The New-York Historical Society.
15. "Return of Artists," *The [New York] Evening Post* (23 October 1848): 2.
16. Inness, Jr., op. cit., p. 21.
17. J. Walker McSpadden, *Famous Painters of America* (New York: Thomas Y. Crowell & Co., 1907), p. 117.
18. Ibid., p. 35.
19. Ibid., p. 105.
20. Passport application no. 1522, 27 February 1851, issued to George Inness by A. C. Kingsland, New York, as recorded at Civitavecchia, Italy, on 19 July 1851. Copy from the collection of Col. Merl M. Moore, Jr., Smithsonian American Art Museum, Washington, D.C.
21. Inness, Jr., op. cit., p. 24.
22. "American Artists Abroad," *Bulletin of the American Art-Union* (August 1851): 80: "Immediately below [Inness], in the same building, Mr. Page continues to produce occasionally an excellent painting. . . . "
23. See above, pp. 25–26.
24. Letters from George Inness to Samuel Gray Ward, New York, 7 January 1852, 21 November 1852, and 30 November 1852, Samuel Gray Ward Papers, bMS Am 1465 (707–709), Houghton Library, Harvard University, Cambridge, Mass.

25. See above, p. 136, n. 133.
26. "Art Intelligence," *Boston Evening Transcript* (15 June 1852): 2. The report from Rome is dated 25 April [1852]. The "hat-tipping" episode is later recounted in Earl Marble, "Anecdotes of Artists," *Baldwin's Monthly* 17:4 (October 1878): 7.
27. Inness 1884, MS, p. 3.
28. "The National Academy," *The [New York] Evening Post* (13 May 1853): 2.
29. Inness, Jr., op. cit., p. 27.
30. Passport Book, U.S. Embassy, log dated 23 July 1852–29 August 1854, line no. 976. Copy from the collection of Col. Merl M. Moore, Jr., Smithsonian American Art Museum, Washington, D.C.
31. Nicolai Cikovsky, Jr., "The Civilized Landscape," in *George Inness* (Los Angeles County Museum of Art, 1985), p. 18, p. 42, n. 21.
32. Henry Ward Beecher, "Landscape Picture," 7 March 1865, inscribed "Before Horticulture Department," in "Sermons, 1860–1865," Henry Ward Beecher Papers, Library of Congress, Box 13, unpaginated.
33. "Art Items," *New-York Daily Tribune* (31 March 1860): 4. (Coleman leaves shortly thereafter for Paris. See letter from Edward V. Valentine to Mann S. Valentine, Jr., 7 June 1860, The Valentine Museum, Richmond, Virginia.)
34. "Art Items," *New-York Daily Tribune* (16 June 1860): 4.
35. Inness, Jr., op. cit., p. 34.
36. See, for example, "Fine Arts. Return of the Artists," *New York World* (26 September 1860): 5. George Ward Nichols, an early supporter of Inness's work and the owner of the Crayon Art Gallery, probably authored the (anonymous) review; see also "Art Items," *The [New York] Evening Post* (3 October 1860): 1, and review by Mrs. Conant, "George Inness," *The Independent* (27 December 1860): 6, in which the author memorably remarks of an Inness landscape, "It is the poet's soul which has thus inspired the painter's hand."
37. "Art Items," *New-York Daily Tribune* (8 December 1860): 6.
38. H. P. S., "A Patriotic Offer," *Boston Evening Transcript* (24 April 1861): [2]. (The only pre-1861 painting entitled *The Mill Stream* is Ireland 45.)
39. "The Spirit of Boston," *The [New York] Evening Post* (19 August 1862): [1].
40. Inness, Jr., op. cit., p. 48.
41. See above, pp. 143, n. 131.
42. George Inness (probable author), "The Sign of Promise," exhibition pamphlet (New York: Snedicor's [*sic*] Gallery, 1863).
43. Maud Honeyman Greene, "Raritan Bay Union, Eagleswood, New Jersey," *Proceedings of the New Jersey Historical Society* 68:1 (January 1950): 1–20; Marie Marmo Mullaney, "Feminism, Utopianism, and Domesticity: The Career of Rebecca Buffum Spring, 1811–1911," *New Jersey History* 104:3–4 (fall/winter 1986): 1–21; Diary of Rebecca Buffum Spring, Department of Special Collections, The Stanford University Libraries, M541, p. 85.
44. See Tom Haydon, "U.S. funds sought to restore Perth Amboy slip," *The [Newark] Star-Ledger* (22 August 1991): 34.
45. Michael John Burlingham, *The Last Tiffany: A Biography of Dorothy Tiffany Burlingham* (New York: Atheneum, 1989), p. 43.
46. Sheldon 1881, p. 30.
47. "Art. Art Notes," *The Round Table* 3:45 (14 July 1866): 438.

48. "Art. Art Notes," *The Round Table* 3:45 (8 December 1866): 311.

49. "Art Items," *The [New York] Evening Post* (13 December 1866): 1: "George Inness has on the easel a large allegorical picture, which he calls 'The Principle of the Cross.' It promises to be a remarkable work of genius, in which the artist attempts to represent the Apocalyptic vision of the New Jerusalem and the River of Life flowing from it for the healing of the nations. Aside from the religious sentiment and the exalted spiritual significance which breathes in every line of this picture, it is exceedingly beautiful as a work of architectural and landscape art."

50. "The Morning News. A Shocking Calamity," *The [New York] Evening Post* (22 April 1880): 1.

51. "The Paris Universal Exposition," *The [Philadelphia] Daily Evening Bulletin* (5 April 1867): 1.

52. "American Artists. George Inness," *Harper's Weekly: A Journal of Civilization* 11:550 (13 July 1867): 433.

53. "Fine Arts," *The [New York] Evening Post* (5 September 1867): [2].

54. George Inness, "Colors and Their Correspondences," *New Jerusalem Messenger* 13 (13 November 1867): 78–79. It constitutes a response to the Reverend Dr. Jonathan Bayley's essay *The Ribband of Blue*. Bayley conducted biblical exegesis on a passage from *Numbers* in which "the Lord" encourages the faithful to wear garments with a "ribband of blue" on the border, which Bayley interpreted to mean that the Lord cares for even the least aspects of our lives. Interpreted in the context of Swedenborgian theology, in which all colors maintain spiritual identities, blue corresponds to faith and red corresponds to love. The color blue tinged with red means, according to Bayley, "all our truth ought to be softened and warmed by love." Inness argues that the ideal color would be blue tinged with both red and yellow (the color that represents the natural, or the external), as this orange hue would embody the "pure, celestial flame that warms as it illumines."

55. "Fine Arts. What the Artists are Doing," *The [New York] Evening Post* (18 May 1868): [2].

56. "Fine Arts," *The [New York] Evening Post* (3 December 1869): [1].

57. Ager became pastor at the Brooklyn church in January 1865; he would serve there for more than forty years. See Louis C. Ager, "Metropolitan New-Church Societies, Brief Sketches of Their Origins: The Brooklyn Society," *The New-Church Messenger* (15 May 1929): 323.

58. Sally M. Promey, "The Ribband of Faith: George Inness, Color Theory, and the Swedenborgian Church," *The American Art Journal* 26:1 & 2 (1994): 44–65

59. E. M. [Earl Marble], "Impetuosity on Canvas," *Boston Daily Evening Transcript* (6 April 1870): [1].

60. Passport (no. 5745) issued to George Inness, "to be accompanied by my wife and four minor children." Department of State, Washington, D.C. Typescript copy from the collection of Col. Merl M. Moore, Jr., Smithsonian American Art Museum, Washington, D.C.

61. "Art Notes," *The [New York] Evening Post* (29 April 1870): [2]: "George Inness sailed for Europe on Saturday last."

62. "Foreign Art Notes," *The [New York] Evening Post* (31 May 1870): [1].

63. Inness, Jr., op. cit., p. 75. See also Calvert, op. cit., p. 48.

64. E. B. G., "Rome . . . Artistic and Local Gossip" (letter from Rome, 19 July [*sic*] 1870), *The [New York] Evening Post* (19 July 1870): [1]: "Healy, Inness and Yewell left very lately."

65. Paul Vevay, "Art Notes," *The [Boston] Daily Evening Transcript* (18 January 1871): 1.

66. "The Leeds Art Gallery. Exhibition of Paintings," *The [New York] Evening Post* (26 January 1871): 2.

67. E. B. G., "Rome. Recent Events in the Eternal City" (letter from Rome, 24 July 1871), *The [New York] Evening Post* (10 August 1871): [1]: "Mr. Inness and family are in Perugia, where are also [Frederick] Crowninshield and [Elihu] Vedder."

68. E. M. [Earl Marble], "The Art Club Exhibition," *The [Boston] Daily Evening Transcript* (27 December 1871): 2.
69. Regina Soria, *Elihu Vedder: American Visionary Artist in Rome (1836–1923)* (Cranbury, N.J.: Associated University Presses, 1970), p. 81.
70. "Artist Life in Rome. Attractions of the City—How American Painters and Sculptors are Engaged," *New-York Daily Tribune* (12 April 1873): 7. See also Soria, ibid., p. 90.
71. H. B. S., "American Artists at Rome," *Boston Evening Transcript* (28 January 1874): [7].
72. Ibid.
73. "Fine Arts," *Appleton's Journal* 12:281 (8 August 1874): 188.
74. "Our Artists Abroad," *Boston Evening Transcript* (22 June 1874): [4].
75. "The Mechanics' Exhibition, Boston," *The [New York] Evening Post* (19 October 1874): 4.
76. "Personal," *Boston Evening Transcript* (30 November 1874): [4].
77. Ireland, op. cit., p. 445.
78. "Art and Artists," *Boston Evening Transcript* (9 March 1875): 6.
79. "Art and Artists," *Boston Daily Evening Transcript* ([Friday] 9 April 1875): 6: "Mr. Inness will read a paper on Saturday night before the Art Club, entitled 'The Logic of the Real, Aesthetically Considered,' which will not only be instructive to those engaged in art studies, but, treated in Mr. Inness's able and energetic manner, will be interesting as well." The *Transcript* adds, "There has been some talk of a succeeding 'talk' by the same artist, he painting a sketch in the meantime as an illustration. This will indeed be a rare treat."
80. Arthur Turnbull Hill, "Early Recollections of George Inness and George Waldo Hill," *New Salmagundi Papers, Series of 1922* (New York: The Library of the Salmagundi Club, 1922), pp. 111–12.
81. "Art and Artists," *Boston Evening Transcript* (1 June 1875): 6. On the Kearsarge House, see "The Summer Exodus, No. V," *Boston Evening Transcript* (28 June 1875): 6, and B., "White Mountain Travel," *Boston Evening Transcript* (13 August 1875): 4. On Monks, see C. S. Pietro, "The Art of John Austin Sands Monks," *The Fine Arts Journal* (Chicago) 35:4 (April 1917): 258–62.
82. "Art and Artists," *Boston Evening Transcript* (7 September 1875): 6.
83. "Art and Artists," *Boston Evening Transcript* (17 September 1875): 6.
84. "Art and Artists," *Boston Daily Traveller* (29 February 1876): 6. In the spring of 1875, Inness and Doll & Richards entered into a business arrangement whereby Inness turned over several paintings to Doll & Richards and allowed them to manage sales of all of his works in return for an advance that eventually came to $6877. (See "Art and Artists," *Boston Daily Evening Transcript* [8 February 1877]: 6.) When Inness sold one painting, *Pine Groves of the Villa Barberini* (1876; The Metropolitan Museum of Art, New York), on his own, Doll brought suit against the artist. Nicolai Cikovsky, Jr., has suggested that the announcement of Inness's imminent trip to California was a ruse to ward off his exasperated dealers. See Nicolai Cikovsky, Jr., *George Inness* (New York: Harry N. Abrams, Inc., 1992), p. 79. The matter was eventually settled in a New York court when Inness turned over *Pine Groves of the Villa Barberini* to Doll & Richards in Boston. For a copy of the settlement paper, signed 19 April 1877, see LeRoy Ireland papers, Archives of American Art, Smithsonian Institution, Washington, D.C., roll 996, frame 8. Doll & Richards held a sale, without reserves, of twenty-six paintings by Inness in their collection on 13 December 1876. See "Art and Artists," *Boston Evening Transcript* (14 December 1876): 6.
85. "Art and Artists," *Boston Evening Transcript* (15 January 1877): 3.
86. Inness, Jr., op. cit., p. 184. On Clarke, see H. Barbara Weinberg, "Thomas B. Clarke: Foremost Patron of American Art from 1872 to 1899," *The American Art Journal* 8:1 (May 1976): 52–83.

87. [Anonymous], "A Painter on Painting," *Harper's New Monthly Magazine* 56 (February 1878): 451–78. Excerpted in "Art and Artists," *Boston Daily Evening Transcript* (18 January 1878): 6.
88. On Tonalism, see Wanda Corn, *The Color of Mood: American Tonalism, 1880–1910*, exhibition catalogue (San Francisco: M. H. De Young Memorial Museum and the California Palace of the Legion of Honor, 1972) and *Tonalism: An American Experience*, exhibition catalogue (New York: Grand Central Art Galleries, 1982).
89. "American Art in Paris," *The [New York] Evening Post* (20 February 1878): 4. The work is identified as *Homestead* in this publication. According to Ireland, Inness also exhibits *St. Peter's Rome, from the Tiber* (Ireland 533) in this exhibition.
90. See "Poems by the Late George Inness, The American Corot," *The Illustrated American* 17:3 (19 January 1895): 1–2. See also C. C. [Clarence Cook], "Fine Arts. National Academy of Design. Fifty-third Annual Exhibition. II," *New York Tribune* (9 April 1878): 2. Although his remarks on Inness's paintings have, in the past, generally been favorable, Cook laments the inclusion of the poems. The condemnation sets off a dialogue, in the *Tribune*, in which Inness identifies Cook's criticism as, essentially, "Whirling wind." See George Inness, "A Poem and a Statue. Mr. Inness Explains his Poem [Letter to the Editor]," *New York Tribune* (11 April 1878): 6. In his rejoinder, Cook reiterates his appreciation of Inness's paintings but also reiterates his condemnation of Inness's poetry, which he calls "sorry stuff." See "Artists and Art Criticism. A Rejoinder from 'C.C.' [Letter to the Editor]," *New York Tribune* (12 April 1878): 2. In his reply, Inness admonishes Cook: "If you cannot praise, at least do not condemn unless it be for reasons given, and let it be done without insult." See "Artists and Critics. George Inness Replies Again to 'C.C.'—Distinction between Deserved Correction and Illogical Abuse [Letter to the Editor]" *New York Tribune* (13 April 1878): 5. In a note that followed Inness's letter, the editor of the *Tribune* criticizes Inness for being "unreasonable."
91. "Personal," *The [New York] Evening Post* (4 June 1878): [2]. According to Rose Inness Hartley, a granddaughter of Inness, her family stayed for the first time in Montclair in 1879. See Interview of Rose Hartley by Miss Gladys Segar, reference librarian at the Montclair Free Public Library, ca. 1940s–52, Inness file, Local History Collection, The Montclair Free Public Library, Montclair, New Jersey.
92. "Personal," *The [New York] Evening Post* (29 October 1878): [2].
93. "The Art Awards," *Boston Daily Evening Transcript* (13 November 1878): 4.
94. E., "Mr. Inness on Art-Matters," *The Art Journal* (American Edition), n.s. 5 (1879): 374–77.
95. "Strong Talk on Art," *The [New York] Evening Post* (3 June 1879): 3.
96. "Studio Notes," *The Art Interchange* 3:1 (9 July 1879): 11.
97. "Studio Notes," *The Art Interchange* 3:5 (3 September 1879): 44.
98. "Fine Arts," *The [New York] Evening Post* (14 October 1879): 1. The *Post* describes Inness's work as follows: "His latest landscape is constructed with reference to a farmer's daughter, just entering womanhood, who timidly crosses a small brook in a meadow of long lush grass, and centres in herself the attention of the spectator by constituting the keynote of the scheme of color, and the principal part of the literary story."
99. "Fine Arts," *The [New York] Evening Post* (17 March 1880): 3. George Inness, Jr., published several of his father's poems in *Life, Art, and Letters of George Inness*: "Exaltation" (pp. 97–98); "Address of the Clouds to the Earth" (p. 101); "Destiny" (pp. 101–4); and "Untitled" (pp. 105–6). For typed copies of the first two poems, in addition to "The Leaves and The Brook," "Love," "Despair," and "The Pilgrim," see George Inness Papers, Archives of American Art, Smithsonian Institution, Washington, D.C., reel 995, nos. 1029–36.

100. Inness, Jr., op. cit., pp. 148–58.
101. Elliott Daingerfield, "Inness, Genius of American Art," *Cosmopolitan* 55 (1913): 519.
102. Sheldon 1882, p. 246.
103. "In Studio and Gallery. Glances at the Work of the Artists," *New-York Daily Tribune* (30 October 1882): 2. See also Where the Artists Work," *New York Daily Tribune* (22 May 1887): 14; "Art News and Comments. The Week in Art Circles," *New York Daily Tribune* (4 March 1888): 11.
104. "Art and Artists," *Boston Daily Globe* (11 November 1883): 11; Inness, Jr., op. cit., pp. 162–64.
105. Inness, Jr., op. cit., p. 164, 167–68.
106. "Art and Artists," *Boston Daily Evening Transcript* (29 January 1884): 6; Inness, Jr., op. cit., p. 177.
107. See above, note 1.
108. E. W. M., "George Inness's Paintings. A Special Exhibition in New York—A Glance at the Works," *Boston Evening Transcript* (14 April 1884): 6. Works loaned for the exhibition include *The Valley of the Shadow of Death* (formerly collection of Fletcher Harper) and *English Oaks* (formerly collection of Henry Ward Beecher).
109. First cited by Diane Pietrucha Fischer, "The Inness Colony of Montclair," *The Montclair Art Colony: Past and Present* (Montclair, New Jersey: The Montclair Art Museum, 1997), p. 9, p. 14, n. 24.
110. See *Off the Coast of Cornwall, England*, 1887, 25¼ x 30", Paine Art Center and Arboretum, Oshkosh, Wisconsin.
111. See above, pp. 145–46. See also "Art and Artists," *Boston Daily Evening Transcript* (11 November 1887): 7.
112. Letter from George Inness to Thomas B. Clarke, 12 August 1888, Rare Books and Special Collections, Princeton University Library, Princeton, New Jersey.
113. "American Artist Honored," *The New-York Times* (20 January 1889): 5 (mentions six paintings); "Art Notes," *The Critic* 265 (26 January 1889): 46.
114. Montezuma [pseud.], "My Note Book," *The Art Amateur* 20:5 (April 1889): 98.
115. "That Picture for Paris Row," *New York Herald* (9 March 1889): 4.
116. "The Fine Arts. Art Notes," *The Critic* (24 August 1889): 92, where Inness is listed as a recipient of a "third," meaning (in this context) third place, medal; see also Montezuma [Pseud.], "My Note Book," *The Art Amateur* (November 1889): 115, where Inness is listed as a winner of a "bronze" medal. See also Annette Blaugrund, et al., *Paris 1889: American Artists at the Universal Exposition* (Pennsylvania Academy of the Fine Arts, in association with Harry N. Abrams, Inc., Publishers, New York, 1989), pp. 173–75.
117. "The George Dinner...George Inness," *The Standard* 7:4 (22 January 1890): 10. See above, p. 150, n.3.
118. "Art and Artists," *Boston Evening Transcript* (25 February 1890): 2. Daingerfield remarked that even after Inness broke his right wrist, he continued to paint with his right hand, although he held his broken wrist with his left hand. See Daingerfield, op. cit., p. 522.
119. Frederic E. Church to Mr. Palmer, Mitchell House, Thomasville, Georgia. Photocopy of letter in Curatorial files for *Georgia Pines* (1890), Smithsonian American Art Museum, Washington, D.C.
120. "Books and Pictures," *New York Herald* (22 February 1891): 26.
121. Ireland, op. cit., p. 28.
122. Marjorie Dakin Arkelian and George Neubert, *George Inness Landscapes: His Signature Years, 1884–1894* (Oakland, California: Oakland Museum of Art, 1987), p. 30.
123. "Art Gossip," *New York World* (10 May 1891): 22.
124. "Art and Artists," *Boston Evening Transcript* (1 April 1891): 4. On Keith, see Brother Fidelis Cornelius, *Keith, Old Master of California* (New York: G. Putnam's Sons, 1942); Henry Atkins, "William Keith,

Landscape Painter, of California," *The International Studio* 33:129 (November 1907): 36–42; and Alfred C. Harrison, Jr., *William Keith: The Saint Mary's College Collection* (Moraga, Calif.: Saint Mary's College of California, 1988).

125. Alfred C. Harrison, Jr., "George Inness and the San Francisco art world in the 1890s," *Antiques* (November 2000): 715–25.
126. George Inness to Thomas B. Clarke, May [1893], Keith-McHenry-Pond Family Papers, The Bancroft Library, University of California, Berkeley, Banc MS, C-B 595, Carton 5.
127. Harrison, op. cit., p. 720; see esp. fig. 4.
128. Letter from George Inness to Thomas B. Clarke, 9 August 1891, Rare Books and Special Collections, Princeton University Library, Princeton, New Jersey.
129. "Fine Arts," *Boston Daily Evening Transcript* (27 March 1893): 6.
130. "In Honor of Inness," *The New York Times* (19 August 1894): 16.
131. George Inness, "Unite and Succeed," *American Federationist* 1:6 (August 1894): 119.
132. See, for example, "Recent Deaths. George Inness, Landscape Painter," *Boston Evening Transcript* (4 August 1894): 9; "George Inness," *The [New York] Evening Post* (7 August 1894): 5; Montgomery Schuyler, "George Inness," *Harper's Weekly: A Journal of Civilization* 38:1965 (18 August 1894): 778.
133. For a description of the funeral, see "Homage to George Inness. Memorial Services in the National Academy of Design," *The New-York Times* (24 August 1894): 8.
134. "Paintings by Inness Sold," *New York Daily Tribune* (13 February 1895): 3; "The Inness Paintings," *New York Daily Tribune* (14 February 1895): 7; "Good Prices for Pictures," *New York Daily Tribune* (15 February 1895): 4.
135. "Members of Orange New Church Society, 1899," manuscript, Church Archives, The New Church (Swedenborgian), New York.
136. "Artist Inness's Widow Expires at Montclair," *Newark Evening News* (7 April 1903): 2:2.

Selected Bibliography

Adams, Henry. "Henry James, William James, John La Farge, and the Foundations of Radical Empiricism," *The American Art Journal* 17:1 (winter 1985): 60–67.

[Anonymous]. "A Painter on Painting," *Harper's New Monthly Magazine* 56 (February 1878): 458–61.

———. "Strong Talk on Art," *The [New York] Evening Post* (3 June 1879): [3].

———. "His Art His Religion," *New York Herald* (12 August 1894), sec. 4:9.

Beecher, Henry Ward. *Star Papers; or, Experiences of Art and Nature*. New York: J. C. Derby, 1857.

Block, Marguerite Beck. *The New Church in the New World*. New York: Swedenborg Publishing Association, 1964.

Calvert, George Chambers. "George Inness. Painter and Personality," *The Bulletin of the Art Association of Indianapolis Indiana. The John Herron Art Institute* 13:5–8 (November 1926): 35–57.

Cikovsky, Jr., Nicolai. "The Life and Work of George Inness." Ph.D. thesis, Harvard University, 1965.

———. *George Inness*. New York: Praeger Publishing, 1971.

———. *George Inness*. New York: Harry N. Abrams, Publishers, 1993.

Cikovsky, Jr., Nicolai, and Michael Quick, eds. *George Inness*. New York: Harper & Row, 1985.

Crenshaw, Karen B. "A Study of George Inness's Painting Technique," unpublished manuscript, c/o Director's Office, Smithsonian American Art Museum, Washington, D.C., n.d.

Croce, Paul Jerome. *Science and Religion in the Era of William James: Eclipse of Certainty, 1820–1880*. Chapel Hill and London: The University of North Carolina Press, 1995.

Daingerfield, Elliott. "George Inness," *The Century Illustrated Monthly Magazine* 95:1 (November 1917): 69–77.

Davidson, Abraham. *The Eccentrics and Other American Visionaries* (New York: E. P. Dutton, 1978).

DeLue, Rachael Ziady. "George Inness: Landscape, Representation, and the Struggle of Vision." Ph.D. thesis, The Johns Hopkins University, 2000.

E. "Mr. Inness on Art-Matters," *The Art Journal* 5 (December 1879): 374–77.

Emerson, Ralph Waldo. "Swedenborg; or, the Mystic," in *Representative Men*. Boston: Phillips, Sampson, and Company, 1854, pp. 95–145.

Feinstein, Howard M. *Becoming William James*. Ithaca and London: Cornell University Press, 1984.

Fischer, Diane Pietrucha. "The 'Inness' Colony of Montclair," in *The Montclair Art Colony: Past and Present*. Montclair, N. J.: Montclair Art Museum, 1997, pp. 8–15.

Fullinwider, S. P. "William James's 'Spiritual Crisis,'" *The Historian* 38:1 (November 1975): 39–57.

Gavin, William Joseph. *William James and the Reinstatement of the Vague*. Philadelphia: Temple University Press, 1992.

Gladish, Robert W. "Tre Amici Artistici: E. B. Browning, Hiram Powers, and William Page in Florence and Rome," *Covenant: A Journal Devoted to the Study of the Five Churches* 1:4 (spring 1998): 273–91.

Habegger, Alfred. *The Father: A Life of Henry James, Sr.* New York: Farrar, Straus and Giroux, 1994.

Hallengren, Anders. *Deciphering Reality: Swedenborg, Emerson, Whitman, and the Search for the Language of Nature.* Minneapolis: The Center for Nordic Studies, 1992.

Hammond, William A. "The Physics and Physiology of Spiritualism," *The North American Review* 110:227 (April 1870): 232–60.

Hill, Arthur Turnbull. "Early Recollections of George Inness and George Waldo Hill," *New Salmagundi Papers. Series of 1922* (New York: The Library of the Salmagundi Club, 1922), pp. 109–15.

Inness, George. "Colors and Their Correspondences," *New Jerusalem Messenger* 13 (13 November 1867): 78–79.

———. "A Plea for the Painters. Letter from the Artist Inness," *The [New York] Evening Post* (21 March 1878): 2.

———. "A Poem and a Statue. Mr. Inness Explains his Poem [Letter to the Editor]," *New-York Tribune* (11 April 1878): 6.

———. "Artists and Critics. George Inness Replies Again to 'C.C.'—Distinction Between Deserved Correction and Illogical Abuse," *New-York Tribune* (15 April 1878): 5.

———. *A Letter from George Inness to Ripley Hitchcock* [23 March 1884]. Mount Vernon, N.Y.: William Edward Rudge, 1928.

———. "The George Dinner. The Great Banquet at the Metropolitan Hotel," *The Standard* 7:4 (22 January 1890): 10.

———. "Unite and Succeed," *American Federationist* 1:6 (August 1894): 119.

———. "Poems by the Late George Inness, The American Corot," *The Illustrated American* 17:3 (19 January 1895): 1–2.

Inness, George (probable author). "The Sign of Promise." Exhibition Pamphlet. New York: Snedicor's [*sic*] Gallery, 1863.

Inness, George, Jr. *Life, Art, and Letters of George Inness.* New York: The Century Co., 1917.

Ireland, LeRoy. *The Works of George Inness: An Illustrated Catalogue Raisonné.* Austin: University of Texas Press, 1965.

James, William. *The Principles of Psychology.* New York: Henry Holt and Company, 1890; reprint, Cambridge, Mass.: Harvard University Press, 1950.

———. *Human Immortality: Two Supposed Objections to the Doctrine.* New York: Houghton Mifflin & Co., 1898.

———. *The Varieties of Religious Experience.* Boston: Longmans, Green, and Co., 1902; reprint, New York: Viking Penguin, 1982.

———. *A Pluralistic Universe.* New York: Longmans, Green, and Co., 1909; reprint, Lincoln and London: University of Nebraska Press, 1996.

Kern, Stephen. *The Culture of Time and Space: 1880–1918.* Cambridge, Mass.: Harvard University Press, 1983.

Lamberth, David C. *William James and the Metaphysics of Experience.* London: Cambridge University Press, 1999.

Larsen, Robin, ed. *Emanuel Swedenborg: A Continuing Vision.* New York: Swedenborg Foundation, Inc., 1988.

Mazow, Leo G. "George Inness: Problems in Antimodernism." Ph.D. thesis, University of Chapel Hill, North Carolina, 1996.

———., with commentaries by Rachael Ziady DeLue. *George Inness: The 1880s and 1890s.* Exhibition Catalogue. Annville, Pa.: Suzanne H. Arnold Art Gallery, Lebanon Valley College, 1999.

Menand, Louis. *The Metaphysical Club.* New York: Farrar, Straus and Giroux, 2001.

Miles, Margaret R. *Image as Insight: Visual Understanding in Western Christianity and Secular Culture.* Boston: Beacon Press, 1985.

Moore, R. Laurence. *In Search of White Crows: Spiritualism and Parapsychology in American Culture*. New York: Oxford University Press, 1977.

Novak, Barbara. *American Painting of the Nineteenth Century: Realism, Idealism and the American Experience*. New York: Harper & Row, Publishers, 1969, 2nd ed., 1979.

———. *Nature and Culture: American Landscape and Painting 1825–1875*. New York: Oxford University Press, rev. ed., 1995.

Page, William Nelson, "Equilibrium of Nature and the Palette—and 'How To Do It," *The Independent* (25 July 1861): [1].

———. "The Art Series: Finite Art The Image of Infinite Creation," *New-York Tribune (Lecture Sheet No. 4)* (1872): 2–3.

———. "The Measure of a Man," *Scribner's Monthly* 17:6 (April 1879): 894–98.

Perry, Ralph Barton. *The Thought and Character of William James*. 2 vols. Boston: Little, Brown, 1935.

Promey, Sally M. "The Ribband of Faith: George Inness, Color Theory, and the Swedenborgian Church," *The American Art Journal* 26:1 & 2 (1994): 44–65.

Rosand, David. *Drawing Acts: Studies in Graphic Expression and Representation.* Cambridge: Cambridge University Press, 2002.

Schapiro, Meyer. *Worldview in Painting—Art and Society (Selected Papers, Vol. V)*. New York: George Braziller, Inc., 1999.

Sers, Philippe. *Kandinsky: Philosophie de L'Abstraction: L'Image Métaphysique*. Geneva: Editions d'Art Albert Skira, 1995.

Sheldon, G. W. "George Inness," *Harper's Weekly Magazine* 26:1322 (22 April 1882): 244–46.

Spalding, J. Howard. "The Spiritual World as Non-Spatial Yet Organic," *Transactions of the International Swedenborg Congress*. London: The Swedenborg Society, 1910, pp. 164–69.

Stavitsky, Gail, et al. *George Inness: Presence of the Unseen*. Exhibition Catalogue. Montclair, N.J.: Montclair Art Museum, 1994.

Stephenson, Jonathan. *The Materials and Techniques of Painting*. London: Thames and Hudson, Ltd., 1989.

Swedenborg, Emanuel. *Heaven and Hell*, trans. by George F. Dole, with an introduction by Colin Wilson. West Chester, Pa.: Swedenborg Foundation, 1976; originally published as *De Coelo et ejus mirabilibus, et de Inferno, ex auditis et visis* (London, 1758).

———. *The Principia; or, The First Principles of Natural Things, Being New Attempts Toward a Philosophical Explanation of the Elementary World*, trans. from the Latin by the Rev. Augustus Clissold, M.A., 2 vols. (London: W. Newbery, 1846); originally published as *Principia rerum naturalium sive novorum tentaminum phaenomena mundi elementaris philosophice explicandi* (London, 1734).

———. *Journal of Dreams*. Edited from the Swedish by G. Klemming, translated by J. J. G. Wilkinson, edited by W. Woofenden. New York: Swedenborg Foundation, 1977.

Taylor, Eugene. *William James on Exceptional Mental States: The 1896 Lowell Lectures*. New York: Charles Scribner's Sons, 1982.

———. "The Interior Landscape: George Inness and William James on Art from a Swedenborgian Point of View," *Archives of American Art Journal* 37:1–2 (1997): 2–10.

Taylor, Joshua C. *William Page: The American Titian*. Chicago: University of Chicago Press, 1957.

Tuchman, Maurice, et al. *The Spiritual in Art: Abstract Paining 1890–1985*. New York: Abbeville Press, 1986.

Very, Frank. *An Epitome of Swedenborg's Science*. Boston: The Four Seasons Company, 1927.

Wilkinson, James John Garth. *Emanuel Swedenborg: A Biography*. Boston: Otis Clapp, 1849.

List of Works

All work are by George Inness,
unless otherwise noted.

PLATES

1. *A Bit of the Roman Aqueduct,* 1852
oil on canvas
39 x 53$\frac{9}{16}$"
High Museum of Art, Atlanta
Purchased with funds from the Members Guild and through exchange, 69.42

2. *Hackensack Meadows, Sunset*, 1859
oil on canvas
18$\frac{1}{4}$ x 26"
On permanent loan from
The New York Public Library,
Stuart Collection 22
Collection of The New-York Historical Society

3. *Landscape*, 1860
oil on paper
16$\frac{1}{4}$ x 24"
National Academy of Design, New York

4. *The Huntsman*, 1859
oil on canvas
30 x 25"
Collection of Robert K. Fitzgerel

5. *Winter Evening, Medfield*, ca. 1860
oil on canvas
10 x 16"
Private collection, New England,
courtesy of Thomas Colville Fine Art

6. *Clearing Up*, 1860
oil on canvas
15 x 25"
George Walter Vincent Smith Art Museum,
Springfield, Massachusetts,
George Walter Vincent Smith Collection

7. *Evening Landscape*, 1862
oil on canvas
48$\frac{1}{4}$ x 66$\frac{1}{4}$"
Permanent Collection, Museum of Art,
Washington State University, Pullman

8. *Sunset,* c. 1860–65
oil on board
10$\frac{1}{4}$ x 14$\frac{1}{2}$"
Private collection, courtesy of Berry-Hill
Galleries, Inc.

9. *Christmas Eve (Winter Moonlight),* 1866
oil on canvas
22 x 30"
Montclair Art Museum, Montclair, New Jersey,
Museum Purchase; Florence O. R. Lang
Acquisition Fund, 1948.29

10. *Winter, Close of Day (A Winter Sky),* 1866
oil on canvas
22 x 30½"
© The Cleveland Museum of Art, 2003
The Charles W. Harkness Gift, 1927.388

11. *The Valley of the Shadow of Death,* 1867
oil on canvas
45⅝ x 72⅞"
The Frances Lehman Loeb Art Center,
Vassar College, Poughkeepsie, New York
Gift of Charles M. Pratt, 1917.1.6

12. *Sunset at Montclair,* 1892
oil on canvas
30 x 45"
Private collection,
courtesy of Berry-Hill Galleries, Inc.

13. *Edge of the Woods,* n.d. (c. 1890)
oil on canvas
22 x 32"
National Academy of Design, New York
Gift of Liza and Michael Moses, 2000

14. *The Trout Brook,* 1891
oil on canvas
30¼ x 45¼"
The Collection of The Newark Museum
Purchase 1965, The Members' Fund
© The Newark Museum

15. *Lake Nemi,* 1872
oil on canvas
30 x 45"
Museum of Fine Arts, Boston
Gift of the Misses Hersey, 1949; 49.412
© 2003 Museum of Fine Arts, Boston

15a. *Catskill Mountains,* 1870
oil on canvas
48¼ x 72¼"
The Art Institute of Chicago,
Edward B. Butler Collection

16. *The Monk,* 1873
oil on canvas
38$\frac{9}{16}$ x 64⅛"
Addison Gallery of American Art,
Phillips Academy, Andover, Massachusetts
Gift of Stephen C. Clark, Esq., in recognition
of the 25th Anniversary of the Addison Gallery
© Addison Gallery of American Art, Phillips
Academy, Andover, Massachusetts.
All Rights Reserved.

17. *Castel Gandolfo,* 1876
oil on canvas
20⅛ x 30⅛"
Portland Art Museum, Oregon
Helen Thurston Ayer Fund

18. *Landscape with Cattle,* c. 1877
oil on canvas
12 x 18⅛"
Private collection

19. *Early Moonrise, Tarpon Springs,* 1892
oil on canvas
32 x 42"
Collection of Fayez Sarofim

20. *Winter Evening,* 1887
oil on canvas
32 x 50"
Private collection

21. *Home at Montclair,* 1892
oil on canvas
30⅛ x 45"
Sterling and Francine Clark Art Institute,
Williamstown, Massachusetts, 1955.10

22. *Autumn Gold,* 1888
oil on canvas
29$\frac{15}{16}$ x 44$\frac{15}{16}$"
Wadsworth Atheneum, Hartford, Connecticut.
Purchased through the gift of
Henry and Walter Keney

23. *Moonrise*, 1888
oil on canvas
29 x 44"
Guild Hall Museum, Easthampton,
New York
Gift of Mrs. Victor Harris

24. *Summer, Montclair (New Jersey Landscape),*
1891
oil on canvas
30¼ x 45"
Sterling and Francine Clark Art Institute,
Williamstown, Massachusetts. Gift of Frank and
Katherine Martucci, 2013.1.17

25. *October Noon,* 1891
oil on canvas
30 x 45"
Courtesy of The Fogg Art Museum,
Harvard University Art Museums,
Bequest of Grenville L. Winthrop
© 2003 President and Fellows of
Harvard College

26. *The Lone Farm, Nantucket*, 1892
oil on canvas
30¼ x 45¼"
The Art Institute of Chicago
Edward B. Butler Collection, 1914.189
© The Art Institute of Chicago

27. *Harvest Moon,* 1891
oil on canvas
30 x 44½"
The Corcoran Gallery of Art, Washington, D.C.
Bequest of Mable Stevens Smithers,
the Frances Sydney Smithers Memorial

28. *Saco Ford: Conway Meadows,* 1876
oil on canvas
38 x 63¼"
Mount Holyoke College Art Museum,
South Hadley, Massachusetts
Gift of Ellen W. Ayer, 1883

29. *The Coming Storm,* 1878
oil on canvas
26 x 39"
Albright-Knox Art Gallery, Buffalo, New York.
Albert H. Tracy Fund, 1900

30. *The Old Barn,* c. 1888
oil on canvas
30 x 45"
Private collection,
courtesy of Thomas Colville Fine Art

31. *Woman with Calf,* 1886
oil on canvas
30 x 40"
Sterling and Francine Clark Art Institute,
Williamstown, Massachusetts. Gift of Frank and
Katherine Martucci, 2013.1.5

32. *Homeward,* 1881
oil on canvas
20¼ x 30¼"
Brooklyn Museum of Art, New York
Gift of the Executors of the Estate of
Colonel Michael Friedsam, 32.827

33. *Indian Summer,* 1894
oil on canvas
30 x 42"
Collection of Fayez Sarofim

34. *Shades of Evening,* c. 1877
oil on canvas
27 x 22"
Private collection

35. *Sunset Glow,* 1883
oil on panel
16 x 24⅛"
Montclair Art Museum, Montclair, New Jersey
Gift of Mrs. Francis M. Weld, 1946.1

36. *Landscape,* 1888
oil on canvas
22⅛ x 27½"
© The Cleveland Museum of Art, 2003
Gift of the Estate of Charles F. Brush, 1929.464

37. *Sunrise,* 1887
oil on canvas
30 x 45¼"
The Metropolitan Museum of Art, New York. Anonymous gift in memory of Emil Thiele, 1954 (54.156). Photograph © 1991 The Metropolitan Museum of Art

38. *Near the Village, October,* 1892
oil on canvas
30 x 45"
Cincinnati Art Museum
Gift of Emilie L. Heine in memory of Mr. and Mrs. John Hauck, 1940.943

39. *Hazy Morning, Montclair,* 1893
oil on canvas
30 x 50"
Collection of The Butler Institute of American Art, Youngstown, Ohio

40. *The Home of the Heron,* 1893
oil on canvas
30 x 45"
The Art Institute of Chicago
Edward B. Butler Collection, 1911.31
© The Art Institute of Chicago

FIGURES

Unless otherwise noted, the names of photographers are unknown.

Fig. 1. Napoleon Sarony (1821–1896)
George Inness, c. late 1870s
albumen print
6 x 4¼"
Culver Pictures, New York

Fig. 2. Thomas Cole (1801–1848)
Subsiding of the Waters of the Deluge, 1829
oil on canvas
36 x 48"
Smithsonian American Art Museum, Washington, D.C.
Gift of Mrs. Katie Dean in memory of Minnibel and James W. Dean and Museum Purchase through S. I. Collections Acquisitions Program

Fig. 3. *The Lackawanna Valley*, c. 1855
oil on canvas
33⅞ x 50¼"
National Gallery of Art, Washington, D.C.
Gift of Mrs. Huttleston Rogers

Fig. 4. Albert Pinkham Ryder (1847–1917)
Toilers of the Sea, c. 1890s
oil on panel
11½ x 12"
The Metropolitan Museum of Art, New York.
George A. Hearn Fund, 15.32
Photo Credit: Image copyright © The Metropolitan Museum of Art.
Image source: Art Resource, NY

Fig. 5. William Page (1811–1885)
Self-Portrait
black and white chalk and graphite on tan wove paper, lined
18 x 14½"
Princeton University Art Museum.
Gift of Frank Jewett Mather, Jr.
© 1970 Trustees of Princeton University
Princeton University Art Museum, Princeton, New Jersey. Photo Credit: Princeton University Art Museum/Art Resource, NY

Fig. 6. Schematic drawing of segments of *Lake Nemi* (Plate 15). © The author

Fig. 7. Schematic drawing of segments of *Castel Gandolfo* (Plate 17). © The author

Fig. 8. Sanford R. Gifford (1823–1880)
Lake Nemi, 1856–57
oil on canvas
39⅝ x 60⅜"

Toledo Museum of Art. Purchased with funds from the Florence Scott Libbey Bequest in Memory of her Father, Maurice A. Scott

Figs. 9a–b. Inness's brushes and paint tubes
Montclair Art Museum, Montclair, New Jersey.
Gift of Mrs. F. H. Hooper, 36.209 A-C

Fig. 9c: Inness's palette
Montclair Art Museum, Montclair,
New Jersey. 88.135

Fig. 10. Henri Matisse (1869–1954)
The Swimming Pool, 1952
Nine-panel mural in two parts:
gouache on paper, cut and pasted, on white painted paper mounted on burlap
a–e, 7' 6⅝" x 27' 9½"; f–i, 7' 6⅝" x 26' 1½"
The Museum of Modern Art, New York.
Mrs. Bernard F. Gimbel Fund.
© 2015 Succession H. Matisse
Artists Rights Society (ARS), New York

Fig. 11. William James (1842–1910)
Self-Portrait, c. 1866
pencil on paper
William James Papers, bMS Am 1092.2, Houghton Library, Harvard University, Cambridge, Massachusetts,
Courtesy of Houghton Library and Alexander R. James

Fig. 12. Martin Johnson Heade (1819–1904)
The Stranded Boat, 1863
oil on canvas
22¾ x 36½"
M. and M. Karolik Collection,
Museum of Fine Arts, Boston

Fig. 13. *William James Participating in a Séance*, c. 1880s, photograph
William James Papers, bMS Am 1092.2, Houghton Library, Harvard University, Cambridge, Massachusetts, Courtesy of Houghton Library and Alexander R. James

Fig. 14. Jonathan Scott Hartley (1845–1912)
George Inness, 1891
bronze
14½ x 10¾ x 5½"
National Academy of Design, New York
Gift of the artist, 1891

Fig. 15. George Inness's home and studio at Eagleswood, Perth Amboy, New Jersey,
(from 1864–67), 1889
photograph
George Inness file
Le Brun Library, Montclair Art Museum,
Montclair, New Jersey

Fig. 16. George Inness's home, 151 Grove Street, Montclair, New Jersey (from 1885–94)
photograph, n.d. (before 1912)
Local History Collection, Montclair Public Library, Montclair, New Jersey

Fig. 17. George Inness's studio (north–west side), 151 Grove Street, Montclair, New Jersey
(from 1885–94)
photograph by W. H. Crocker, c. 1890
Local History Collection, Montclair Public Library, Montclair, New Jersey

Fig. 18. George Inness's studio (north side), 151 Grove Street, Montclair, New Jersey
(from 1885–94)
photograph, n.d. (before 1912)
Local History Collection, Montclair Public Library, Montclair, New Jersey

Fig. 19. George Inness, Jr. (1854–1926)
George Inness Sketching Outside His Montclair Studio
c. 1889
oil on canvas board
14½ x 15¼"
Montclair Art Museum, Montclair, New Jersey.
Museum Purchase 1945.10